Nepal's Investment Climate

Nepal's Investment Climate

Leveraging the Private Sector for
Job Creation and Growth

Gabi G. Afram and Angelica Salvi Del Pero

THE WORLD BANK
Washington, D.C.

1 2 3 4 15 14 13 12

This volume is a product of the staff of The World Bank with external contributions. The findings, interpretations, and conclusions expressed in this volume do not necessarily reflect the views of The World Bank, its Board of Executive Directors, or the governments they represent.

The World Bank does not guarantee the accuracy of the data included in this work. The boundaries, colors, denominations, and other information shown on any map in this work do not imply any judgment on the part of The World Bank concerning the legal status of any territory or the endorsement or acceptance of such boundaries.

ISBN (paper): 978-0-8213-9465-6
ISBN (electronic): 978-0-8213-9466-3
DOI: 10.1596/978-0-8213-9465-6

Library of Congress Cataloging-in-Publication Data
Afram, Gabi G. (Gabi George) Nepal's investment climate : leveraging the private sector for job creation and growth / Gabi G. Afram and Angelica Salvi Del Pero.
    p. cm.
  Includes bibliographical references.
  ISBN 978-0-8213-9465-6 — ISBN 978-0-8213-9466-3 (electronic)
  1. Investments, Foreign—Nepal. 2. Labor market—Nepal. 3. Nepal—Economic conditions.
4. Nepal—Economic policy. I. Salvi Del Pero, Angelica. II. World Bank. III. Title.
  HG5720.9.A3A47 2012
  330.95496—dc23

                                                                        2011052343

Cover painting: Soledad Salamé, courtesy of the World bank Art Program
Cover design: Naylor Design

Contents

Boxes

Figures

Tables

Acknowledgments

This report was prepared by a World Bank team led by Gabi Afram, under the guidance of Susan G. Goldmark and Ivan Rossignol. Angelica Salvi Del Pero led the quantitative analysis and survey analysis and provided substantial compilation and editing support. The report team also included Sara Al Rowais, Ina Hoxha, Hiau Looi Kee, Lisa N. Overbey, and Ceren Ozer. Specific chapters benefited from detailed comments from Maitreyi B. Das, Aurora Ferrari, Michael Haney, Surendra Govinda Joshi, Mehnaz Safavian, and Sabin Raj Shrestha, while the overall report benefited from the advice and comments of Tatiana Nenova, Irina Niederberger, and John F. Speakman.

The report was based on five Enterprise Surveys that were conducted by Solutions Consultants P. Ltd., and administered by Arvind Jain and Jorge Luis Rodriguez Meza. The report also used five background studies, which were commissioned by the IFC. Irina Niederberger was the Project Manager, Sayef Tanzeem Qayyum (NICRP, IFC Nepal) was the Task Leader, and Shyamal Krishna Shrestha (NICRP, IFC Nepal) coordinated, prepared, and edited these five studies. Birgit Hansl helped manage the preparation for the Enterprise Survey. The IFC Nepal funded the editing and publication of this report.

The report's peer reviewers were Hisanobu Shishido (World Bank) and Andrew H.W. Stone (World Bank). The report benefited from extensive discussions, interactions, suggestions, and insights from the Ministry of Industry, Commerce and Supplies; the Ministry of Finance; Nepal Rastra Bank (NRB); the Ministry of Labor and Transport; the Federation of Nepalese Chambers of Commerce and Industry (FNCCI); the Confederation of Nepalese Industries (CNI); and the Nepal Tourism Board (NTB); as well as various associations active in the private sector in Nepal, and other related institutions.

Abbreviations

CAAN	Civil Aviation Authority of Nepal
CBS	Central Bureau of Statistics
C/D	Credit/Deposit Ratio
CIB	Credit Information Bureau
CICL	Credit Information Company Limited
DSA	Debt Sustainability Analysis
EU	European Union
FDI	Foreign Direct Investment
FI	Financial Institution
FSO	Financial Sector
FX	Foreign Exchange
FY	Fiscal Year
GDP	Gross Domestic Product
GNI	Gross National Income
GoN	Government of Nepal
ICA	Investment Climate Assessment
ICD	Inland Clearance Depot
ILO	International Labour Organization
IMF	International Monetary Fund
IT	Information Technology

MFDB	Micro Finance Development Bank
MFI	Micro Finance Institution
MFN	Most Favored Nation
MIS	Monitoring and Information System
MOCS	Ministry of Commerce and Supplies
MOF	Ministry of Finance
MOICS	Ministry of Industry Commerce and Supplies
MOTCA	Ministry of Tourism and Civil Aviation
MSME	Micro, Small, and Medium Enterprises
MW	Megawatt
NEA	Nepal Electricity Authority
NGO	Nongovernmental Organization
NLFS	Nepal Labor Force Survey
NLSS	National Living Standards Survey
NPC	National Planning Commission
NRB	Nepal Rastra Bank
OLS	Ordinary Least Squares
PPP	Public-Private Partnerships
SEZ	Special Economic Zone
SME	Small and Medium Enterprise
ST	Secured Transactions
TEPC	Trade and Export Promotion Center
TIA	Tribhuvan International Airport
TTRI	Trade Tariff Restrictiveness Index
U.K.	United Kingdom
U.S.	United States
VAT	Value Added Tax
VGF	Viability Gap Fund
WTTC	World Travel and Tourism Council

Structure of the Report

The Executive Summary and the Report Highlights present the main results and findings about the investment climate in Nepal. Chapter 1 presents background information on the Nepalese economy and the macro environment under which Nepalese firms operate and discusses the characteristics of formal firms in Nepal's private sector. Chapter 2 provides an overview of the investment climate faced by Nepalese firms. Chapter 3 follows with an analysis of private sector enterprise performance and labor productivity in Nepal. Investment climate issues in the three main factor markets—infrastructure, access to finance, and the labor market—are then analyzed in Chapter 4, Chapter 6, and Chapter 7, respectively, while Chapter 5 provides an analysis of the investment climate for informal firms. Output markets are then examined by looking at opportunities for international trade in Chapter 8. Tourism, one of the sectors with best potential for growth, is explored in Chapter 9. Appendix 1 describes the methodology of the various surveys undertaken, while Appendix 2 summarizes the main findings of the Employee Survey.

Executive Summary

Why Is the Nepal Investment Climate Assessment Important?

The objective of the Nepal Investment Climate Assessment (ICA) is to evaluate the investment climate in Nepal in all its dimensions and promote policies to strengthen the private sector. The investment climate is made up of many dimensions that shape the opportunities for investments, employment creation, and growth of private firms. Such dimensions include factor markets, product markets, infrastructure services, and the macroeconomic, legal, regulatory, and institutional framework.

The Nepal ICA delivers a number of important results. It provides evidence-based data on the obstacles faced by the private sector and on its performance and characteristics. In doing so, it quantifies the reality within which the private sector operates (thereby complementing the Doing Business dataset, which quantifies rules and regulations). Furthermore, the Nepal ICA provides a tool to inform and provide evidence-based input to the workings of public-private dialogue vehicles, such as the recently established Nepal Business Forum (NBF). Finally, it provides an opening for sectoral and cross-sectoral reforms and a substantial basis for a private sector development strategy for Nepal.

The main sources of information for this ICA are three surveys. The first survey (Enterprise Survey) covered registered micro enterprises and

1

enterprises with five employees or more in the manufacturing and services sectors in urban areas. In addition to the Enterprise Survey, an Employee Survey and Informal Survey were simultaneously conducted. Overall, between March 2009 and June 2009, data were collected for 486 registered establishments, 120 unregistered establishments, and 392 employees. Information from the surveys is supplemented with information from other sources, including five specially-commissioned Background Studies on Labor Issues, the Informal Sector, Strategic Partnerships with India and China, Tourism, and the Agri-sector; the Doing Business Report; analytical reports by the World Bank, the International Monetary Fund, other international organizations, and the Government of Nepal (GoN); and academic papers and reports.

One of the advantages that the World Bank's Enterprise Surveys have over other firm-level surveys is that similar surveys have been conducted in a wide range of countries. It is therefore possible to benchmark Nepal against other countries with respect to both firm performance and measures of the investment climate. Throughout the report, firm performance and the investment climate in Nepal are benchmarked against other countries in the South Asia region and countries with comparable economies, locations, and factor endowments from different regions: Bhutan, Bolivia, the Lao People's Democratic Republic (PDR), and Mongolia. Subsequent to the completion of the Enterprise Survey, stakeholder workshops and focus group discussions were conducted throughout the drafting of the ICA to inform and validate the report's results.[1]

What Do the Survey Results Say about the Investment Climate in Nepal?

The report's key finding is that while there are some niche sectors growing and expanding employment in Nepal (including tourism and certain educational and other services), there are many constraints to the investment climate in Nepal that are hindering the development and growth of the private sector. In particular, political instability, poor infrastructure, poor labor relations, poor access to finance, and declining exports plague Nepal's private sector. To overcome many of these issues and move forward, many reforms are needed. Given the extent of the challenge, effective Public-Private Dialogue is required so that the government and the private sector can work in partnership to address these constraints.

The 2009 ICA shows that Nepal's private sector is starting to reap some dividends from the cessation of armed conflict in terms of employment generation. Employment in the private sector increased by almost 4 percent a year between FY2005/06 and FY2007/08. Tourism has rebounded, while dealing with regulations, paying taxes, and obtaining business permits in Nepal is becoming less complex.

Against these promising signs, a daunting set of challenges remain. Political instability and infrastructure (especially for transport and electricity) **represent the two main challenges.** Ninety percent of the firms consider political instability to be a major or very severe obstacle; for electricity, the proportion is 57 percent. Political instability is the top obstacle across all industries, while transport, electricity, and corruption are problematic for many sectors. Labor regulations are more critical for the manufacturing sector and for large firms, whereas access to finance is more often an issue for tourism, informal, and micro enterprises.

The effects on business confidence and economic performance are visible: production costs are high and business operations and trade are often disrupted. The extent of the political instability and the frequency of electricity shortages translate into real costs to the private sector. Losses due to civil unrest (44 days a year on average) and electricity shortages (of up to 27 percent of total sales for firms with more than five employees) are prohibitively high.

What Next? Developing Nepal's Private Sector for Job Creation and Growth

The pervasiveness and impact of political instability in Nepal makes the investment climate in the country comparable more to Afghanistan than other countries in the region or the comparator countries used in the analysis. While this comparison is unflattering, it is true. Political instability has stifled growth and limited Nepal's ability to exploit its hydropower and tourism potential. Interestingly, many firms do not perceive access to land and finance as major obstacles. This could be a reflection of lack of dynamism: Nepalese firms are simply not planning to invest, expand, and grow in their unstable and unpredictable environment. The peace dividend is not difficult to measure. As the surveys show, ending civil unrest alone would give back to enterprises 44 working days a year! The effects on economic activity, investment, growth, and job creation could be potentially huge.

These political instability costs add to the already daunting weak infrastructure costs. Electricity shortages alone cost Nepalese firms a staggering 27 percent of their annual sales. Add labor market costs (in terms of trade union action and inflexibility of hiring and firing) with governance costs (informal payments are common) and it becomes hard to dispel the perception that the private sector in Nepal operates and survives against many odds and despite the challenging business environment.

Not surprisingly then, private enterprises in Nepal, with a few exceptions, are almost overwhelmingly non-exporters; they are not investing or expanding, nor are they accessing finance. They generally do not invest in skills and training of their employees, and are not innovative. Indeed, most of the employment in Nepal is in the informal sector, which is generally not linked to the formal firms. The formal firms, in their turn, are not connected to any regional or global value chains. Therefore, despite the substantial growth in services over the past decade, much of the country's employment is still in low-productivity agriculture.

These structural problems cause low levels of savings and investment, resulting in low job creation, which lead millions of Nepalese to seek temporary employment elsewhere. It is believed that one-third of the male population in Nepal is abroad. The high rate of migration has resulted in high remittance inflows, which now account for a quarter of the economy. Despite serious unemployment and underemployment, in real terms, labor costs have risen due to the influx of remittances. The emerging picture is of an uncompetitive, non-exporting, remittance-dependent economy that is becoming increasingly reliant for its growth on external remittance flows instead of its internal dynamism and economic activity.

Thus, the Nepalese economy is stuck in a cycle where lack of investment opportunities and jobs drive people to migrate, resulting in remittance flows, which are mainly channeled to consumption and asset bubbles. This liquidity inflates prices of goods and assets and increases costs to the productive job-creating sector. Competitiveness and contracts are lost and the amount of exports and tradable activities decrease, prolonging the cycle of mediocre and jobless growth at home (Dutch Disease).

In order for Nepal to improve productivity and shift economic activity from the less productive (rural economy and low-cost manufacturing) to more productive sectors (services, tourism, niche manufacturing), private investment (including foreign direct investment (FDI)) has to be expanded, while innovation and exports need to be encouraged. To do so, the country's political uncertainties and factor market issues (above all, infrastructure deficiencies but also access to finance and labor market issues) need to be addressed. This will help create jobs, reduce production costs, and increase the country's declining competitiveness. Addressing these constraints takes time and requires leadership and vision.

Public-Private Dialogue is key to ensuring that all stakeholders are onboard and in agreement on how to move forward. Some reforms can be dealt with earlier, such as reforms to processes and regulations that could help the informal sector, reforms that can enhance access to finance, and reforms to labor regulations and relations (that would stop labor issues from being a problem as firms begin to grow and export)—while others require time. In particular, a strategy to improve transport and electricity infrastructure is sorely needed. Implementation of such improvement strategies is likely to be long term, partly because of the difficult topographic characteristics of the country and partly because of the complex issues that have led to the present situation. The NBF could be the vehicle for such dialogue. However, the GoN will still need to address directly some of the investment climate constraints, in particular those relating to law and order and poor security because they cannot be sorted out by any other party.

Choices will have to be made and not all sectors can grow and become competitive. Quick wins, related to the country's potential in tourism and hydropower, and economic linkages to the growing economies of India and China, should be identified and pursued. However, adopting certain policies involve trade-offs in a world of limited resources. For example, a land-locked, poor infrastructure country experiencing Dutch Disease might find it hard to develop low-cost manufacturing. Choices will have to be grounded in reality and in the country's priorities. However, the right labor laws and adequate power supply in an industrial zone close to the Indian border, coupled with a transit deal with either India or Bangladesh, can still create a favorable environment for the growth of such industries. But maybe it would be simpler to focus on developing the information and technology (IT) sector by improving telecommunication infrastructure. This kind of discussion needs a forum that brings together all stakeholders.

The remainder of the report attempts to provide a complete analysis of the investment climate for the private sector in Nepal, along with a discussion of possible recommendations to address some of the business environment constraints. Given that political instability dwarfed all other issues, needless to say, this should be uppermost on the minds of both politicians and policymakers. However, many other reforms could still be implemented to improve the investment climate for the struggling Nepalese private sector.

Summary of Recommendations

The table below presents a summary of the policy recommendations that follow from the findings of this ICA for Nepal, and that are described in detail in both the summary report and the main report. The recommendations are prioritized into short-term and medium/long-term recommendations (Table 1).

Table 1 Summary of Policy Recommendations

Sector	What needs to be done	How?
Short term		
Law and order and stability	Address the law and order situation (including armed gangs, violence, extortion, and intimidation), which drives away business and scares entrepreneurs	• The GoN needs to take the lead on the law and order and security situation because no other party can handle this • The political class and the opinion makers need to turn the focus from politics to the economy and to development
Governance and institution building	Institution building needs to be supported as institutions remain very fragile (especially nascent ones)	• Support by development partners (in terms of capacity building, technical assistance, and funding) to reformers within the Nepalese government is needed to help build institutions
Finance	Financial stability is paramount for the health of the private sector, and needs to be maintained	• Rigorous supervision and monitoring by the Nepal Rastra Bank (NRB) • Develop a crisis management framework
Finance	A broad range of assets should become acceptable as collateral	• Operationalize the secured transaction registry envisaged by the Secured Transaction Act • Create a registration database in which a public record of obligations secured by movable property can be made
Finance	Broaden the reach of the Credit Information Bureau (CIB)	• Expand the coverage of the CIB through improved management and information systems (MIS) at both the CIB and participating financial institutions (FIs) • Provide services to small and medium enterprises (SMEs) to help them access credit from banks more cheaply and rapidly
Services sector	Promote the development of service sectors like IT and medical colleges, which are technically high value-added and are not easily unionized or susceptible to government interventions	• Undertake a value-chain analysis to understand the structure and players in these sectors, the reasons behind their recent success, and how to help them • Develop and implement a sector promotion strategy and an investment promotion plan

(continued next page)

Table 1 (continued)

Sector	What needs to be done	How?
External sector	Improve access to external markets	• Reduce non-tariff barriers to trade and improve related regulatory framework
External sector	Reduce infrastructural constraints	• Bring shipping lines to Inland Clearance Depot • Improve airport warehouse
Tourism	Invest in tourism-related infrastructure	• Develop the Himalayan trail, new trekking areas, and more hotels to provide investment opportunities and short-term growth to the tourism sector
Tourism	Develop skills of labor force	• Develop targeted training to improve quality of service • Pilot the introduction of tourism as part of school curriculum
Medium/Long term		
Infrastructure	Strategically expand, maintain, and rehabilitate the country's road network	• Set up viability gap funds with government and donor resources to finance expansion of low volume road network • Identify commercial corridors with potentially high traffic for private sector investment and public–private partnerships (PPPs)
Infrastructure	Develop electricity supply through developing private hydropower provision	• Improve the investment climate for private hydropower developers by establishing a "one-window" agency to facilitate hydropower development • Improve utilization of existing capacity by improving water storage
Finance	Enhance access to finance	• Design technical assistance and financial literacy training programs for SMEs to develop bankable proposals and keep better accounts • Allow warehouse receipts to act as collateral • Reduce the cost of remittance services
Finance	Develop the appropriate regulatory framework for mobile banking	• Issue NRB guidelines on mobile phone banking • Make Unstructured Supplementary Service Data (USSD) mobile phone platform (as opposed to the Short Message Service (SMS)-based platform) available through mobile phone operators to allow developments in mobile phone banking

Labor	Improve monitoring of labor issues and disputes	• Encourage direct dialogue between employers and labor to break the link with politically motivated industrial action • Introduce independent labor inspection to help government in resolving labor disputes • Create new labor court branches to increase efficiency in dealing with labor cases
Labor	Reduce non wage costs of labor by increasing flexibility	• Review the Bonus Act of 1973 to provide flexibility to employers and more wage differentiation to employees • Introduce employment contract system to provide employers with more options for formally employing workers • Pilot flexible labor regimes in special economic zones
Tourism	Invest in tourism-related infrastructure to enhance accessibility to tourism resources and establishments	• Develop selected small airfields within Nepal • Develop better connecting nodes between road and air travel • Invest in energy efficiency measures • Reform approval/licensing processes to attract FDI • End subsidized parking fees for domestic airlines
Tourism	Improve implementation of existing laws and regulations	• Build capacity in tourism-related government institutions • Collect comprehensive data on hotel/guesthouse/lodge occupancy to prepare a proper marketing strategy • Resolve the issues of land ownership rights and cumbersome court procedures to encourage FDI
Tourism	Promote quality and environmental certification	• Develop proper regulation and monitoring of certifications to expand opportunities in eco-tourism, etc.
External sector	Reduce red tape	• Develop and enact comprehensive capacity building program for Customs Department • Amend Export-Import Act and enact the Trade Promotion Act for trade facilitation

(continued next page)

Table 1 (continued)

Sector	What needs to be done	How?
External sector	Reduce constraints to exports	• Set technical standards, phyto-sanitary measures, intellectual property rights, and domestic services regulation • Promote better quality standards • Address non-tariff barriers for exporting to India
Informal sector	Improving productivity and working conditions of informal firms is an important component of private sector development and of the growth and poverty reduction agenda	• Strengthen linkages to the formal sector • Promote human capital development through better educational attainment and active labor market interventions, such as training and skill-development programs • Simplify registration procedures and reduce entry costs • Promote better access to finance, especially through microfinance programs
Regulations and licensing	Ease the regulatory burden for large firms in order to help them grow and generate employment	• Simplify the process of dealing with regulations and taxes as much as possible, in particular, the number of payments and the time involved in paying taxes

Source: Authors.

Note

1. Sector-specific value-chain analysis is very important to identify growth potential within Nepal's private sector landscape. While the data collected through the Nepal Enterprise Survey does not typically allow for such analysis, such an exercise should nonetheless be undertaken in earnest to complement the ICA report.

Report Highlights

At the end of a rough and rugged one-lane road near the edge of a crowded and congested urban area lies the Shresthra Garments Factory—a somewhat derelict early 90s construction, where the machinery is old and some of the capacity lies idle. Power supply is patchy, and on the best of days, does not exceed 50 percent of the production time. Only half of the workers are there because many are taking part in a strike to demand better wages, while the others couldn't make it to work because yet another bandh *was announced the night before. The factory still produces good quality garments, but many of the foreign contracts are long gone since buyers abroad found cheaper and more reliable sources. Some people in the nearby villages and cities still buy part of the factory's production, but as their migrant relatives send them more funds from Qatar, they increasingly buy imported garments. Therefore, the owner has no intentions to expand operations and has shelved plans to acquire more land and access more funding. At the nearby, more recent, Poudel Garments Factory, the owner has just acquired (with relative ease) the permits to import fabrics for making hiking gear. The production of the latter has expanded, with the increase in tourism, and the owner has increased employment at the factory. This is the story of the private sector in Nepal: pockets of success buoyed by growing activity and employment in certain sectors (especially tourism), which are operating against many odds (political uncertainty, poor infrastructure, poor labor relations and regulations, declining exports, corruption, and rampant informality).*

Introduction

After a decade-long conflict and civil unrest, Nepal's political parties signed a Comprehensive Peace Agreement in 2006, which paved the way for Constituent Assembly elections in 2008. The transition to peace and prosperity is, however, complex and prolonged. Civil unrest and the ensuing political uncertainty have adversely affected business confidence and economic performance—already constrained by poor infrastructure and rigid labor regulations.

Despite continued political uncertainty, macroeconomic stability has been maintained and Nepal's gross domestic product (GDP) has grown by 4.5 percent on average during the four years since the end of the conflict.[1] The exchange rate peg to the Indian Rupee and, thus far, prudent fiscal policy have anchored the relative macroeconomic stability.

Poverty incidence has also declined and social indicators are improving. Although Nepal's per capita income (of around US$400) and human development indicators lag behind the rest of the South Asia region, there have been improvements in health and education outcomes and the poverty level has come down significantly (from 42 percent in 1995/96, to around 31 percent in 2004, to a 2010 estimate of less than 20 percent)[2]—largely driven by substantial remittance inflows (estimated at more than 25 percent of GDP).

In addition, as the Enterprise Survey shows, employment generation in the private sector also increased by almost 4 percent a year between FY2005/06 and FY2007/08. Tourism has rebounded and its contribution to GDP is expected to grow. Furthermore, dealing with regulations, paying taxes, and obtaining business permits in Nepal is relatively easy.

Still, Nepal is severely constrained by its transport and electricity infrastructure, which is generally underdeveloped and poorly maintained. The effects on business confidence and firm performance are visible: production costs are high and business operations and trade are often disrupted, contributing to a decline in the contribution of manufacturing activity to employment and GDP. This is important, since despite the substantial growth in services over the past decade, much of the country's employment is still in low-productivity agriculture. The private sector is further challenged with rigid labor market regulations (and poor labor relations), which curb employment growth, as well as with limited access to finance (where eligibility barriers and lack of appropriate products curtail the use of financial services).

In order for Nepal to improve productivity and shift economic activity from the less productive (rural economy and low-cost manufacturing) to more productive sectors (services, tourism, niche manufacturing), private investment (including FDI) has to be expanded, while innovation and exports need to be encouraged. To do so, the country's political uncertainties and factor market issues (above all infrastructure deficiencies, but also access to finance and labor market issues) need to be addressed. These will help create jobs, reduce production costs, and increase the country's declining competitiveness. Addressing these constraints takes time and requires leadership and vision. Public-Private Dialogue is key to ensuring that all stakeholders are onboard and that there is an agreement on how to move forward. Some reforms can be dealt with earlier (including reforms to processes and regulations that could help the informal sector, as well as reforms that can enhance access to finance and labor relations), while others require time. In particular, a strategy to improve transport and electricity infrastructure is sorely needed. In this case, implementation is likely to be long term, partly because of the difficult topographic characteristics of the country and partly because of the complex issues that have led to the present situation.

In the absence of a good investment climate, Nepal's economy will remain stuck in a cycle where lack of jobs drives people to migrate, resulting in remittance flows that are mainly channeled to consumption and asset bubbles. This liquidity inflates prices of goods and assets and increases costs to the productive job-creating sectors, which lose competitiveness and contract, prolonging the cycle of slow, jobless growth at home.

The Nepal Enterprise Survey and Investment Climate Assessment

The objective of the Nepal Investment Climate Assessment (ICA) is to evaluate the investment climate in Nepal in all its dimensions and promote policies to strengthen the private sector. The investment climate is made up of many dimensions that shape the opportunities for investments, employment creation, and growth of private firms. Such dimensions include factor markets, product markets, infrastructure services, and the macroeconomic, legal, regulatory, and institutional framework.

The report provides an assessment of the prevailing business environment and of the performance of private firms in the manufacturing and

services sectors in urban areas of Nepal, based on the enterprise and employee surveys. These surveys are a standardized instrument to measure and compare the investment climate conditions in a country, focusing on the microeconomic and structural dimensions (Box 1). The report also provides information on which dimensions of the investment climate are seen as a reform priority by the private sector.

Box 1

Methodology

Data underpinning the analysis in ICAs are collected through Enterprise Surveys. For the Nepal ICA, three main surveys were conducted. An Enterprise Survey was conducted in urban areas and covered micro enterprises and enterprises with five employees or more in the manufacturing and services sectors; sampling was designed to have a representative sample of firms in the tourism industry. In addition to the Enterprise Survey, an Employee Survey and an Informal Survey were simultaneously conducted. Overall, between March 2009 and June 2009 data were collected for 486 registered establishments, 120 unregistered establishments, and 392 employees. The Enterprise Survey sample is representative of the urban manufacturing and services industries and was collected through a stratified random sampling with replacement based on a block enumeration exercise that led to the enumeration of 6,755 establishments for the survey fieldwork. Information from the surveys is supplemented with information from other sources, including five Background Studies on: Labor Issues, the Informal Sector, Strategic Partnerships with India and China, Tourism, and the Agri-sector; the Doing Business Report; analytical reports by the World Bank, the International Monetary Fund, other international organizations, and the GoN; and academic papers and reports.

One of the advantages that the World Bank's Enterprise Surveys have over other firm-level surveys is that similar surveys have been conducted in a wide range of countries. It is therefore possible to benchmark Nepal against other countries with respect to both firm performance and measures of the investment climate. Throughout the report, firm performance and the investment climate in Nepal is benchmarked against other countries of the South Asia region and countries with comparable economies, locations, and factor endowments from different regions: Bhutan, Bolivia, Lao PDR, and Mongolia. Subsequent to the completion of the Enterprise Survey, stakeholder workshops and focus group discussions were conducted throughout the drafting of the ICA to inform and validate the report's results.

The Nepal Enterprise Survey 2009 follows-up on an Enterprise Survey conducted in 2000,[3] for which 223 firms in the manufacturing sector were surveyed across the country. The main investment climate obstacles that afflict Nepal today were already critical at the time of the 2000 Enterprise Survey. The 2000 survey found that—while the market-oriented policy reforms and trade agreements with India initiated by Nepal in the early 1990s had dramatic effects in terms of GDP growth and manufacturing sector performance—the post-reform growth trends did not prove sustainable after the mid-1990s. Poor implementation of reforms, bureaucratic burden, and continued political and policy uncertainty were to blame. Government policy and its implementation were the greatest obstacles to doing business in Nepal; inadequate demand for products, poor access to finance, and inadequate infrastructure services were secondary obstacles.

Key Features of the Nepalese Private Sector

The Nepalese economy is still dependent on a highly volatile agricultural sector, which accounts for 36 percent of GDP and 74 percent of the workforce. Growth has, however, been driven by the services sector, which now accounts for 49 percent of GDP (Figure 1). The industrial sector's contribution to GDP has, instead, declined to around 15 percent over the past few years with an annual growth rate in FY2008/09 of –0.4 percent. Within services, wholesale and retail trade and transportation services have been the key contributors to GDP growth.

A strong dependence on remittances exacerbates the country's structural weaknesses, resulting in an erosion of competitiveness in an increasingly vulnerable macro-financial environment. Indeed, over the past two decades, while other South Asian countries transformed their economies and expanded their manufacturing base and competitiveness, Nepal's performance has deteriorated. Since the mid-1990s, other South Asian countries such as Bangladesh, India, and Sri Lanka have all experienced significant growth in the services sector (Figure 2). However, in parallel, unlike Nepal, they also managed to achieve value added growth in industry and particularly in the manufacturing sub-sector for most years. In contrast, Nepal achieved only meager value added growth in all sectors, but particularly performed worse in manufacturing (Figure 2).

Structurally, small retail firms dominate the Nepalese private sector. Among registered non-agricultural enterprises, retailers account for 60 percent of the firms; beyond retail, the prevalent industries are

Figure 1   **Nepalese Real GDP Composition by Sector, FY2008/09**
percent

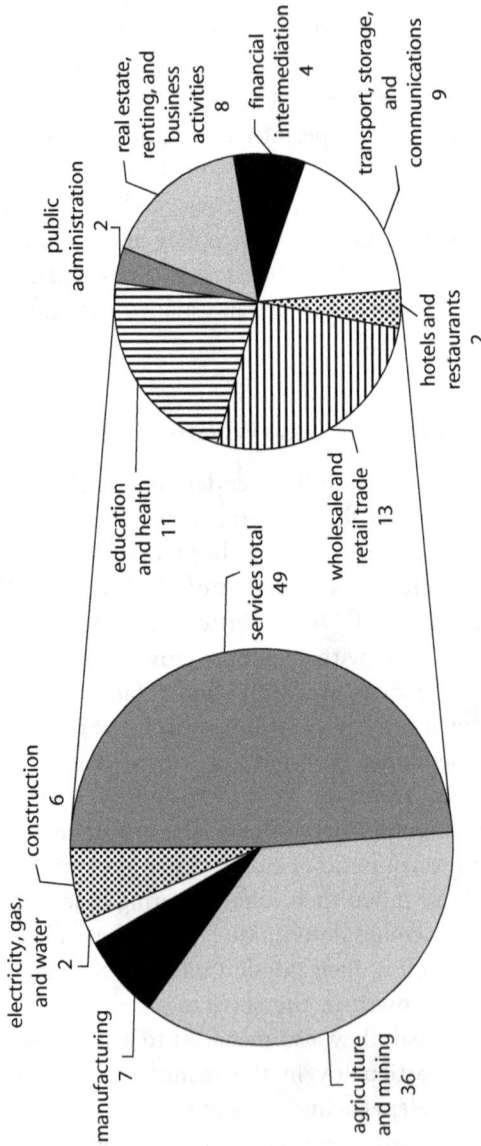

real estate, renting, and business activities
8

financial intermediation
4

transport, storage, and communications
9

public administration
2

hotels and restaurants
2

education and health
11

wholesale and retail trade
13

services total
49

construction
6

electricity, gas, and water
2

manufacturing
7

agriculture and mining
36

Sources: NRB 2009, 2010; World Bank staff calculations.

Figure 2   Value Added Growth by Sector 1995–2008, Selected South Asian Countries

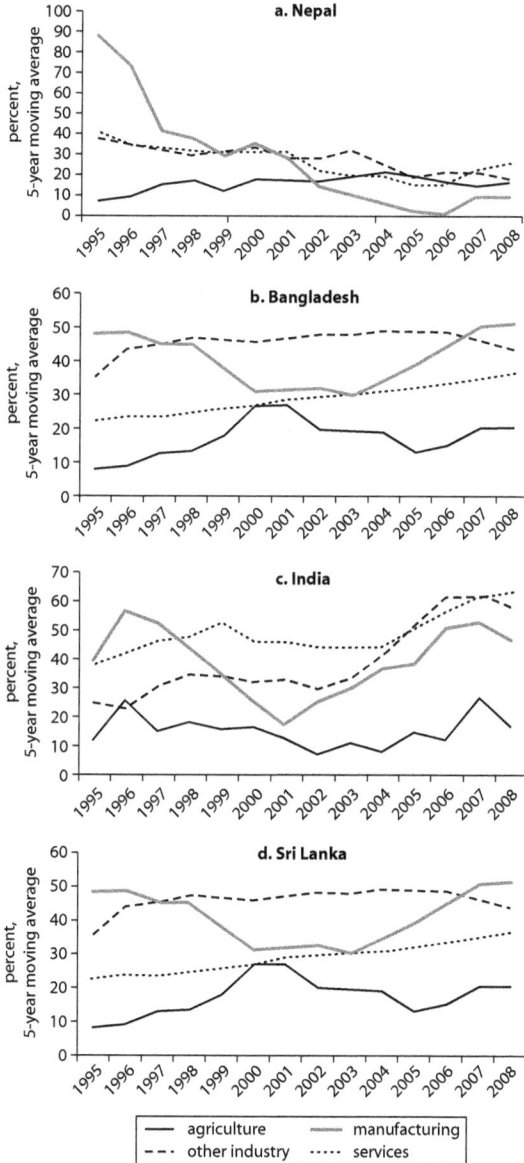

Source: World Bank 2009d.
Note: Sectoral value added growth rates are calculated as 5-year moving averages based on constant US$ in 2000 prices.

manufacturing and hotels and restaurants. **Enterprises are concentrated in the Central region, especially manufacturing firms.** Sixty-four percent of the firms are located in the Central region, 20 percent in the West, and 16 percent in the East.

The average size of formal firms in the private sector is very small.[4] The private sector is characterized by informality—it is estimated that 70 percent of workers are employed in the informal sector—and by the prevalence of micro firms. Outside the agricultural sector, firms with less than five employees account for 65 percent of informal firms and 70 percent of the registered firms.

According to the survey, most Nepalese firms are middle-aged firms. The average firm has been operating for 9.6 years but manufacturing firms are on average older (11.4 years). Most Nepalese firms are between five and 20 years old (Figure 3). Only 10 percent of the firms are more than 20 years old and 25 percent are less than five years old. This means that either fewer firms have entered the market over the past five years than the preceding five-year period, or that their survival rate is much lower. In either case, it shows that the business environment for the entry and survival of new firms has worsened over time since the early 1990s.

Employment generation in the whole private sector (including micro-enterprises) increased by almost 4 percent per year between FY 2005/06 and FY 2007/08. This is a sign of resilience in Nepal's private sector. In

Figure 3   Distribution of Registered Firms in Nepal by Age of Firm

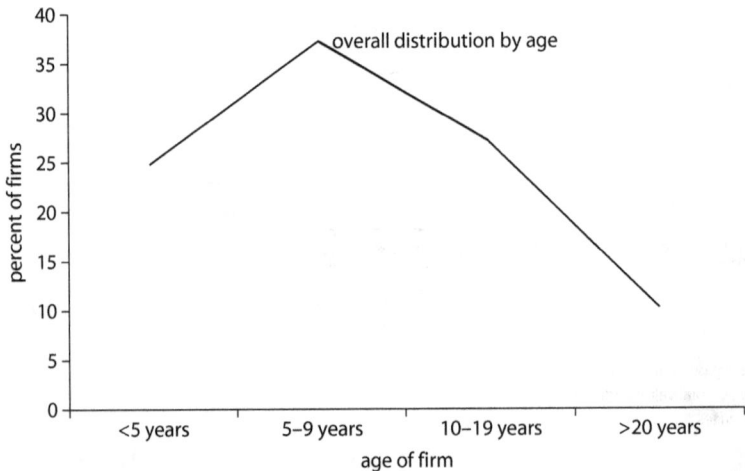

Source: Nepal Enterprise Survey 2009.

addition to showing initial gains from the end of the armed conflict (peace dividend), the private sector is expanding employment (albeit from a low start, as the average number of employees per firm is much smaller than in comparator countries).[5]

However, labor productivity has been lagging as a result of the conflict and infrastructure limitations.[6] Indeed, a cross-country comparison of the performance of Nepalese firms with firms in comparator countries confirms that the country's private sector performance is poor (Table 2). Furthermore, firms are on average smaller in size and the incidence of exporters is much lower. On the other hand, Nepal is competitive in terms of labor costs, having the lowest unit labor cost average among comparator countries—thanks to low total labor cost per worker.

When including micro-firms, it becomes clear that while sales and employment have increased over the past two years, labor productivity has actually contracted. Performance in terms of labor productivity varies across industries, regions, and sizes. Not surprisingly, productivity is highest in the Central region, among larger firms, among exporting firms, and in the retail sector. However, overall productivity is declining, driven by a decline in the retail sector, the Central region, among micro-enterprises, and among non-exporters.

The empirical analysis conducted for this report shows that firms with more fixed assets perform better both in terms of total sales and in terms of labor productivity. Being open to international markets—such as being exporters or having foreign ownership/capital—also improves performance.

In terms of the impact of a number of investment climate dimensions, better access to finance is associated with higher sales and higher labor productivity, while electricity outages are associated with poorer performance on both these counts.

The poor investment climate also discourages innovation and technology adoption. Only 0.5 percent of manufacturing firms have patents registered abroad and 9 percent have patents registered in Nepal; even among large firms, the proportion is only 4 and 9 percent, respectively. Fewer firms use email and websites than in any of the comparator countries except for Lao PDR and Bangladesh (Figure 4).

Leading Constraints for Nepalese Firms

In addition to firm performance, ICAs collect information on the business climate dimensions that are perceived to be the most constraining obstacles to the growth and operations of firms. Although most of the

Table 2 Cross-Country Comparisons of Firm Performance

	Sales		Labor productivity		Employment		Direct exporter
	Average (thousand 2005 US$)	Average annual growth rate	Average (thousand 2005 US$)	Average annual growth rate (%)	Average number	Average annual growth rate	% firms
Nepal	415	8.7%	22	2.4	14	6.5%	3.8
Bhutan	1,804	26.8%	106	12.4	25	15.0%	8.4
Bangladesh	1,780	3.8%	12	4.8	179	6.2%	6.1
Lao PDR	494	3.7%	29	4.4	23	1.2%	9.5
Mongolia	1,367	35.9%	23	22.3	40	15.6%	7.6

Source: World Bank Enterprise Surveys, latest available year.

Notes: Data is based on the most recent available survey; however, average sales and labor productivity are converted in 2005 prices to make them comparable. Sample restricted to firms with 5+ employees in sectors surveyed in most countries in the comparator group, i.e. manufacturing, retail, wholesale, hotels and restaurants, transport, and travel agencies.

Figure 4 Indicators of Innovation and Technology for Nepal and Comparator Countries

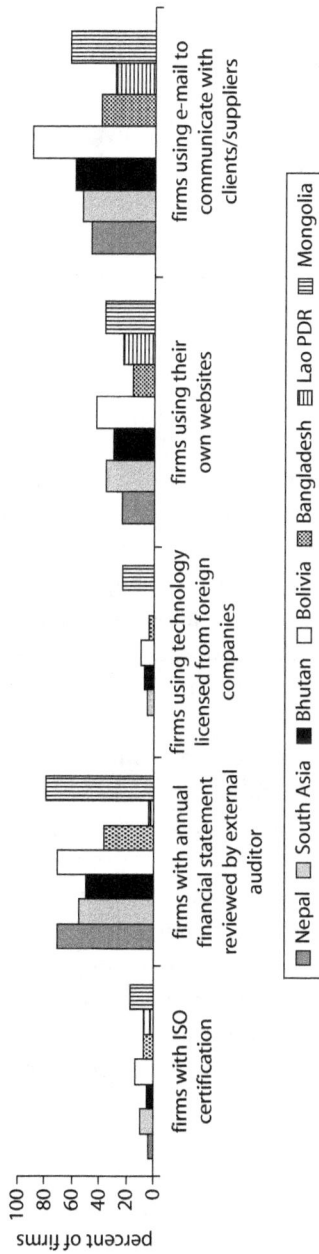

percent of firms

firms with ISO certification

firms with annual financial statement reviewed by external auditor

firms using technology licensed from foreign companies

firms using their own websites

firms using e-mail to communicate with clients/suppliers

Nepal ▨ South Asia ▨ Bhutan ☐ Bolivia ▨ Bangladesh ▥ Lao PDR ▤ Mongolia

Source: World Bank Enterprise Surveys, latest available year.

Note: Comparison restricted to firms with 5+ employees in sectors surveyed in most countries in the comparator group, i.e., manufacturing, retail, wholesale, hotels and restaurants, transport, and travel agencies.

questions are quantitative (such as how many times did power go out in the previous month, how much do the firms spend on security, and how much time do senior managers spend dealing with regulation), managers are also asked what they see as the biggest problem that they face. Although there are many problems with questions on firm perceptions, it is natural to start any analysis of the investment climate by looking at what firm managers said were the biggest problems that they faced. Objective data on many of these issues are discussed later in this section and in greater detail in the rest of the report.

Political instability and electricity supply are unambiguously regarded as the most important obstacles in Nepal. Ninety percent of the firms consider political instability to be a major or very severe obstacle; for electricity the proportion is 57 percent (Figure 5). By comparison, in Afghanistan (the only other country in South Asia where enterprises were asked about political instability) political instability is considered as the most important constraint by only 16 percent of firms and electricity by 18 percent.[7] Political instability is the top obstacle across all industries in Nepal, while transport, electricity, and corruption are especially problematic for the tourism industry; labor regulations are instead more critical for the manufacturing sector, and informal competition is especially felt by firms in services other than retail and tourism. Access to finance is more often an issue for manufacturing and retail industries. The perception of the investment climate also varies depending on the firm's size; large firms perceive the investment climate to be poorer, especially in terms of labor regulations and taxes.

A cross-country comparison shows that Nepal is doing worse than comparator countries or the South Asia region in electricity and transportation, whereas it is doing better with respect to tax rates and tax administration, labor skills, functioning of the courts, and business licensing and permits (Figure 6). Political stability was not surveyed in most comparator countries and therefore cannot be compared.

These perceptions stem from real costs and losses that firms experience and are, therefore, more than just perceptions. Indeed, Nepalese firms bear higher aggregate costs associated with the poor investment climate than any of the comparator countries for the dimensions directly relating to infrastructure (losses due to power outages, losses due to breakage or spoilage) and to crime and vandalism (Figure 7). Therefore, these costs are real and not just perceptions.[8]

The real costs of the conflict (political instability) and the poor investment climate in Nepal become evident once the number of days lost to

Figure 5 Perception of Obstacles Constraining the Investment Climate in Nepal

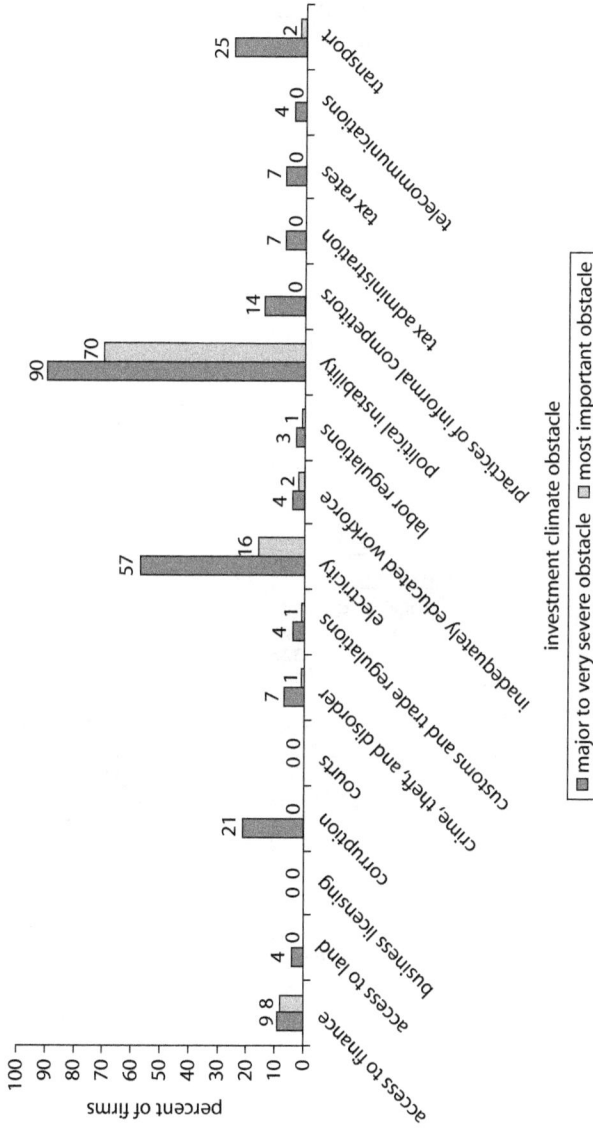

percent of firms

access to finance 9 8
access to land 4
business licensing 0
corruption 21
courts 0
crime, theft, and disorder 7 1
customs and trade regulations 4 1
electricity 57 16
inadequately educated workforce
labor regulations 4 2
political instability 3 1
practices of informal competitors 90 70
tax administration 14 0
tax rates 7 0
telecommunications 4 0
transport 25 2

investment climate obstacle

■ major to very severe obstacle ■ most important obstacle

Source: Nepal Enterprise Survey 2009.

Figure 6   Investment Climate Obstacles Perceived as Major to Very Severe in Nepal and Comparator Countries

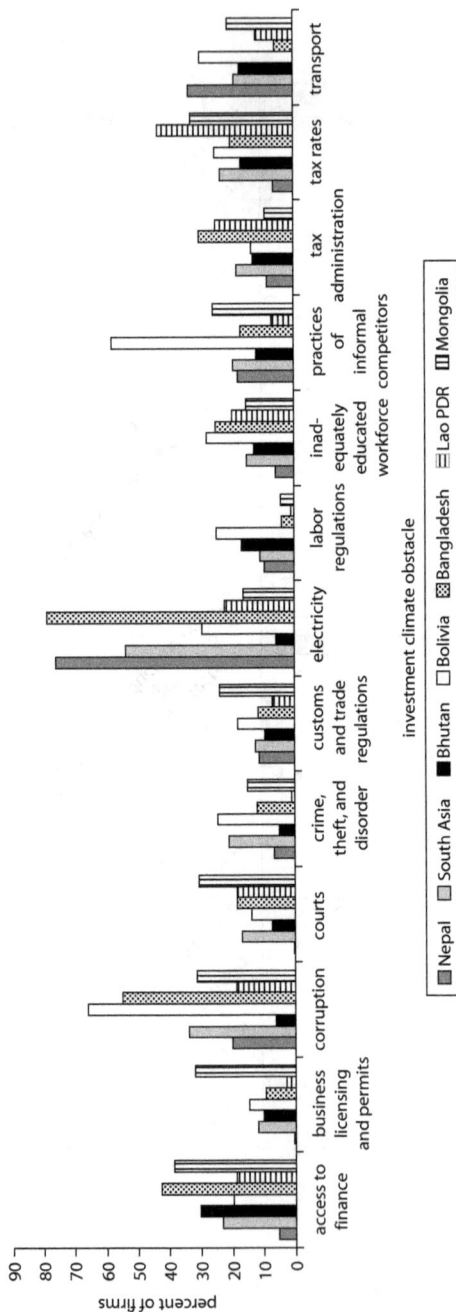

Source: World Bank Enterprise Surveys, latest available year.

Note: Comparison restricted to firms with 5+ employees in sectors surveyed in most countries in the comparator group, i.e., manufacturing, retail, wholesale, hotels and restaurants, transport, and travel agencies. Political instability is not included among compared investment climate obstacles because it was not surveyed in comparator countries.

Figure 7   Costs Associated with Investment Climate Weaknesses in Nepal and Comparator Countries

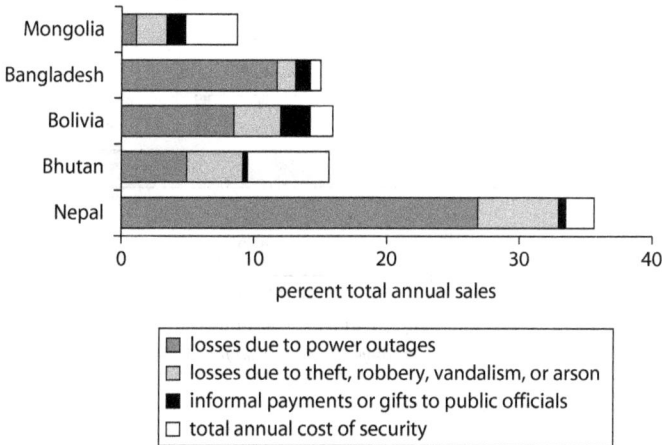

percent total annual sales

■ losses due to power outages
▨ losses due to theft, robbery, vandalism, or arson
■ informal payments or gifts to public officials
□ total annual cost of security

Source: World Bank Enterprise Surveys, latest available year.
Note: Comparison restricted to firms with 5+ employees in sectors surveyed in most countries in the comparator group, i.e. manufacturing, retail, wholesale, hotels and restaurants, transport, and travel agencies.
Losses due to civil unrest and trade union actions are not included in this chart because enterprises were asked to report on them as number of days lost rather than as a proportion of annual sales.

civil unrest and trade union actions is added (where Nepalese firms lose a total of 55 working days) (Figure 8). This added burden on the private sector is daunting, especially when coupled with losses due to power outages and crime.

The next sections of the report benchmark Nepal against comparator countries on both objective and perception data on the investment climate. This chapter focuses mostly on those areas of the investment climate that firms said were a serious problem or on areas where the objective data leads to a similar conclusion. It also provides a summary of other aspects of the business environment and markets (factor and product markets) that are of importance to the Nepalese private sector. More details, findings, and analysis are discussed in the rest of the report.

The Main Issues with the Investment Climate in Nepal

Poor Electricity and Roads Hinder Competitiveness and Growth

Extensive and effective infrastructure is key to the competitiveness and growth of an economy; without proper infrastructure, firms cannot use modern production technologies and cannot connect to their input and output markets; production costs are high and competitiveness declines.

Figure 8   Average Number of Days Lost in Nepalese Firms Due to Labor Issues

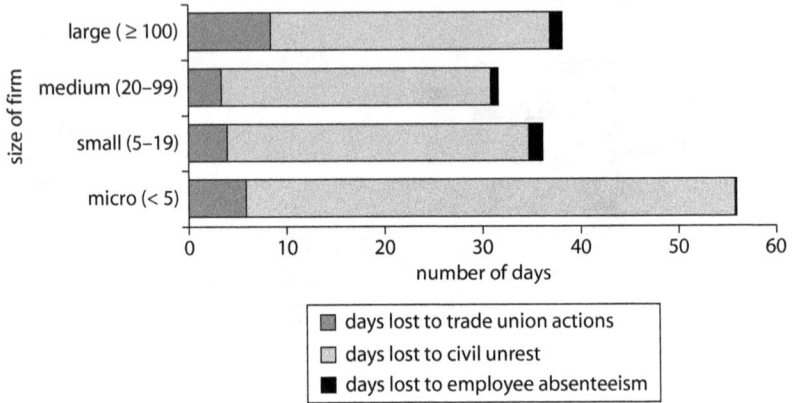

Source: Nepal Enterprise Survey 2009.

Poor infrastructure also negatively affects the business environment and discourages foreign investments, hampering the mix of economic activities that can develop in the economy.

Nepal's infrastructure is underdeveloped and poorly maintained, especially with regard to power generation and transportation. Although the country operates at much below its hydropower generation potential, the electricity supply is insufficient, unreliable, and expensive. Ninety-nine percent of the firms experience frequent power outages, which cost them 22 percent of annual sales. Transport infrastructure is also insufficient and unreliable, especially road transport where 2 percent of consignment value is lost on average due to breakage and spoilage during transport. In Afghanistan, on the other hand, firms on average lose just 6 percent of annual sales due to power outages and 3 percent during transport. Furthermore, in Nepal, the conflict has caused physical destruction of existing infrastructure and has discouraged investments. While the government's spending for infrastructure development is similar to other South Asian countries as a portion of GDP, in absolute terms, such investments are insufficient and have been decreasing over time.

Electricity supply in Nepal is inadequate, unreliable, and expensive. Over the years, Nepal's demand for electricity has increased, but per capita consumption is still the lowest in the region, due to low coverage and insufficient supply. Nearly all firms regularly suffer power outages, with an average of 52 outages per month, each lasting 4.9 hours (Figure 9). There is, however, potential for improvement; Nepal's

Figure 9   Power Outages and Water Shortages per Typical Month in Nepal and Comparator Countries

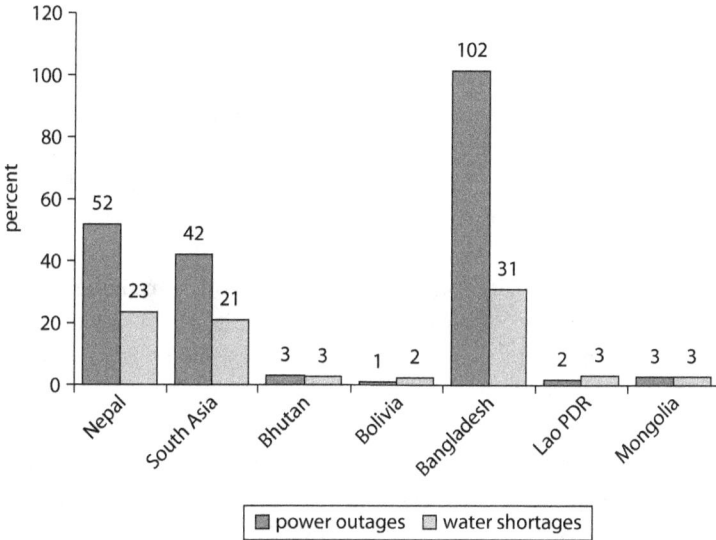

Source: World Bank Enterprise Surveys, latest available year.
Note: Comparison restricted to firms with 5+ employees in sectors surveyed in most countries in the comparator group, i.e., manufacturing, retail, wholesale, hotels and restaurants, transport, and travel agencies.

installed generation capacity is much lower than its hydropower generation potential and existing capacity is underutilized. Nepal could export energy to India and Bangladesh if its connection to India is improved.

In order to cope with irregular power availability, some firms use generators. The proportion of firms that own or share generators, however, is not particularly high in Nepal (at 15.7 percent of firms with five or more employees), especially considering that the average number of power outages in Nepal is much higher than in comparator countries. On average, 26 percent of the electricity used by the establishments comes from generators, which is generally more expensive than electricity from the national grid.

The inadequate and unreliable electricity supply in Nepal and the low electrification rate can be attributed to a number of reasons, including: high transmission and distribution losses, piecemeal expansion of the national grid, the high cost of power purchase agreements, inefficiencies at the Nepal Electricity Authority, and underutilization of the existing capacity. In addition, the conflict and post-conflict instability, the monopoly that characterized the hydropower sector in the past, governance problems, and the failure to see India as a viable destination for electricity exports, all discouraged investments to develop more than a very small part of the country's potential. While solving these problems is a long-term endeavor that needs to start now and requires a broad program of public support and funding for enhanced power supply, the investment climate for private hydropower developers can be improved in the short-term, for example by establishing a "one-window" agency to facilitate hydropower development. At the moment, Nepalese private hydropower developers suffer many obstacles (such as in obtaining licenses and permits, etc.).

Transport infrastructure is also inadequate and unreliable. Nepal's road density, at 0.6 km of road per 1,000 people, is the lowest in the region. More than half of the population lacks year-round ready access to roads and about 90 percent of Nepal's roads are concentrated in the lowland Terai. Disruptions in traffic on the main highway or connected roads frequently occur because of a lack of alternate routes, leading to losses in trade and shortages of essential commodities. Transport strikes and protests also often cause disruptions in transportation. Air transport is thriving and attracts significant private sector participation, while the railway network is almost non-existent. The transport system is also inefficient due to the poor condition of roads and obsolete transport services. More than one-third of the road network is not in trafficable condition and most of the vehicles are old and obsolete. There are also problems with syndicates and a lack of competition in the transport operators sector.

As a result, transport costs are high in Nepal. According to the Doing Business Report, the cost of exporting and importing a container is much higher in Nepal than in Bangladesh, India, and Pakistan. Pre-shipment transport costs in Nepal are estimated to be twice those of competitors in the region. In the manufacturing sector, 1.4 percent of shipments to domestic markets are lost due to breakage and spoilage (Figure 10).

Development of transport infrastructure is critical in Nepal. Nepal needs to increase funding to strategically expand, maintain, and rehabilitate its road network. Efforts should be made to connect all districts by all-season roads. These roads are low volume roads requiring low investment for an affordable and safe transport system. **The private sector could have a role in providing better transport services**. However, current volumes of trade traffic do not seem to demand high volume roads, limiting their investment appeal to the private sector. Therefore, viability gap funding should be explored and a Viability Gap Fund set up with government and donor resources. This effort should be complemented by an

Figure 10   Percentage of Shipments to Domestic Markets Lost Due to Breakage or Spoilage in Nepal and Comparator Countries

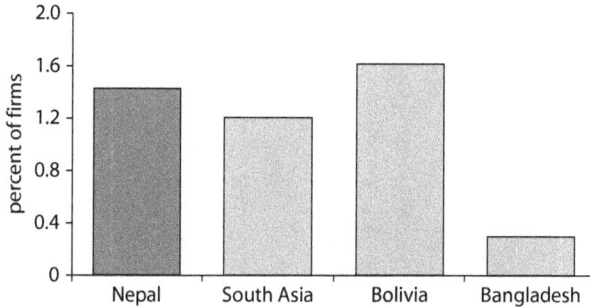

Source: World Bank Enterprise Surveys, latest available year.
Note: Comparison restricted to firms with 5+ employees in sectors surveyed in most countries in the comparator group, i.e., manufacturing, retail, wholesale, hotels and restaurants, transport, and travel agencies.

attempt to identify commercial corridors with potentially high traffic for private sector investment and PPPs. In addition, a detailed analysis and study of PPP options and funding modalities suitable for Nepal, given the low turnover, country risks, and capacity constraints of the local investors, should be undertaken. This should be coupled with more education on PPP options and funding modalities.

Access to Finance for Firms Needs to Be Expanded

Financial development is an important component of a country's ability to grow, and access to finance at the firm level is important for firm productivity and survival. Indeed the analysis of the performance of Nepalese enterprises shows that higher reliance on banks for borrowing working capital—as opposed to internal funds or informal sources—is linked to better performance.

While Nepal's financial sector is broad and expanding, firms' access to finance remains limited. Only 74 percent of the firms have a bank account and 39 percent have a line of credit or a loan from a financial institution. Most firms rely on internal funds to finance the bulk of their investments and their working capital needs. Very few firms use banks to finance investments (12 percent) and expenses (16 percent) (Figure 11). **As a result, registered firms consider access to finance as the third most important obstacle.** However, only 9 percent of the firms perceive it to be a major or severe constraint. Access to finance is a constraint especially for micro, small, and medium size

Figure 11   Access to Finance in Nepal and Comparator Countries

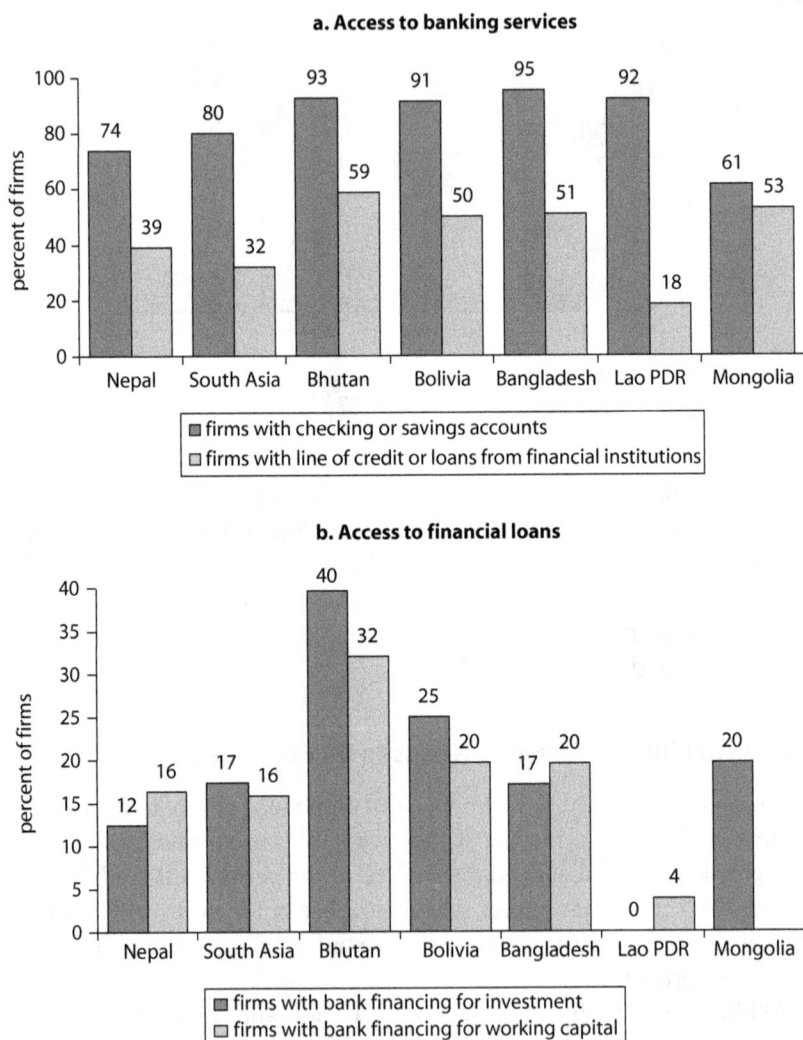

a. Access to banking services

- firms with checking or savings accounts
- firms with line of credit or loans from financial institutions

b. Access to financial loans

- firms with bank financing for investment
- firms with bank financing for working capital

Source: World Bank Enterprise Surveys, latest available year.
Note: Comparison restricted to firms with 5+ employees in sectors surveyed in most countries in the comparator group, i.e., manufacturing, retail, wholesale, hotels and restaurants, transport, and travel agencies.

enterprises (MSMEs). Large firms have good access to finance but still often choose not to resort to banks to finance their investments and operational expenses.[9]

In FY2007/08, only **23 percent of Nepalese firms applied for a loan.** Fifty-seven percent indicated that they had no need for a loan (in itself an indication that firms are not growing or investing beyond what their internal sources allow them to, reflecting a certain lack of dynamism and growth), 9.5 percent cited interest rates as being too high, another 9 percent cited high collateral requirements, 8 percent cited application procedures as being too burdensome, and 15 percent cited other reasons (Figure 12).

The reasons for limited access are complex, but include weak financial infrastructure (the absence of an operating registry to record liens on movable assets and the fact that the credit bureau only covers loans larger than Nrs 1 million), inability of banks to provide profitable lending to MSMEs at acceptable costs, and more subtle barriers such as eligibility criteria (by some measures Nepal has the highest number of documents required to access financial services) and lack of appropriate financial products (the most popular bank product, overdrafts, is inappropriate for many small businesses). MSMEs (the majority of firms in Nepal) are instead burdened by high collateral requirements and resort to internal sources of funding (which are invariably limited). The result is a suboptimal equilibrium of supply of and demand for financial services.

Collateral requirements on loans are part of the problem of access to finance. The main reason for scarce use of bank loans lies in excessive

Figure 12   Reasons Nepalese Firms Did Not Apply for a Line of Credit
percent of firms

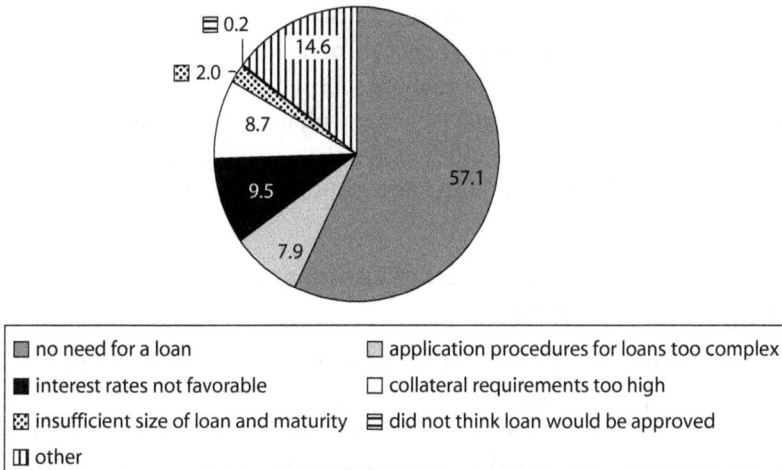

no need for a loan
interest rates not favorable
insufficient size of loan and maturity
other

application procedures for loans too complex
collateral requirements too high
did not think loan would be approved

Source: Nepal Enterprise Survey 2009.

Table 3   Strategies to Increase Access to Finance

What needs to be done	How?
Broaden the range of assets acceptable as collateral	• Operationalize the secured transaction registry envisaged by Secured Transaction Act • Create a registration database in which a public record of obligations secured by movable property can be made
Deepen the reach of the Credit Information Bureau (CIB)	• Expand the coverage of the CIB through improved MIS at both the CIB and participating FIs. • Provide services to MSMEs to help them access credit from banks more cheaply and rapidly
Enhance the financial literacy of MSMEs	• Design technical assistance and financial literacy training programs for MSMEs to develop and present bankable proposals and to keep better accounts
Develop the appropriate regulatory framework for mobile banking	• Issue NRB guidelines on mobile phone banking • Instruct mobile phone operators to make available USSD platform (as opposed to the SMS-based platform)

Source: Authors.

loan requirements: not only do banks require on average the highest values of collateral when compared to comparator countries (260 percent of the loan amount), they most commonly require personal assets of the owner as the type of collateral. Seventy percent of firms have partially or fully collaterized this way, (typically land and/or buildings of the owner). Further, there is a discrepancy between the type of collateral used by firms and the assets purchased.

To help lenders increase small business lending, the government could develop an enabling environment that makes small business lending safer, cheaper, and faster. This can be achieved by broadening the range of assets acceptable as collateral, deepening the reach of the CIB, downscaling commercial banks' lending, enhancing the financial literacy of MSMEs, and developing the appropriate regulatory framework for mobile banking. Table 3 presents some strategies to this end.

Rigid Labor Regulations Require Easing and Labor Relations Need Improving

There are three main interconnecting labor market issues in Nepal. First and foremost, labor is part of the political stability story in post-conflict Nepal. The labor supply is increasing at a time when conflict has ended and jobs need to be created for restless young entrants to the market. In addition, much of the employed labor is unionized and politicized, and takes part in politically motivated industrial action (which typically involve strikes and lock-outs). The second labor market issue that is very important for Nepal's economy is labor migration. The Nepalese labor market and economy have both been transformed by exponential growth in the number of Nepalese migrants. Finally, rigid labor rules and regulations and poor labor relations are a major source of grief for large firms. Furthermore, the discussion on labor issues needs to distinguish between the job-seekers and job-holders. Nepalese workers insist on rigid labor regulations; therefore, job-holders in the domestic market are generally well-protected; at the same time, such rigid regulations, when coupled with highly unionized labor, prevents sufficient job creation at home and forces many job-seekers to go abroad and work in much worse conditions.

The labor market has witnessed an increase in labor supply due to the demographic transition, the cessation of the armed conflict, and a reduction in labor demand following the recent economic crisis. The unemployment rate is relatively low (estimated at 2.8 percent by the 2008 Nepal Labor Force Survey); however, underemployment is very high (6.7 percent of the labor force), and unpaid/contributing family members comprise 44 percent of the workforce. An increasing share of the active labor force in Nepal is finding work abroad and the flow of remittances sent back to Nepal by migrant workers constitutes a significant proportion of GDP. The main push factors behind international migration from Nepal have been the armed conflict—especially after 2001—and limited private sector employment growth.

Nepal has one of the most rigid regulatory frameworks in South Asia. Nepal ranks 150 out of 181 countries in the world according to *Doing Business* data in terms of the flexibility of labor regulations. Such rigid regulations reduce incentives to hire workers through formal contracts, resulting in high levels of unpaid work and underemployment.

Labor laws also provide for minimum wages with very little differentiation across skill levels; as a result, labor productivity and investments in human capital are low. In firms with five employees or more, one-fourth of the workers have a primary school level education or less and another 38 percent have a general secondary school degree. Manufacturing firms in Nepal have a low share of skilled workers employed in the production process (58 percent) (Figure 13), and only 7 percent of the firms offer formal training to permanent full-time employees.

Figure 13   Total Number of Skilled and Unskilled Production Workers per Firm in Nepal and Comparator Countries

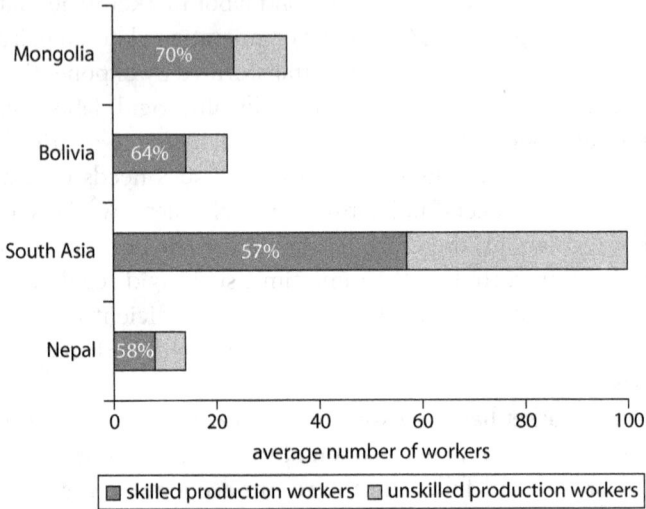

Source: World Bank Enterprise Surveys, latest available year.
Note: Comparison restricted to firms with 5+ employees in sectors surveyed in most countries in the comparator group, i.e., manufacturing, retail, wholesale, hotels and restaurants, transport, and travel agencies. Skilled workers are shown as a percentage of total workers.

Regardless of the sector, size is what matters when it comes to labor regulations. Fifty-five percent of large firms consider labor regulations a major or very severe obstacle (compared to 3 percent overall) and 26 percent of large firms consider an inadequately educated workforce as a major or very severe obstacle (compared to 4 percent overall). At the same time, larger firms are more likely to offer formal training (45 percent of them do) and have higher labor productivity, on average. Labor regulations, therefore, discourage firm growth. In fact, firms are on average small (employing 6.4 workers) and in the three years before the 2009 Enterprise Survey, the average annual growth rate in employment was 3.9 percent; but 75 percent of the firms did not increase the number of permanent workers at all.[10]

Despite the established legislative and institutional arrangements, industrial relations in Nepal are deteriorating due to a lack of capacity of the government to enforce the arrangements and monitor compliance on the part of both employers and employees. Trade union activities are on the rise, disrupting productivity. Unions are mainly active in medium and especially in large firms, but the participation rate tends to be high in all firms that have them; 64.7 percent of the firms lost working days due to trade union actions (with an average loss of 15.8 working days).

Table 4   Strategies to Ease Labor Regulations and Improve Labor Relations

What needs to be done	How?
Reduce non-wage costs of labor by increasing flexibility	• Review the Bonus Act 1973 to provide flexibility to employers and relax mandatory requirements • Introduce employment contract system to provide employers with more options for employees with more wage differentiation • Pilot flexible labor regimes in special economic zones
Improve monitoring	• Encourage direct dialogue between employers and labor to break the link with politically motivated industrial action • Introduce independent labor inspection to help the government resolve labor disputes • Create new labor court branches to increase efficiency in dealing with labor cases

Source: Authors.

Political problems and wages were the main disputed issues that led to trade union action.

Rigid regulations discourage employment growth. The rigid regulations that characterize Nepal's labor market—and in particular the guarantee of employment and restriction against laying off workers included in the Labor Act of 1992—reduce incentives to hire workers through formal channels. Provisions for minimum wages and a narrowing wage gap between skilled and unskilled workers take away incentives to improve labor productivity and accumulate human capital.

Policies aimed at introducing some flexibility in the labor market that would reduce non-wage costs for employers, allow for better monitoring, and improve labor relations, should be enacted to provide incentives to workers and firms to improve human capital (Table 4). Investments for training by firms and greater educational attainment among Nepal's labor force should also be encouraged.

Governance, Regulations, Licensing, and Informality

The single aspect of the investment climate that most deeply affects firms in Nepal is political stability. For 89 percent of the firms, business operations were disrupted by political changes and instability; 90 percent of the firms perceive political instability to be a major or very severe obstacle and 69.6 percent ranked it as the most important obstacle. Political instability is an equally severe problem across industries, regions, and firm sizes and ages.

Corruption is seen as a major obstacle by one in five firms (the fourth major or very severe constraint after political instability, electricity, and transport). On the one hand, 63 percent of the firms perceive the court system to be fair and uncorrupted. On the other hand, Nepal scores poorly in Transparency International's Corruption Perception Index 2009[11]—143 out of 180 countries and second to last among its comparator countries. This discrepancy could be explained by the unfortunate fact that firms are so used to paying bribes (which are generally inexpensive), that it has become part of their business and they do not perceive it as a big issue. By this measure, Nepal appears to be doing better than Afghanistan, which ranks second to last in Transparency International's Corruption Perception Index 2009 and where more than half of the firms (54 percent) see corruption as a major issue and only 17 of the firms see the court system as uncorrupted.

However, the Enterprise Survey reveals that the amount of time spent dealing with regulations and obtaining permits and licenses is often lower than in comparator countries (Figure 14). Dealing with regulations is more difficult for large firms. On average, 7 percent of the firms perceive tax rates and tax administration to be a major obstacle, but the proportions are 24 percent and 35 percent, respectively, among large firms.

To help ease the regulatory burden for large firms, dealing with regulations and taxes should be simplified as much as possible, in particular, the number of payments and the time involved in paying taxes and the time and procedures required to obtain construction permits. Alleviating the regulatory burden on large firms, and on registered firms in general, is also important in order not to discourage informal firms from registering and small firms from growing. Finally, predictability in the interpretation of laws and regulations is lacking and needs to be improved.

Informality is pervasive in Nepal's non-agricultural sector, mainly for two reasons: 1) the inability of the formal sector in Nepal to generate enough employment and economic activity, and 2) the poor investment climate in Nepal. Having such a large informal sector presents challenges to policy makers with regard to working conditions, legal and social protection of workers, productivity growth, training and skills development, and foregone tax revenues (informal firms in Nepal are less productive, employ less, and grow less than formal ones). Informal firms also lack incentives to formalize. According to the 2008 Labor Force Survey, the informal economy in Nepal accounts for 70 percent of total non-agricultural employment. During the last nine years, the

Figure 14   Time Spent Obtaining Licenses and Dealing with Regulations in Nepal and Comparator Countries

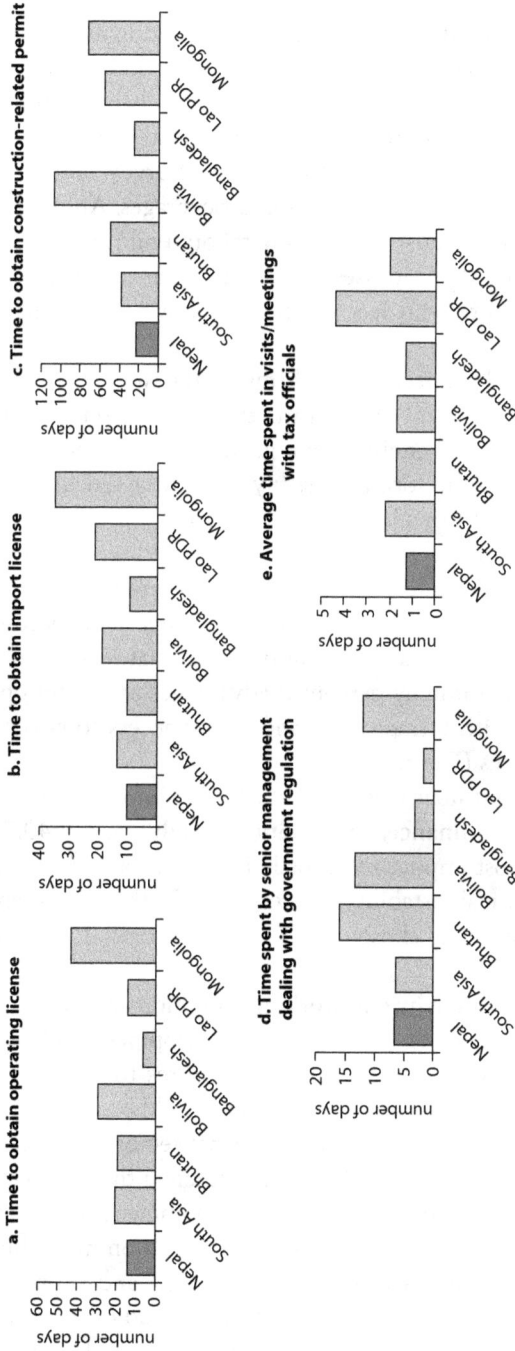

a. Time to obtain operating license

b. Time to obtain import license

c. Time to obtain construction-related permit

d. Time spent by senior management dealing with government regulation

e. Average time spent in visits/meetings with tax officials

Source: World Bank Enterprise Surveys, latest available year.

Note: Comparison restricted to firms with 5+ employees in sectors surveyed in most countries in the comparator group, i.e., manufacturing, retail, wholesale, hotels and restaurants, transport, and travel agencies.

population employed in the non-agricultural informal sector grew by 29.3 percent. The survey data show limited downstream linkages to other firms and, therefore, limited linkages to formal firms, hindering the sector's ability to play a role in the supply chain for the formal sector. Most informal firms are very small and mostly employ unpaid workers. In the Nepal 2009 Informal Enterprise Survey sample, 48 percent of the firms produced or sold food and beverages. Another 21 percent were in the apparel industry, including tailors, embroiderers, and apparel producers. Informal businesses are predominantly owned by a single owner (90 percent) who has, on average, low educational attainment and little training.

Only half of the unregistered firms in the survey would like to be registered. For 46 percent of the firms, the main reason for not registering is because they see no benefit from registration. Thus, most informal firms choose not to become formal possibly so as to avoid many of the constraints that formal firms face (labor regulations would be the main culprit). Other common reasons for not registering are the difficulties involved in obtaining information on the registration process and the fees involved in the registration process. On the other hand, access to finance is the main advantage that informal firms associate with formal registration; two other commonly perceived advantages are better opportunities for negotiation with formal firms and better access to government programs and services (Figure 15).

The main investment climate obstacles for informal firms are lack of demand, access to finance, and political instability. For 40.7 percent of the firms, the most important obstacle faced is lack of demand. Access to finance and political instability are, respectively, the second and the third obstacles, having being chosen by 25.4 percent and 23.7 percent of the firms (Figure 16).

Improving productivity and working conditions of informal firms is an important component of private sector development and of the growth and poverty reduction agenda. While measures to bring informal firms into the formal sector are important, they should be coupled with efforts to improve the performance of the informal sector. In particular: i) linkages to the formal sector should be strengthened through technical assistance (provided by small business development agencies and NGOs focusing on small and micro-businesses) focused on marketing and business planning, as well as through strengthened and simplified contract enforcement. The latter would support the spread of subcontracting and franchising, which can be prime avenues for linkages with formal

Figure 15   Improvements Nepalese Firms Believe Could Be Obtained by Registering

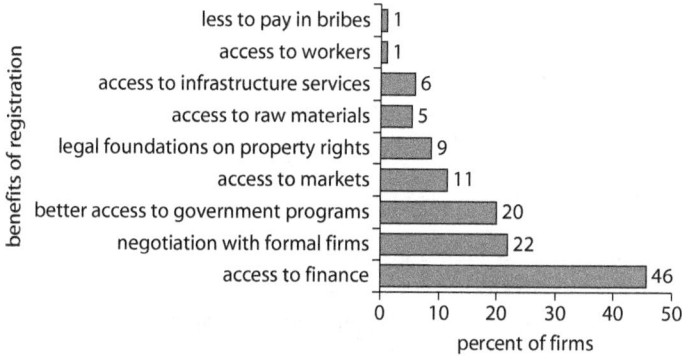

Source: Nepal Enterprise Survey 2009.

Figure 16   Investment Climate Obstacles Ranked Most Important for Informal Firms in Nepal

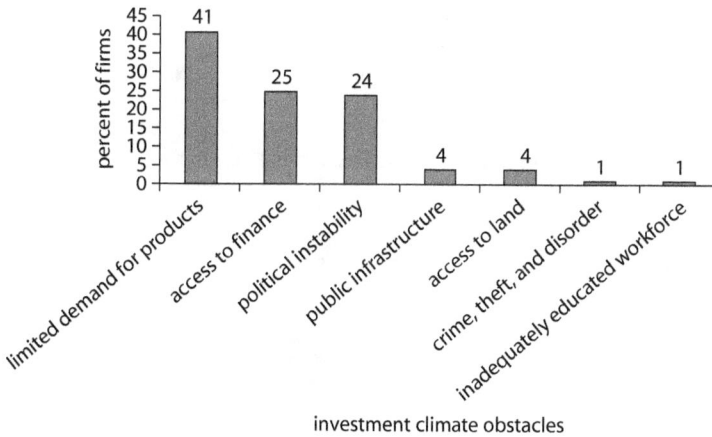

Source: Nepal Enterprise Survey 2009.
Note: Percent of firms ranking obstacle as most important.

enterprises. Linkages to the formal sector can help informal firms obtain more credit and access to more advanced technologies; ii) human capital development should be promoted through better educational attainment and through active labor market interventions, such as training and skill-development programs, which can be provided by the government or

NGOs and the private sector; iii) registration procedures should be simplified and entry costs reduced, especially in terms of information about registration procedures, which are usually designed for medium and large firms; and iv) better access to finance should be promoted, especially through microfinance programs that target business, and through establishment of a movable collateral registry.

Developing Nepal's External Sector

The external sector in Nepal accounts for only 47 percent of GDP and exports are concentrated in low value-added, low growth segments, and are limited to a few markets. Ninety percent of Nepal's exports go to three countries (India, the United States, and Germany). The country's location, low productivity, high tariffs, lengthy customs procedures (time to clear customs is high for importers and imports appear to elicit informal payments), and poor transportation infrastructure hinder export growth. As a consequence, only 3.8 percent of enterprises export their products; even within manufacturing, exporters only amount to 7 percent of the firms (Figure 17). On the other hand, in Afghanistan, 6 percent of non-micro firms are exporters.

Figure 17   Percentage of Exporting and Importing Firms in Nepal and Comparator Countries

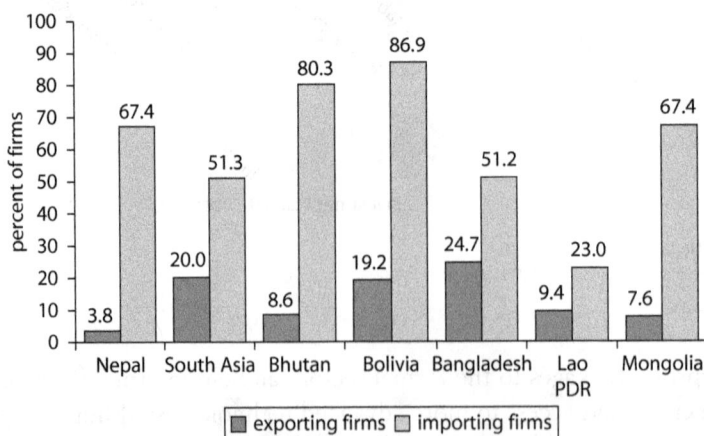

Source: World Bank Enterprise Surveys, latest available year.
Note: Comparison restricted to firms with 5+ employees in sectors surveyed in most countries in the comparator group, i.e., manufacturing, retail, wholesale, hotels and restaurants, transport, and travel agencies.

Compared to the average firm, exporters are typically larger, older, have higher labor productivity, and are more technologically advanced because they are more likely to use technology licensed from foreign-owned companies, have internationally-recognized quality certifications, and register more patents in Nepal.

Road is by far the main means of transport used by exporters in the manufacturing industry. 92.2 percent of the exports for manufacturing firms were transported by road, 2.7 percent by air, and 5.1 percent by sea. Air transport of exported goods is limited to enterprises located in the Central region where the Tribhuvan International Airport in Kathmandu is located. However, transportation is a major obstacle for exporting due to poor road infrastructure and low airfreight capacity, coupled with high transport costs. Exporters and importers also face breakage or spoilage losses, which can be ascribed to poor transport infrastructure and/or poor management of the transportation system. The most important obstacles in transportation are strikes for road transport, and airfreight capacity and airport customs for air transport.

Given its location, Nepal is dependent on China and India in terms of trade, aid, investment, tourism, and remittances. In particular, Nepal trades over 60 percent of its total imports and total exports with India, which is also the most important destination for work migrants. This is not surprising given Nepal's geographical position and non-trade links to both countries. However, these relations are lopsided with Nepal facing a huge trade deficit and attracting very little investment.

Only a marginal part of the bilateral trade between China and India goes through Nepal. Nepal has been unable to become part of a global production network or be inserted into regional value chains precisely because of the deterioration of its business environment. Most of the bilateral trade between India and China travels by sea; the land route through Nepal could significantly reduce transport time and costs for some routes, but political stability as well as transport infrastructure and services need to be improved.

The external sector in Nepal is small and suffers from low productivity, high tariffs, and poor transportation infrastructure. Nepal needs to exploit its economic relations with India and China and become a part of regional value chains. In order to do this, it will be necessary to improve terms of trade and to either increase exports (both in value and volume) of existing products or identify new products with potential for export to China and India. Another strategic option would be to take advantage of the proximity to India and China and strengthen the trade sector in order

Table 5   Strategies to Increase Trade with India and China

What needs to be done	How? (see main report for details)
Short-term policies	• Bring shipping lines to Inland Clearance Depot (dry-port) • Improve airport warehouse
Medium-term policies	• Develop and enact comprehensive capacity building program for Customs Department • Address labor issues (no work no pay)
Long-term policies	• Amend Export-Import Act and enact the Trade Promotion Act for trade facilitation

Source: Authors.

to become a transit economy between these two countries. A number of reforms can be undertaken in the short-, medium-, and long-term to reach these objectives (Table 5).

Tourism Sector and Potential for Future Growth

Nepal has abundant tourism potential owing to its natural beauty; bio-diversity; ethnic, linguistic, and social diversity; and historical and cultural wealth. Tourist arrivals in Nepal have grown from just over 6,000 in 1962 to over half a million in 2007—despite a decade-long conflict, which left prime tourist attractions damaged and underdeveloped. Tourism is also a key service export for Nepal, with foreign exchange earnings amounting to 1.3 percent of GDP. Tourism firms also tend to be more productive than the average private sector firm in Nepal. India is Nepal's largest source for international visitor arrivals (23 percent of total air arrivals) mainly because of direct access, liberal travel arrangements, and convertibility of the Indian currency; the EU, the UK, France, and Germany are consistent sources of long-haul traffic.

Tourism firms are more productive and perform better than the private sector firms overall. Private firms associated with the tourism industry—hotels and restaurants and travel agencies—are mostly micro enterprises (52 percent), younger enterprises, and mostly in the Central region. Despite being mostly micro-firms, tourism firms employ on average more workers (14 workers) than the overall private sector in Nepal (six workers). This is driven by the fact that the larger tourism firms (especially hotels and restaurants) tend to be quite larger than the average large private sector firm.[12] Therefore, labor productivity, as measured by average sales per worker, is 1.6 times higher for tourism firms than the rest of the private sector firms. Also, unlike the rest of the private sector, although employment growth has stagnated, productivity growth has rebounded strongly with the end of the armed conflict over the past three years, and has risen by an annual average of 18.6 percent.

Most tourism firms expect to expand their activities, especially travel agencies, and have made investments to improve their competitiveness either by upgrading their classification, improving their facilities, or upgrading services provided to clients (Figure 18). However, only 1.5 percent of the firms have an internationally recognized quality certification.

For Nepal's tourism sector to reach its full potential, it must address infrastructure constraints in the medium and long term. Nepal's road network is underdeveloped and airports in the mountainous regions are in need of further investment. Over two thirds of the tourism firms surveyed complain that their clients face transportation difficulties in getting to their establishments; firms in the Western region are especially concerned by transportation difficulties. Moreover, 97 percent of the firms report suffering losses due to transportation difficulties.

Figure 18   Percentage of Nepalese Tourism Firms Investing to Improve Competitiveness

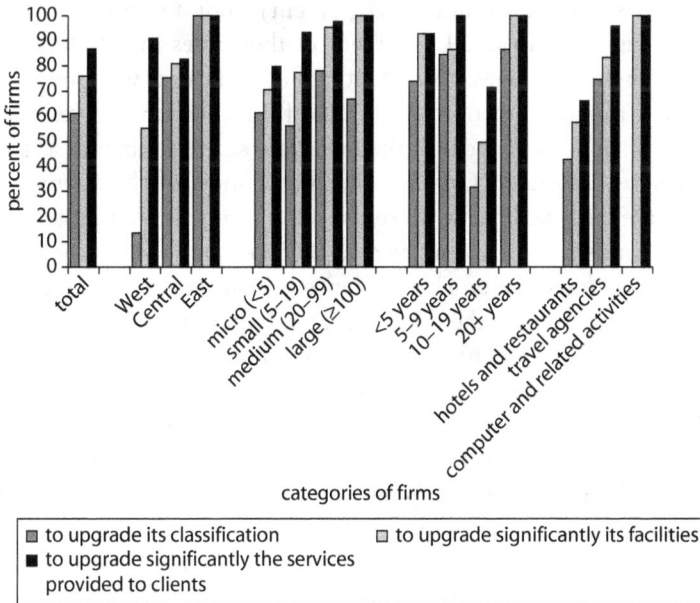

Source: Nepal Enterprise Survey 2009.

Table 6   Strategies to Strengthen the Tourism Sector

What needs to be done	How?
Invest in tourism-related infrastructure to enhance accessibility to tourism establishments	• Develop selected small airfields within Nepal • Develop better connecting nodes between road and air travel • Invest in energy efficiency measures • Reform licensing/approval processes to attract FDI
Develop skills of labor force	• Develop targeted training to improve quality of service • Pilot the introduction of tourism as part of school curriculum
Improve implementation of existing laws and regulations	• End subsidized parking fees for domestic airlines • Build capacity in tourism-related government institutions • Conduct comprehensive data collection on hotel/guesthouse/lodge occupancy to prepare a proper marketing strategy • Resolve the issues of land ownership rights and cumbersome court procedures to encourage FDI
Promote quality and environmental certification	• Develop proper regulation and monitoring of certifications to expand opportunities in eco-tourism, etc.

Source: Authors.

Almost all of the tourism firms consider acute shortages of electricity a major or severe constraint (97.7 percent)—not a surprise, given that tourism firms lost up to 31.3 percent of their sales in FY2007/08 as a result of these shortages. Availability of an educated workforce is also considered a significant obstacle for the firms. Due to the very limited access to finance, 11 percent of the firms rate access to finance as a major or very severe obstacle. On the other hand, most of the tourism firms sampled are fairly satisfied with services for immigration, tourism regulation, and tourism centers. On average, 32.5 percent of the tourism firms choose to pay for security. The incidence is higher among large and older firms as well as firms in the Central region (where most of the firms sustained costs of over 5 percent of their sales for security services).

Developing Nepal as an attractive, safe, and sustainable tourism destination requires a holistic approach wherein the government, the private sector, and PPPs work collectively. The government's new tourism policy highlights the need to identify new tourism destinations, develop tourism-related infrastructure, provide reliable service delivery to tourists, and enhance the quality of such services. This can be achieved through attracting investments, both private and foreign, into the sector, and enhancing the capacity of the sector by: i) proper tourism planning through PPPs; ii) capacity building in tourism related public institutions to ensure competitive airline regulation, tourism marketing, licensing of tourism establishments, etc.; and iii) support for micro and small enterprises, which bear the burden of infrastructure constraints and instability disproportionately. Table 6 presents specific recommendations for some of the main obstacles facing tourism firms in Nepal.

Notes

1. All GDP data are from the Nepal Rastra Bank. Data were compiled from the archive of Nepal Rastra Bank Recent Macroeconomic Situation Reports (NRB 2009, 2010) to create a monthly time-series database, which was used for the analysis in this ICA. http://www.nrb.org.np/ofg/press.php?tp=recent_macroeconomic&&vw=15.

2. Poverty rates are calculated based on the National Living Standards Survey (NLSS). Dates refer, therefore, to the data collection period. The first NLSS was carried out between June 1995 and June 1996 and the second NLSS was conducted between April 2003 and April 2004 (CBS 1996, 2004).

3. World Bank 2000.

4. The average size of the non-micro firms (the firms with 5 employees and more) is only 14.1 employees (much less than all comparator countries, see Table 1), while the overall average for the whole private sector is six employees.

5. When excluding micro-enterprises, the average annual employment growth rate for Nepalese firms increases to 7 percent.

6. Given Enterprise Survey data limitations, no total factor productivity (TFP) calculations or cross-country comparisons of productivity among exporting firms were possible. In addition, given that there are no time series data, the analysis can only observe correlations and associations, and not causation.

7. Therefore, in Afghanistan, despite the chronic lack of security and protracted hostilities outside the main cities, the fact that there was a stable government in the main urban centers seems to be important for enterprises.

8. Indeed, the study team observed that some of the firms that were enumerated a couple of months earlier were shut down when the enumerators went to conduct the interview. The manufacturing enterprises located in the industrial area of Kathmandu, especially, were closed or were in the process of being shut down due to excessive load shedding (power outages) and political problems.

9. In Afghanistan, despite its much less developed financial sector, 73 percent of non-micro firms have a bank account, however, unlike Nepal, only 3 percent have a credit line or loan and a meager 0.7 percent of firms' investments are financed by banks.

10. The number of employees is computed on the basis of the number of full-time workers, both permanent and temporary (the latter weighted by the number of months they were employed in the firm). Employment growth, instead, only takes into consideration full-time permanent workers, due to the lack of data on the number of temporary workers in the past.

11. Source: http://www.transparency.org/policy_research/surveys_indices/cpi/2009/cpi_2009_table.

12. In addition, tourism firms show very limited growth in size over the life of the firm—remaining mostly within the same initial size group for most of their lives.

CHAPTER 1

Introduction

Since the civil unrest ended in 2006, Nepal's gross domestic product (GDP) growth rate has averaged 4.5 percent and relative macroeconomic stability has so far been maintained primarily through prudent fiscal management. However, downside risks lie ahead. This chapter analyzes the macro-environment in which Nepalese firms operate. It shows that agriculture remains the largest employer whereas the services sector has been the growth driver. It also highlights how a strong dependence on remittances exacerbates the country's structural weaknesses, resulting in an erosion of competitiveness, and in an increasingly vulnerable macro-financial environment. It concludes by highlighting the importance of building a stronger private sector and the role it plays in accelerating and diversifying the sources of economic growth.

Macroeconomic Environment: Resilient Economy Despite Political Uncertainty, but Risks Lie Ahead

After a decade of conflict and civil unrest, Nepal's political parties signed a Comprehensive Peace Agreement in 2006, which paved the way for Constituent Assembly elections in 2008. The transition to peace and prosperity is, however, complex and prolonged. **The civil unrest and the ensuing political instability have adversely affected business confidence** and economic performance—already constrained by poor infrastructure and rigid labor regulations.

Despite continued political uncertainty, macroeconomic stability has been maintained and GDP has grown by 4.5 percent on average during the four years since the end of the conflict (NRB 2009, 2010).[1] The exchange rate peg to the Indian Rupee and prudent fiscal policy thus far have anchored relative macroeconomic stability, while remittance inflows, which exceed a quarter of GDP, have ensured that a comfortable level of international reserves could be maintained despite a widening trade deficit (NRB 2009, 2010).

Poverty incidence has declined and social indicators are improving (Table 1.1). Although Nepal's per capita income (of around US$400) and human development indicators lag behind the rest of the region (*indeed, Nepal remains the poorest and slowest growing economy in South Asia*), there have been improvements in health and education outcomes and the national poverty level has come down significantly (from 42 percent in 2000 to around 31 percent in 2008 and to a 2010 estimate of less than 20 percent) (World Bank and CBS 2010)—largely driven by substantial remittance inflows.

However, the difficult investment climate, due to the prolonged conflict, continuing political uncertainties, and violence with impunity, as well as the absence of key reform implementation, has limited the potential peace dividend, and growth has come down. GDP growth, which rose to 5.3 percent in FY2007/08, immediately after the arrival of peace, quickly came down to the 3–3.5 percent range, the level of average growth during the insurgency (the period from 2000 to 2007) (NRB 2009, 2010). The country's economic potential (which could be abundant in terms of hydropower, agriculture, and labor supply) remains untapped.

Table 1.1   Poverty and Social Indicators

	Nepal		South Asia	
	2000	*2008*	*2000*	*2008*
Population below poverty line (US$1.25/ day, %)	41.8	30.9	34.3	28.6
GNI per capita (US$)	220.0	400.0	751.0	1,469.0
Gross primary enrollment (%)	116.7	123.9	104.0	105.9
Infant mortality (per 1,000 live births)	62.9	43.1	58.8	45.2
Human Development Index	0.5	0.6	0.6	0.6

Source: World Bank 2010a.
Note: South Asia includes Bangladesh, Bhutan, India, Maldives, Nepal, Pakistan, and Sri Lanka. Afghanistan is excluded due to lack of data.

Fiscal policy has been generally prudent but is gradually becoming expansionary. Nepal's fiscal prudence has been an important anchor of macroeconomic stability, and given weaknesses in external and financial sectors, needs to remain so. However, there is room for improvement in terms of quality of spending. The budget deficit increased by around 13.8 percent in FY2009/10 to reach 3.3 percent of GDP and continues to rise (NRB 2009, 2010). Historically, low deficits were a product of low budget utilization due to capacity constraints. But in recent years, thanks to reforms in revenue administration, strong customs receipts, and increased value-added tax (VAT) collection, strong performance in revenue collection has also been a key contributor to low fiscal deficit levels. Revenues rose from 12 percent of GDP in FY2006/07 to 14.8 percent in FY2008/09. The expansion in tax and duty collections reflected higher consumption, supported by remittances from abroad. While Nepal's public debt level at 40 percent of GDP is well below its comparators, and is assessed as only a modest level of debt distress[2], the possibility of a worsening external position would require that the domestically financed deficit remain at current levels (NRB 2009, 2010).

Monetary policy on the other hand has been accommodative, allowing a near 30 percent money growth over the past two years. Lax monetary policy kept the interest rate structure negative in real terms from FY2006/07 to FY2008/09 (NRB 2009, 2010). It was lower than the Indian rates most of that time, exerting pressure toward shifting Nepalese Rupees into Indian Currency holdings—especially when confidence in the Nepalese Rupee weakened.

Nepal's financial sector has grown rapidly in recent years in an environment of limited central bank supervision, loose bank licensing policy, and rapidly inflating asset prices. While some of this growth is a reflection of the deepening of the system, rapid proliferation of banking sector licenses and credit expansion have coincided with sharp increases in real estate and stock prices, which took place after FY2006/07 when the peace process began: average prices of commercial property have increased six times from 2007 to January 2010. In the absence of other investment opportunities, commercial bank credit is largely extended to the real estate sector and construction activities. Credit to real estate increased by 127 percent, while credit to housing rose by 25 percent year on year through January 2010. Credit to the construction sector doubled from FY2006/07 to FY2008/09. Loans under other categories are also linked to land—in fact 70 percent of all commercial bank loans are collateralized by real estate (NRB 2009, 2010).

However, the proliferation of financial institutions and the rapid growth of credit have not translated into an easing of credit constraints for firms in Nepal. This is the case across the urban-rural divide and even among firms based in the Central Region, which tend to be located closer to financial institutions.

The trade deficit in FY2009/10 increased to around 28.8 percent of GDP. It has widened considerably over time as imports grew by 28 percent and 33 percent in FY2008/09 and FY2009/10, respectively, while exports declined by 9.7 percent and grew by only 14.2 percent over the same period. In fact, imports as a share of GDP have become almost four times as large as exports, as the GDP share of exports has continuously declined over the last eight years (NRB 2009, 2010). The fall in exports was mainly due to fall in demand, partly due to an appreciating currency. The overall increase in imports is due to the increase in imports of oil, gold[3], and consumer goods, fueled by strong remittance growth (Figure 1.1).

High remittances offset the high trade deficit and are keeping the economy afloat, but the dependence on remittances is increasing the economy's vulnerability. Inflows grew by 42.5 percent and 47 percent in FY2007/08 and FY2008/09, respectively (allowing real national disposable income to grow by around 8 percent a year). However, in FY2009/10 the year on year growth rate of remittances dropped to 10.5 percent—a significant slowdown (NRB 2009, 2010).

The widening current account deficit, slowing remittance growth, and capital flight as a result of deteriorating confidence in the economy, contributed to a 13 percent decline in international reserves in the first half

Figure 1.1   Nepal Trade Balance and Current Account Balance, 2000–09
percent of GDP per fiscal year

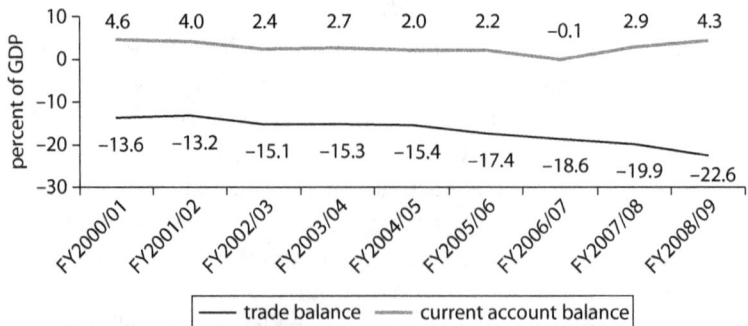

Source: NRB 2009, 2010; World Bank staff calculations.

of FY2009/10 (NRB 2009, 2010). Reserves came down from nine months to five months of imports of goods and services during the period. This reserve loss precipitated an IMF program, and was partially reversed by the end of FY2009/10.

Financial sector vulnerability has also increased because high levels of remittances, in the absence of adequate productive investment opportunities, poured into the real estate sector creating a domestic bubble. Commercial banks and other financial institutions appear to have funded a significant portion of speculative activities and are exposed to real estate lending. A fall in real estate prices could strain these institutions and rapidly erode depositor confidence.

Growth Dynamics: Growth Driven by Consumption and Services

The services sector has been the engine of growth in Nepal over the past decade because industry has stagnated and manufacturing has actually declined. While low productivity agriculture keeps a large portion of the population employed, migration is changing the employment pattern and real wages are rising—further jeopardizing the industrial and agricultural sectors.

In the past two decades, while other South Asian countries transformed their economies and expanded their manufacturing base and competitiveness, Nepal's economic performance has deteriorated. As can be seen in Figure 1.2, from the mid- 1990s onward, other South Asian countries such as Bangladesh, India, and Sri Lanka all have experienced significant value added growth in the services sector. However, in parallel, unlike Nepal, they also managed to achieve value added growth in industry, particularly in the manufacturing sub-sector for most years (Figure 1.2). In sharp contrast, Nepal achieved only meager value added growth in all sectors, but particularly performed worse in manufacturing (World Bank 2010a).

Services

The services sector is the largest contributor to Nepal's GDP with 49 percent, followed by agriculture and mining (36 percent) and industry (15 percent). The services sector has been the recent engine of growth. Its contribution to GDP has risen from 30 percent in the 1990s to around 50 percent currently (Figure 1.3a). The sector grew

Figure 1.2   Value Added Growth by Sector 1995–2008, Selected South Asian Countries

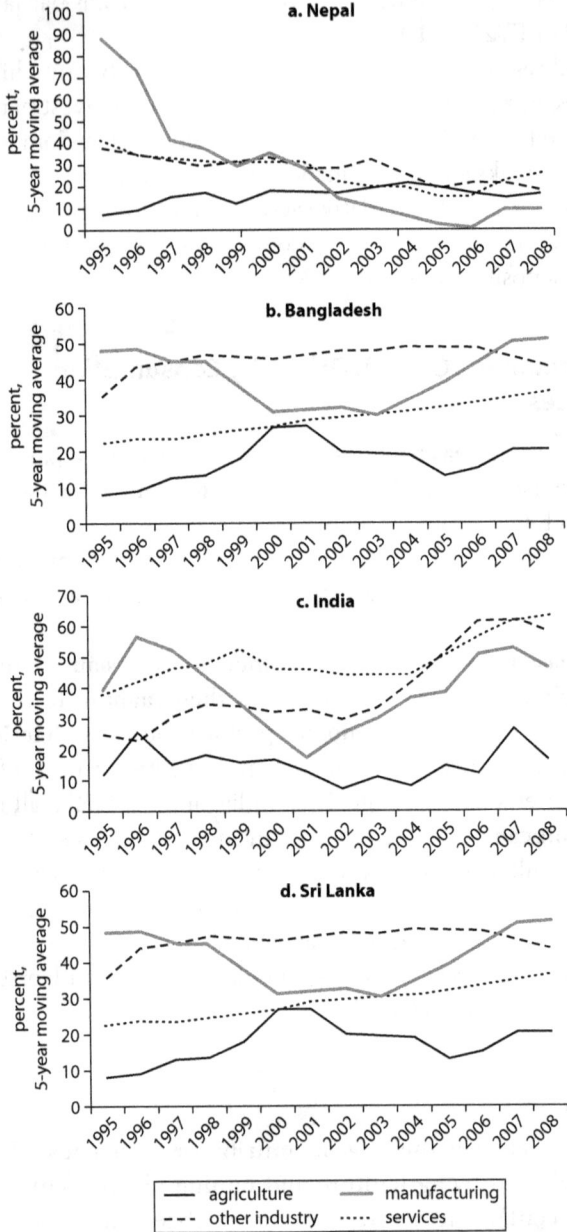

Source: World Bank 2010a.
Note: Sectoral value added growth rates calculated as 5-year moving averages based on constant US$ in 2000 prices.

Figure 1.3   Composition of Real GDP in Nepal, 1990–2008, and Sector Growth Rate, FY2002–FY2009

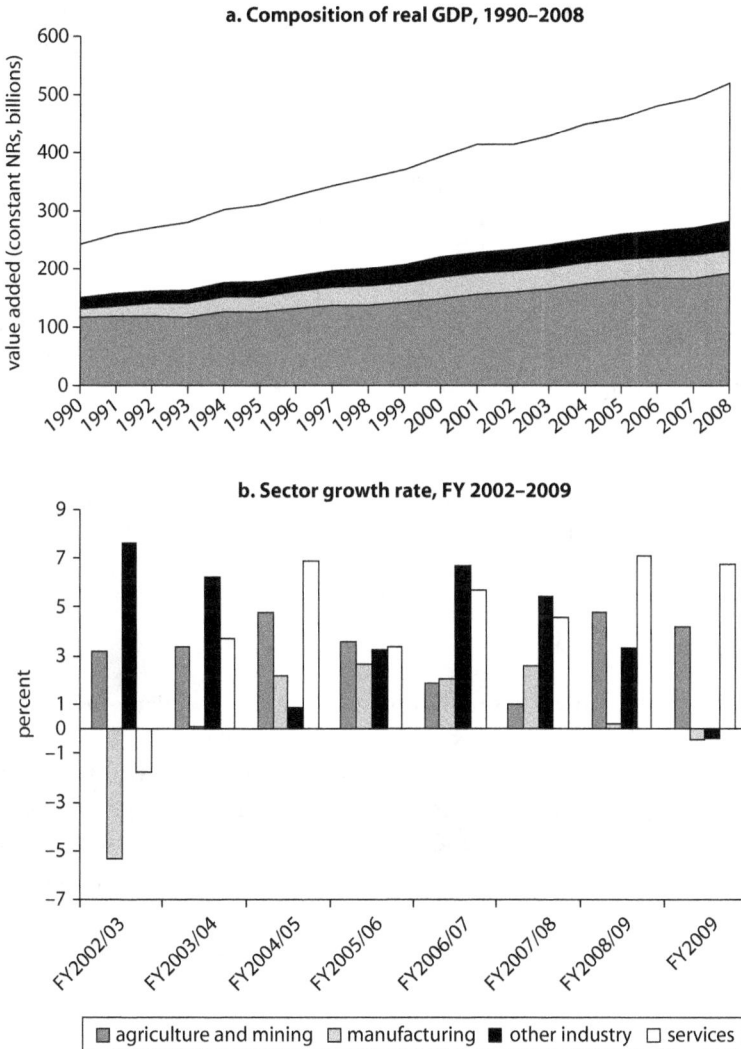

a. Composition of real GDP, 1990–2008

b. Sector growth rate, FY 2002–2009

agriculture and mining   manufacturing   other industry   services

Sources: World Bank 2010a.

by an average of 6 percent since FY2006/07 (Figure 1.3b). However, services account for only 15.3 percent of adult employment (World Bank 2010a).

Within the services sector, wholesale and retail trade, and transportation services have been the key contributors to GDP growth. Wholesale and retail trade constituted 13 percent of GDP in FY2008/09 and its contribution to real GDP growth was on average the highest in the past two years. The transport, storage, and communications sub-sector (9 percent of GDP) was the second largest contributor to real GDP growth. Despite the importance of tourism for Nepal's economy, the direct contribution of the hotels and restaurants sub-sector to Nepal's GDP is only 2 percent, and its contribution to GDP growth was 0.08 percent in FY2008/09 (Figure 1.4) (NRB 2009, 2010).

The two key service sub-sectors that benefited from the influx of remittances are financial intermediation and real estate activities. Financial intermediation constitutes 4 percent of GDP and has grown rapidly over the past five years. Real estate renting and business activities constitute 8 percent of GDP and have been growing over time. On the social service delivery front, education activities constituted 6 percent of GDP and have been a significant contributor to GDP growth with an average of 0.5 percent over the last decade. The education sector will continue to be an important sector for real GDP growth especially given the demand for private education services supported by remittance inflows (NRB 2009, 2010).

Agriculture

Nepal's GDP growth strongly depends on highly volatile agricultural growth. Agriculture accounts for 36 percent of GDP, and employs about 74 percent of the workforce (NRB 2009, 2010). The agricultural sector has significant linkages to industrial production; the manufacturing sector processes a large share of agricultural products, such as pulses, jute, sugarcane, tobacco, and grain. Agricultural production in Nepal, as in the rest of the South Asia region, is largely rain fed and therefore output is highly volatile. For example, due to prolonged drought and unseasonal rains, paddy production (21 percent of agricultural output) fell by 11 percent in FY2009/10, profoundly impacting the economy and pushing a large number of Nepalese to the edge of hunger.[4]

Industry and Manufacturing
Industry has made a limited contribution to GDP. The industrial sector's share remained constant at 16–17 percent, and in the past few years declined to 15 percent. Industry's share is very low even when compared to rest of the South Asian countries which, like Nepal, are mainly growing on the back of the services sector. Industrial growth,

Figure 1.4   Nepalese Real GDP Composition by Sector, FY2008/09
percent

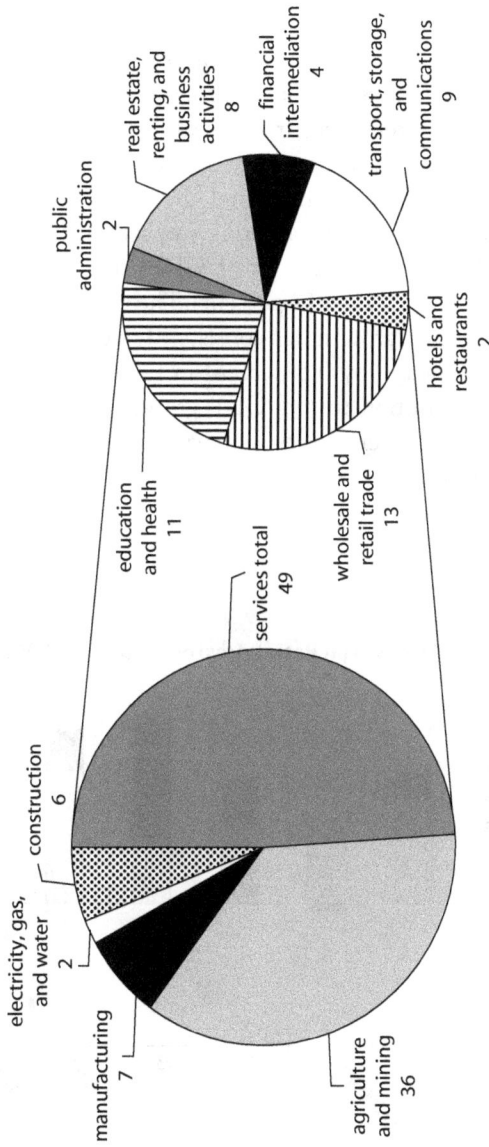

real estate, renting, and business activities
8

financial intermediation
4

transport, storage, and communications
9

public administration
2

hotels and restaurants
2

education and health
11

wholesale and retail trade
13

services total
49

construction
6

electricity, gas, and water
2

manufacturing
7

agriculture and mining
36

Source: NRB 2009, 2010; World Bank staff calculations.

particularly the manufacturing sub-sector, has been in a dramatic decline from the already very low base Nepal started from: In FY2008/09, the growth of this subsector was almost zero and it declined by 0.4 percent in FY2009/10 (Figure 1.3b) (World Bank 2010a).

The industrial sector's contribution to GDP growth declined in FY2007/08 and FY2008/09. The political instability, poor governance, supply bottlenecks stemming from weak infrastructure (power shortages, transportation disruptions), frequent strikes (*bandhs*), and testy labor relations have been detrimental to the industrial sector's performance, particularly the manufacturing sub-sector. Industrial sub-sectors include manufacturing (7 percent of GDP), construction (6 percent), and electricity, gas, and water (2 percent). The manufacturing sub-sector's contribution to GDP growth has consistently declined, and the absolute output level contracted by 0.5 percent in FY2008/09. The construction sub-sector's contribution to real GDP growth on average has been the most significant in recent years and was the sole source of industrial sector contribution to real GDP growth in FY2008/09 (Figure 1.5) (NRB 2009, 2010).[5]

Figure 1.5   Real GDP Growth (at Basic Prices) by Industry, FY2001/02–FY2008/09

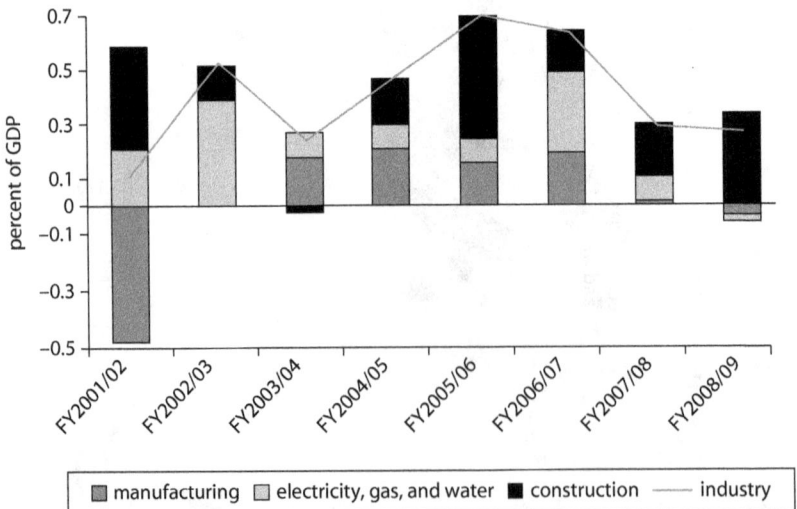

Sources: NRB 2009, 2010; World Bank staff calculations.

Consumption-Driven Demand Fueled by Remittances

On the demand side, Nepal's economy has recently become dependent on remittances, which are predominantly channeled to consumption and purchase of assets such as real estate, rather than savings and productive investment. A simple growth accounting exercise by expenditure reveals that Nepal's economic growth is mostly consumption driven (Table 1.2 and Figure 1.6).[6] Consumption's share of GDP is around 94 percent (NRB 2009, 2010). Investment (gross capital formation) and exports have played either an insignificant role or, for some years (see Table 1.2), detracted from the growth process. The implication has been an erosion of competitiveness in export-oriented sectors as non-tradable prices (including wages) increase, a decline in the manufacturing sector, and exponential growth of imports.[7] The Enterprise Survey results support the data on loss of competitiveness in Nepal, particularly relating to export-oriented manufacturing firms. This implies the need to pursue a growth strategy that involves developing the services sector and service exports (such as education/health services and information technology (IT) services).

Structural Weaknesses Increase Vulnerability/Risks

Nepal's economy faces a number of structural problems that are key impediments for investment and businesses: political uncertainty, violence, security concerns, and poor infrastructure (especially electricity and transportation) top the list of these problems. Poor infrastructure not only raises the overall cost of production, but also affects firms' competitiveness and exports. The government's weak implementation capacity limits its ability to address infrastructure issues head-on. Other areas where structural weaknesses and issues are keeping the investment climate from improving include inadequate policy reforms (such as labor regulations, power tariffs, public-private partnership (PPP) frameworks), corruption, and institutional weaknesses.

These structural problems cause low levels of savings and investment, which are both a source of weakness as well as a symptom of the structural problems. Both private and public investments are low, even by regional standards. Gross domestic savings are about 11 percent of GDP, while FDI flows on average remain below 0.06 percent of GDP (NRB 2009, 2010).

Poor investment opportunities in turn result in low job creation (coupled with strong demand for labor from abroad), which lead millions of Nepalese to seek temporary employment elsewhere.[8] It is

Table 1.2 Real GDP Growth (at Producers' Prices) by Expenditure, FY2001/02–FY2008/09

Growth accounting	FY02	FY03	FY04	FY05	FY06	FY07	FY08	FY09	FY09 GDP share
Real GDP growth	0.1	3.9	4.7	3.5	3.4	3.3	5.3	4.7	100
Consumption	3.3	3.5	1.8	5.7	3.3	3.1	6.7	4.2	94
Gross capital formation	–3.0	1.2	3.3	0.2	2.1	0.5	1.3	1.3	23
Exports	–5.2	–0.8	1.9	–0.5	–0.2	0.1	–0.5	5.2	18
Imports	5.0	0.0	–2.3	–1.9	–1.9	–0.3	–2.2	–6.0	–34

Sources: NRB 2009, 2010; World Bank staff calculations.

Figure 1.6   Real GDP Growth (at Producers' Prices) by Expenditure, FY2001/02–FY2008/09

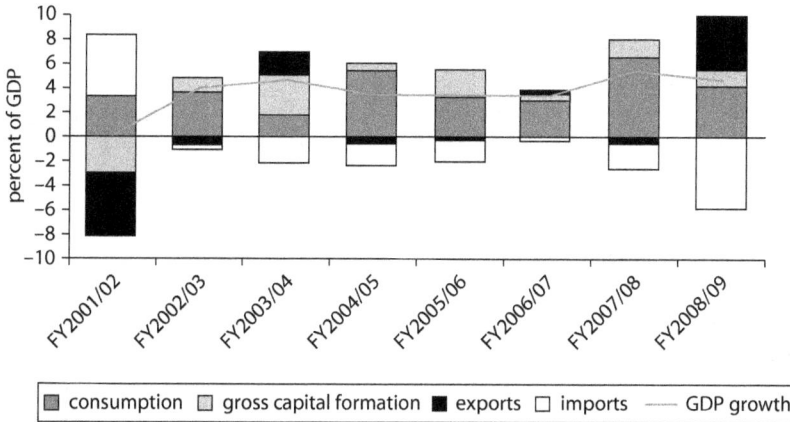

Sources: NRB 2009, 2010; World Bank staff calculations.

believed that one-third of the male population in Nepal is abroad, mostly in India.[9] The unemployment rate (estimated by the 2008 Labor Force Survey was a low 2.1 percent) is not meaningful, as underemployment is widespread and inadequately measured in Nepal and in the rest of South Asia. The high rate of migration has resulted in high remittance inflows. Despite serious un-and-under-employment, in real terms, labor costs have gone up due to the influx of remittances and hikes in public sector wages in the past few years (CBS 2008).[10]

Thus, the Nepalese economy is stuck in a cycle where lack of investment opportunities and jobs drive people to migrate, resulting in remittance flows that are mainly channeled to consumption and asset bubbles. Liquidity resulting from remittance flows inflates prices of goods and assets and increases costs to the productive job-creating sectors. These sectors lose competitiveness and contract, and experience a decline in exports and tradable activities, prolonging the cycle of mediocre and jobless growth at home (Dutch Disease). Further, with remittances, policy makers are not made accountable for good policy, therefore, policy does not improve, job creation remains low, and migration occurs further—a vicious cycle.

Furthermore, after years of excess liquidity, the decline in reserves and economy-wide liquidity squeeze have exposed Nepal's financial sector weaknesses. The financial sector has overextended itself in recent years in an environment of abundant liquidity fed by remittances, proliferation of financial institutions, and weak supervision. Rapid credit growth has fueled asset booms rendering the banking system, and with it, the rest of the economy, vulnerable to significant credit and liquidity risks. Thus, going forward, the key risk to Nepal's economy stems from potentially weaker remittance flows. Weaker remittance flows could herald a fall in real estate prices, which could strain financial institutions and erode depositor confidence. In addition, weaker remittance flows could lead to a further widening of the current account deficit, putting pressure on reserves and the exchange rate peg.

Finally, an added and more recent concern is the emerging loss of fiscal discipline as policy makers and bureaucrats succumb to political pressures.

Looking Ahead

Building a stronger private sector is essential for accelerating economic growth, diversifying its sources, and creating gainful employment opportunities. It is also a key instrument for sustained poverty reduction.

Remittances allow receiving households not only to increase their consumption levels, but also to build up savings for investment both when migrants are overseas and when they return. In order for these hard earned incomes to be saved and invested in Nepal, the investment climate needs to improve. Given that the remittances are private flows from individuals to households, governments often have little or no direct influence on how these funds will be used. Therefore, an improved investment climate is the best way to encourage the channeling of these large volumes of flows into productive sectors of Nepal's economy and the strengthening of the country's growth prospects in the long run.

Microenvironment: Characteristics of the Formal Urban Private Sector

Characteristics of the formal private sector in urban Nepal can be analyzed through the Nepal Enterprise Survey 2009, a representative survey of registered manufacturing and services enterprises. The survey covers a broad range of business-environment topics including access to finance, corruption, infrastructure, crime, competition, and performance measures. Information on characteristics of the firms and their performance is also collected. Data were collected for 486 registered establishments in urban areas of Nepal from March 8, 2009 to June 15, 2009,[11] through a sampling process stratified by industry, region, and size. The sample includes both micro firms and firms with 5 or more employees in the following sectors: manufacturing, retail, tourism, and other services. A slightly different sample instrument was administered to each sector.[12]

The formal non-agricultural private sector in Nepal consists mainly of retailers. 60.1 percent of the firms in the Nepal Enterprise Survey 2009 (Appendix 1) are retailers; the other two most common industries are manufacturing and hotels and restaurants (12.3 percent and 15.0 percent of the enterprises, respectively). Other industries represented in the survey are transportation and travel agencies, wholesale, auto sales, computing, and telecommunications (Figure 1.7).

Enterprises are concentrated in the Central region, especially manufacturing firms. Overall, sixty-four percent of the firms are located in the Central region, 20 percent in the West, and 16 percent in the East. Manufacturing accounts for a larger share of the private sector in the Central region, whereas tourism is concentrated in the West (Figure 1.8).

The average size of formal firms in the private sector is very small. Only 3 percent of the firms have twenty employees or more; 0.4 percent have 100 employees or more. On the other hand, 70 percent of the firms have less than five employees (i.e., they are micro enterprises).[13]

Figure 1.7   Distribution of Registered Firms in Nepal by Industry
percent of firms

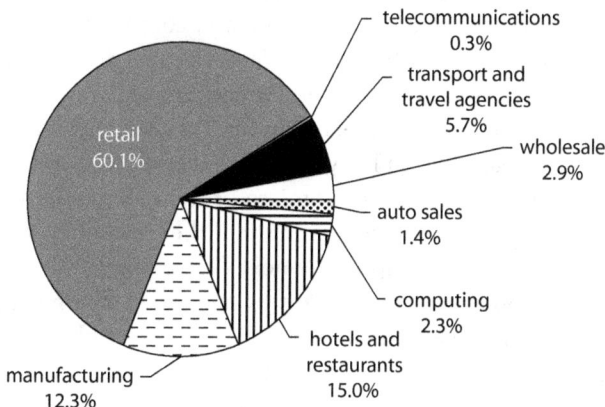

- retail 60.1%
- telecommunications 0.3%
- transport and travel agencies 5.7%
- wholesale 2.9%
- auto sales 1.4%
- computing 2.3%
- hotels and restaurants 15.0%
- manufacturing 12.3%

Source: Nepal Enterprise Survey 2009.

Figure 1.8   Distribution of Registered Firms in Nepal by Region

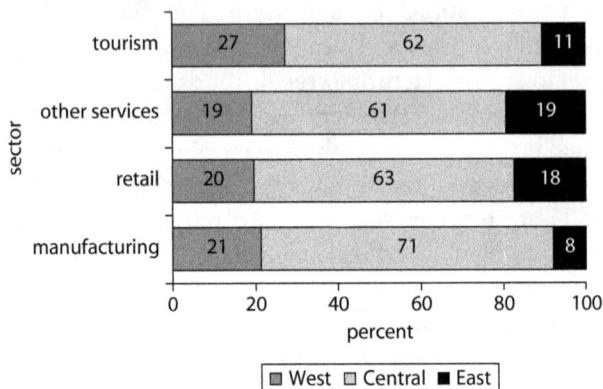

Source: Nepal Enterprise Survey 2009.

Firm size varies considerably across sectors. The average firm is smallest in the retail industry. However, even within the manufacturing sector, 93 percent of the firms employ less than 20 workers. Large firms are found only in the manufacturing and tourism sectors (Figure 1.9).

Even among comparator countries, firms in Nepal are on average small in terms of employment. Cross-country comparisons of Enterprise Surveys have to exclude micro enterprises because of lack of data in some countries, so the dominance of micro firms in Nepal cannot be assessed in an international and regional setting. Even the proportion of small firms, however, is much larger than in any of the comparator countries and the proportion of medium and large firms is smaller (Table 1.3). The share of retail over other industry is also larger than in other countries. On the other hand, while the share of hotels and restaurants is larger than in comparator countries, this could be due to a sampling bias that reflects the specific interest that the 2009 Nepal Enterprise Survey took in the tourism sector.

The average firm has been operating for 9.6 years but manufacturing firms are on average older (11.4 years). The distribution of firms by age groups also shows that the share of micro firms among older firms is not smaller than among the rest, suggesting that there could be very limited transition from one size group to the next (Table 1.4).

The distribution of registered firms by age shows that most Nepalese firms are more than five years and less than 20 years old. Only 10 percent of the firms are more than 20 years old and 25 percent are less than 5 years old (Figure 1.10). This means that either fewer firms have entered the market over the last five years than during the preceding five-year period, or that their survival rate is much lower. In either case, it shows

Figure 1.9   Distribution of Registered Firms in Nepal across Sectors by Size

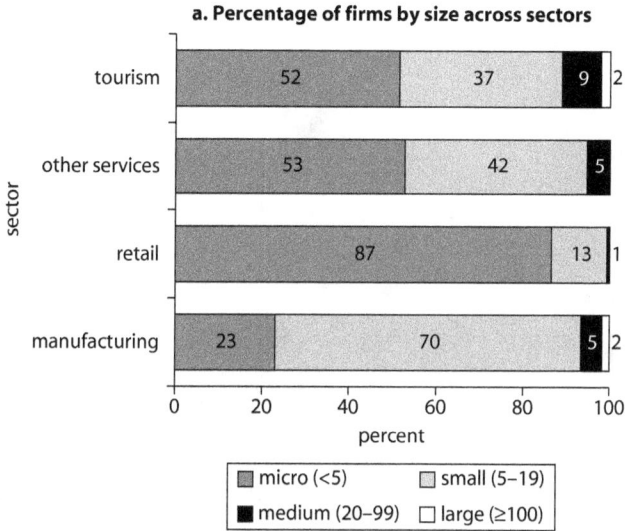

a. Percentage of firms by size across sectors

sector				
tourism	52	37	9	2
other services	53	42	5	
retail	87	13	1	
manufacturing	23	70	5	2

percent (0, 20, 40, 60, 80, 100)

☐ micro (<5)   ☐ small (5–19)
■ medium (20–99)   ☐ large (≥100)

b. Percentage of total firms by size (number of workers)

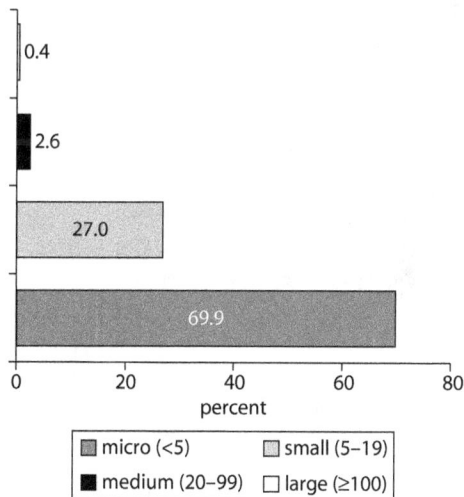

	0.4
	2.6
	27.0
	69.9

percent (0, 20, 40, 60, 80)

☐ micro (<5)   ☐ small (5–19)
■ medium (20–99)   ☐ large (≥100)

Source: Nepal Enterprise Survey 2009.

that the business environment for the entry and survival of new firms has worsened over time since the early 1990s.

The most common legal form adopted by private formal firms in Nepal is sole proprietorship. 82.3 percent of the firms in the formal sector are sole proprietorships, another 14.8 percent are privately held lim-

Table 1.3 Distribution of Firms by Size and Sector for Nepal and Comparator Countries

	Nepal	South Asia	Bhutan	Bolivia	Bangladesh	Lao PDR	Mongolia
Size							
Small (5–19)	85.3	59.5	71.9	55.3	40.6	76.5	44.6
Medium (20–99)	13.2	23.9	21.0	39.0	30.0	19.9	46.5
Large (100 and over)	1.5	16.6	7.1	5.8	29.4	3.6	9.0
Sector							
Textiles	3.0	9.3	—	—	18.0	2.5	1.7
Leather	—	6.4	—	—	16.0	—	—
Garments	2.5	13.0	—	19.7	12.4	14.2	3.9
Food	6.5	12.4	3.6	20.1	14.4	4.2	14.1
Metals and machinery	7.3	6.3	4.8	—	5.9	—	2.5
Electronics	—	4.7	3.2	—	3.7	—	—
Chemicals and pharmaceuticals	2.2	4.7	—	9.6	9.8	1.4	—
Wood and furniture	4.9	5.2	14.0	—	0.7	9.4	—
Non-metallic and plastic materials	6.3	5.4	6.4	3.3	3.2	4.2	3.6
Auto and auto components	—	5.1	—	—	—	—	—
Other manufacturing	—	13.6	—	14.0	0.6	1.7	8.3
Retail and wholesale trade	34.8	25.0	23.6	20.1	5.3	37.5	29.0
Hotels and restaurants	17.9	8.4	4.8	—	3.8	15.0	10.8
Other services	12.2	10.2	10.8	5.7	1.1	4.2	8.6
Other	—	19.3	26.0	7.5	5.0	3.6	15.8

Source: World Bank Enterprise Surveys, latest available year.

Note: Sample restricted to firms with 5+ employees. The industry classification reflects the standardized classification used for international comparison in the Enterprise Survey website http://www.enterprisesurveys.org/; the classification used in Figure 1.5 reflects the classification used within this report. — = not available.

Table 1.4   Age Distribution of Registered Firms by Size

	<5 yrs	*5–9 yrs*	*10–19 yrs*	*20+ yrs*	*Total*
Micro (<5)	64.8	75.5	68.4	66.6	70.0
Small (5–19)	33.6	22.9	27.1	25.5	27.0
Medium (20–99)	1.6	1.6	3.8	5.4	2.6
Large (>=100)	0.0	0.0	0.7	2.5	0.5
Total	100.0	100.0	100.0	100.0	100.0

Source: Nepal Enterprise Survey 2009.

Figure 1.10   Distribution of Registered Firms in Nepal across Sectors by Age of Firm

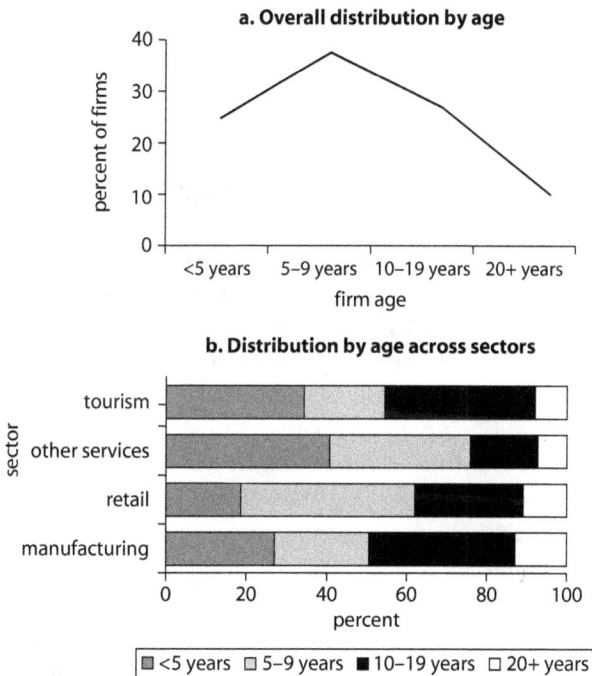

Source: Nepal Enterprise Survey 2009.

ited liability companies, 2.4 percent are partnerships, and 0.5 percent are publicly listed companies. Within the manufacturing sector, limited liability companies are fairly common (43 percent) but even here, publicly listed companies account for less than 2 percent of the firms.

Private, domestic individuals own 99 percent of private sector firms; private foreigners own the remaining 1 percent. There is no significant

Table 1.5   Management and Ownership: Female Participation and Experience, Nepal and Comparator Countries

	% of firms with female participation in ownership	% of firms with female top manager	Average years of experience in the firm's sector
South Asia	15.6	7.1	14.8
Bhutan	31.3	—	16.1
Bolivia	41.1	—	18.5
Bangladesh	—	16.1	13.6
Lao PDR	39.1	—	11.8
Mongolia	52.0	36.4	14.1
Nepal	28.3	17.9	13.4

Source: World Bank Enterprise Surveys, latest available year.
Note: Comparison restricted to firms with 5+ employees in sectors surveyed in most countries in the comparator group, i.e., manufacturing, retail, wholesale, hotels and restaurants, transport, and travel agencies.
— = question not included or data not available.

participation from the government in the private sector. The incidence of foreign ownership is much larger than average (5 percent) in the tourism industry, while none of the enterprises operating in the services sector, outside tourism or retail, reported foreign participation.

Firm managers and owners are predominantly male. Overall, 28.3 percent of the firms have female participation in their ownership and only 17.9 percent of the firms have a woman as a top manager. The presence of women in management is slightly stronger in services other than retail and tourism (27.3 percent). Nepal compares favorably with regional and comparator countries on female participation rates (Table 1.5).

The average manager has 12.4 years of experience. In the manufacturing sector, managers have on average a few more years of experience (15.9 years). Managerial experience is low by international standards. Restricting the comparison to firms with five employees or more, managers in Nepal are found to have the lowest average experience among Nepal's comparator group. Presence of women is, instead, around the average of the comparator group.

Notes

1. All GDP data are from the Nepal Rastra Bank. World Bank staff compiled data from the archive of Nepal Rastra Bank Recent Macroeconomic Situation Reports to create a monthly time-series database, which was used for the analysis in this ICA. http://www.nrb.org.np/ofg/press.php?tp=recent_macroeconomic&&vw=15.

2. The Joint Bank-Fund Debt Sustainability Analysis (DSA) of 2010 found that Nepal is under moderate debt distress. Nepal's external debt indicators are comfortably within the DSA thresholds with a net present value (NPV) of debt-to-GDP ratio of 21.7 percent, and an NPV of debt-to-exports-and -remittances ratio of 63 percent.

3. The hike in gold imports was attributed to deteriorating confidence in the economy, as well as incentives to take advantage of a wedge that existed between the India and Nepal import tariff rates when India increased the import tariff on gold imports.

4. According to the World Food Program, in the last three years, as a result of high food prices, the global financial crisis, a lack of agricultural investment, frequent and severe natural disasters, and ongoing political instability, the number of highly food insecure people in Nepal has tripled and now stands at more than 3.7 million.

5. For the purposes of growth accounting by expenditure, real GDP at producers' prices is used. In Nepal, the indicator of choice to track overall GDP growth is GDP at producers' prices. However, in order to apply growth accounting by sector, this section utilizes real GDP at basic prices. The difference between the two indicators arises because GDP at producers' prices includes total taxes minus subsidies on products (this line is reported as an independent line entry in GDP statistics). In Nepal, GDP by sectoral composition (e.g., agriculture, industry, services) is reported only in basic prices. Real GDP of Nepal at basic prices grew by 3.8 percent in FY09, while GDP at domestic prices grew by 4.7 percent.

6. GDP data (by demand/expenditure categories) has shortcomings as compilation methods heavily rely on fixed ratios derived from outdated surveys or ad hoc assumptions. In Nepal, household consumption expenditure estimates are based on extrapolations of the Nepal Living Standards Survey of 2003/04. Officially recorded remittance flows have increased from around US$800 million to over US$2.7 billion and have profoundly changed consumption patterns; however, the assumptions behind the GDP calculations have not changed. Therefore, the current consumption is very likely to be underestimated in the national accounts, and as a result, the residual, the change in stocks (which is added to the gross capital formation), is overestimated. The residual in Nepal GDP data in recent years can be as high as 8–11 percent of GDP, which is much higher than levels seen in other countries in the region (1–4 percent). Figure 1.6 adjusts the change in stocks to a historical average of 3 percent of GDP; adding the excess of the residual to the consumption.

7. "Dutch Disease" is a term used to explain erosion of external competitiveness and a decline in manufacturing that occurs when there are large foreign exchange inflows into an economy. The term originated in the Netherlands, which had large inflows of sales' proceeds following the discovery of North

Sea gas. Higher disposable incomes (due in this case to remittance inflows) expand demand, driving prices of non-tradable goods and services to rise in relation to externally determined prices of tradable goods. These higher prices lead to an expansion of the non-tradable sector and contraction of the tradable sector. By definition, an increase in the price of non-tradable goods relative to the price of tradable goods translates into real exchange rate appreciation.

8. Most migrants are low-skilled migrants working abroad temporarily and sending remittances back home, which are mostly used for consumption.

9. This is supported by the results of a 2009 migration survey in Nepal. The forthcoming publication, "Nepal Issues of Large-scale Migration and Remittances: Migration Survey of 2009 and Beyond" (World Bank) provides in-depth information on migration dynamics in Nepal.

10. In theory, it could be argued that migration directly reduces labor supply in countries where migrants originate. Also, the increase in household income due to remittances may lead to a further decrease in labor supply as households substitute more leisure for work. A shrinking labor supply, in turn, puts upward pressure on wages, which raise production costs; higher costs can lead to a further contraction of the tradable sector.

11. Registered firms were defined as being registered with the Inland Revenue Department, i.e., having a PAN/VAT number.

12. Given the stratified design, sample frames containing a complete and updated list of establishments as well as information on all stratification variables (firm size, industry, and region) are required to draw the sample for the Enterprise Surveys. Initially a sample frame was sought from the Government of Nepal and from appropriate trade associations, but the lists that were obtained were deemed incomplete and potentially out of date. It was therefore decided to undertake block enumeration, i.e., the contractor would physically create a list of establishments from which to sample. In total, the contractor enumerated 6,755 establishments for the survey fieldwork (the block enumeration elicited firms for both the Enterprise Survey and the Informal Survey).

13. The analysis is adjusted for sampling weights to account for the over sampling of large firms in the survey.

CHAPTER 2

Overview of the Investment Climate in the Formal Private Sector in Nepal

This chapter provides an overview of the investment climate constraints and issues for the formal private sector in Nepal. Political instability is the first and foremost investment climate obstacle in Nepal for 70 percent of the firms, followed by electricity. Transportation, corruption, and access to finance are also considered significant or severe obstacles by many Nepalese firms. On the other hand, labor regulations are a pressing issue for manufacturing firms. Customs, access to land, regulations, and permits are seldom considered to be major or very severe obstacles for business. These investment climate issues have changed since the last enterprise survey for Nepal in 2000 (Box 2.1).

Political instability[1] and electricity are unambiguously perceived as the most important investment climate obstacles in Nepal. Over two-thirds of the enterprises (70 percent) perceive political instability to be the most important obstacle to their operations while electricity is the main obstacle for 16 percent of the firms. Access to finance comes third, being perceived as the most important obstacle by 8 percent of the enterprises. The blue bars in Figure 2.1 report the proportion of firms that ranked each dimension of the investment climate as the main obstacle to their business.

Based on the perception of the entrepreneurs, a clear priority should be given to achieving political stability[2] and to improving the country's power infrastructure. The red bars in Figure 2.1 represent the proportion of firms that rate each dimension of the investment climate as a major or

Figure 2.1 Perception of Obstacles Constraining the Investment Climate in Nepal

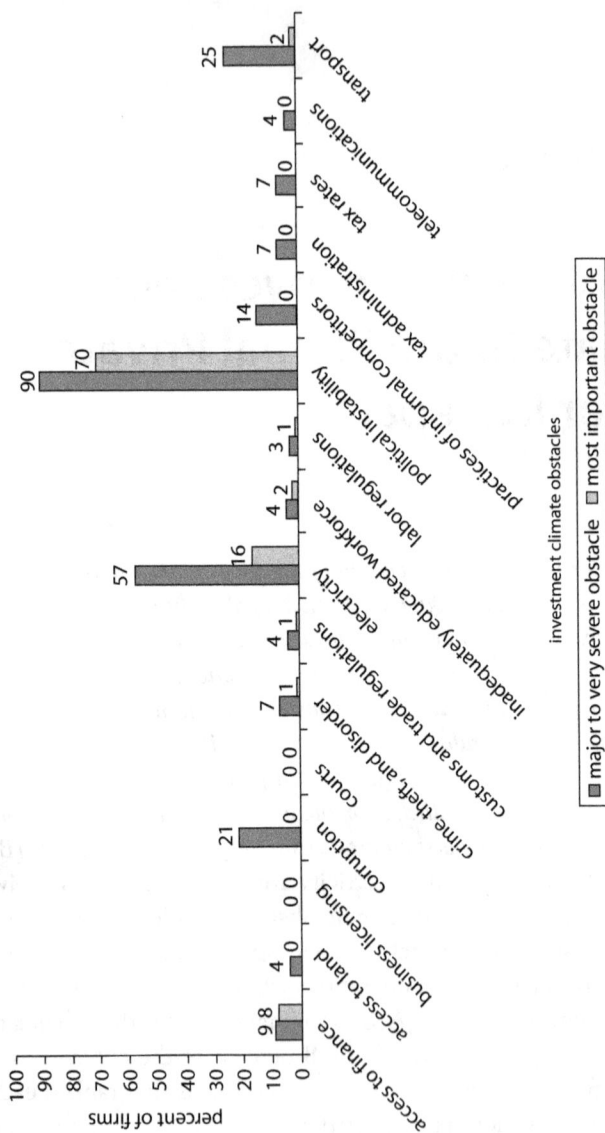

investment climate obstacles

■ major to very severe obstacle   □ most important obstacle

Source: Nepal Enterprise Survey 2009.

very severe obstacle. By this measure, many dimensions of the investment climate are problematic: first and foremost political instability and electricity, but also transportation, corruption, and competition from the informal sector. Compared to the South Asia region or comparator countries, Nepal is doing worse in electricity and transportation, whereas it is doing better with respect to tax rates and tax administration, labor skills, functioning of the courts, and business licensing and permits (Figure 2.2).

Perceptions of the investment climate vary across industries. Comparing the proportion of firms that rate obstacles as major or very severe, we can compare the investment climate across industries (Figure 2.3). While political instability is the top obstacle across the board, transport, electricity, and corruption are especially problematic for the tourism industry; labor regulations are the fourth major obstacle within the manufacturing sector, and informal competition is especially felt by firms in services other than retail and tourism. Labor regulations are the most important obstacles only for manufacturing firms. Access to finance is more of an issue for the manufacturing and retail industries (Figure 2.4).

Perceptions also change according to firm size. Overall, large firms perceive the investment climate to be worse; in particular, labor regulation is a major to very severe obstacle for more than half of the large firms

---

Box 2.1

Results of the Nepal Manufacturing Enterprise Survey of 2000

While no fully-fledged investment climate assessment had been previously conducted for Nepal, an enterprise survey in 2000 covered 223 firms in the manufacturing sector across the country. The main investment climate obstacles Nepal faces today were already critical at the time. The 2000 survey found that while the market-oriented policy reforms and trade agreements with India initiated by Nepal in the early 1990s had dramatic effects in terms of GDP growth and manufacturing sector performance, the post-reform growth trends did not prove sustainable after the mid-1990s. Poor implementation of reforms, bureaucratic burden, and continued political and policy uncertainty were to blame. Government policy and its implementation were the greatest obstacles to doing business in Nepal; inadequate demand for products, poor access to finance, and inadequate infrastructure services were in second place.

Source: World Bank 2000.

Figure 2.2   Investment Climate Obstacles Perceived as Major to Very Severe in Nepal and Comparator Countries

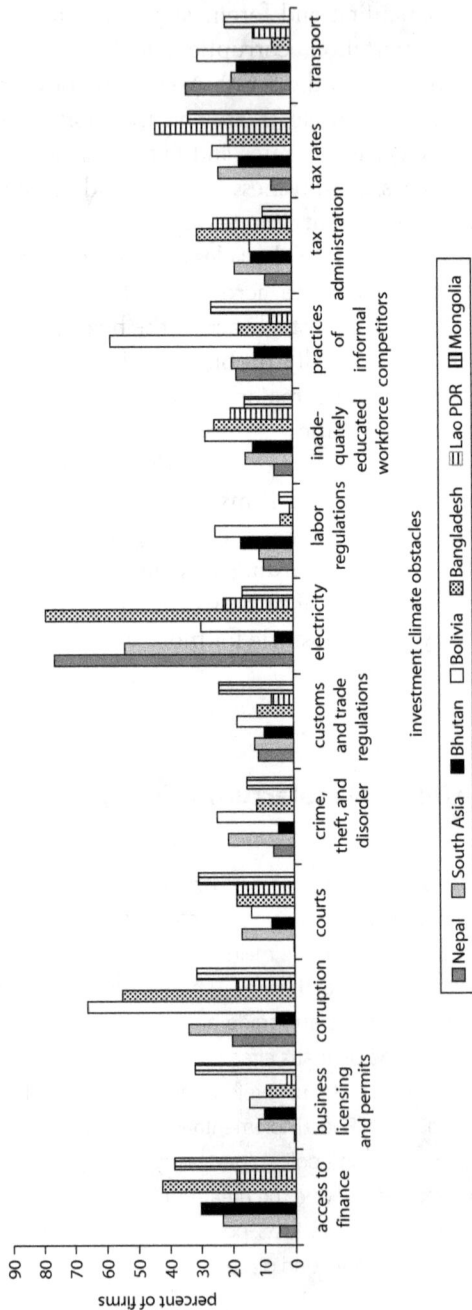

investment climate obstacles

Legend: Nepal ▨ South Asia ■ Bhutan ☐ Bolivia ▨ Bangladesh ▤ Lao PDR ▥ Mongolia

Source: World Bank Enterprise Surveys, latest available year.

Note: Comparison restricted to firms with 5+ employees in sectors surveyed in most countries in the comparator group, i.e, manufacturing, retail, wholesale, hotels and restaurants, transport, and travel agencies. Political instability is not included among compared investment climate obstacles because it was not surveyed in comparator countries.

Figure 2.3   Perception of Obstacles to the Investment Climate in Nepal as Major or Severe by Industry

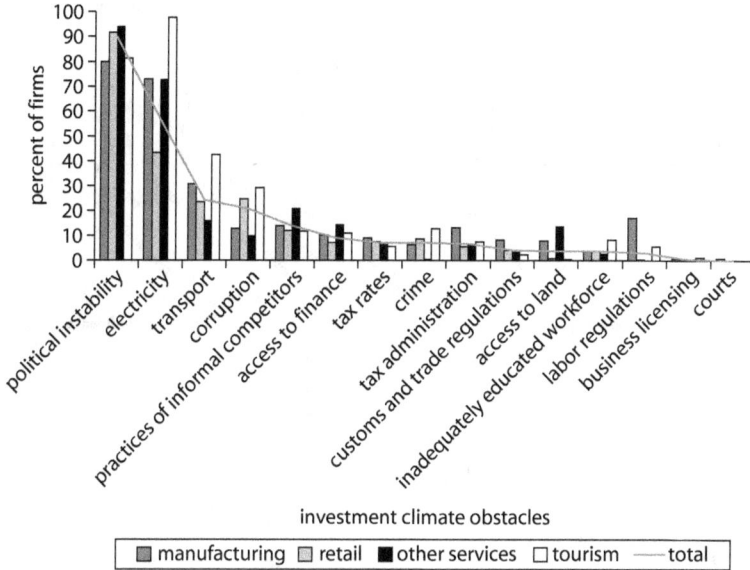

investment climate obstacles

manufacturing   retail   other services   tourism   —— total

Source: Nepal Enterprise Survey 2009.

(Figure 2.5). Tax rates and tax administration are also a relevant problem for large firms, but not for the other size groups.

Exporting firms are considerably less constrained by political instability than non-exporters: 36 percent of the exporters perceive political instability as a major or very severe constraint compared to 92 percent of the non-exporters. This is likely to be co-determined by size, as most exporters are large firms (Figure 2.6). Tax rates and tax administration and especially labor regulations are instead more constraining for exporters.

Enterprises managed by women, on the other hand, are more constrained than others by access to land and to skilled workers as well as by competition by informal firms. In other dimensions of the investment climate, women entrepreneurs do not perceive themselves to be more constrained than men.

Factor Markets

Infrastructure
Over 99 percent of the firms suffered power outages and on average firms suffered 57.3 outages per month each lasting 4.9 hours (Table 2.1). Outages

Figure 2.4   Nepalese Firms by Sector Rate Most Important Investment Climate Obstacles

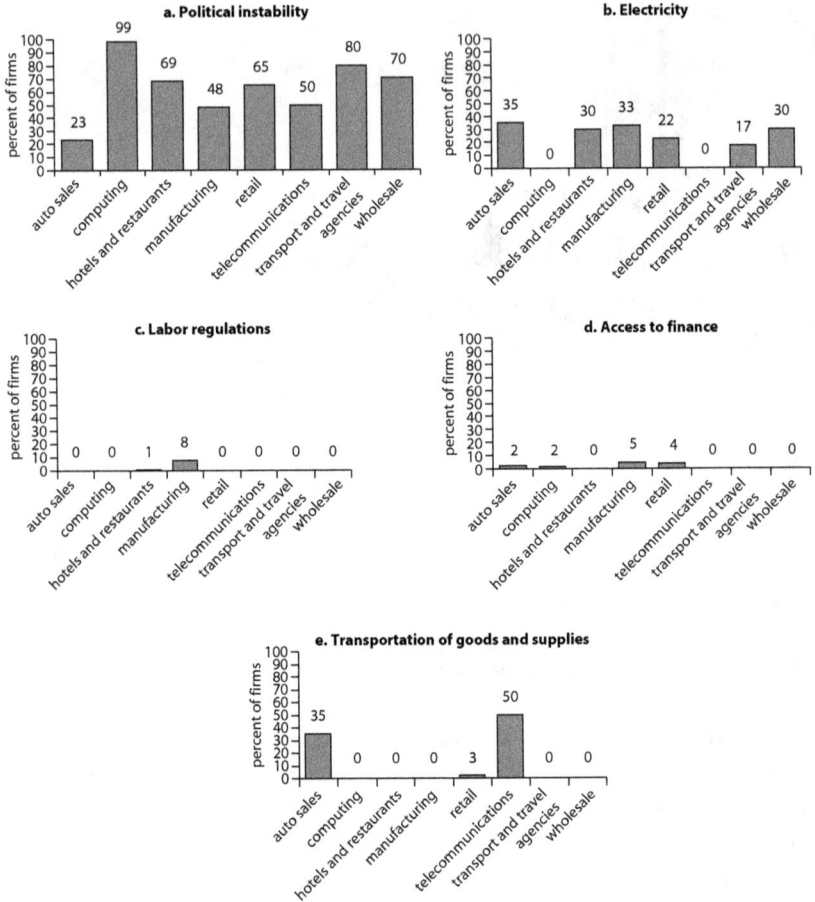

Source: Nepal Enterprise Survey 2009.

result in losses that amount on average to 22.1 percent of the firm's annual sales. In a country with a large hydropower potential, this is striking, especially when compared to Bhutan, which exports hydropower to India. In response to power outages, firms can purchase or share a generator; however, despite the very strong impact of power shortages, only 11.2 percent of manufacturing firms in Nepal own a generator (Table 2.1).

Larger firms and firms in the Eastern region perceive electricity as a greater obstacle. Also, over 80 percent of the firms in telecommunications, wholesale, transport, and travel agencies find electricity to be a major or

Figure 2.5   Perception of Obstacles to the Investment Climate in Nepal as Major or Severe by Size of Firm

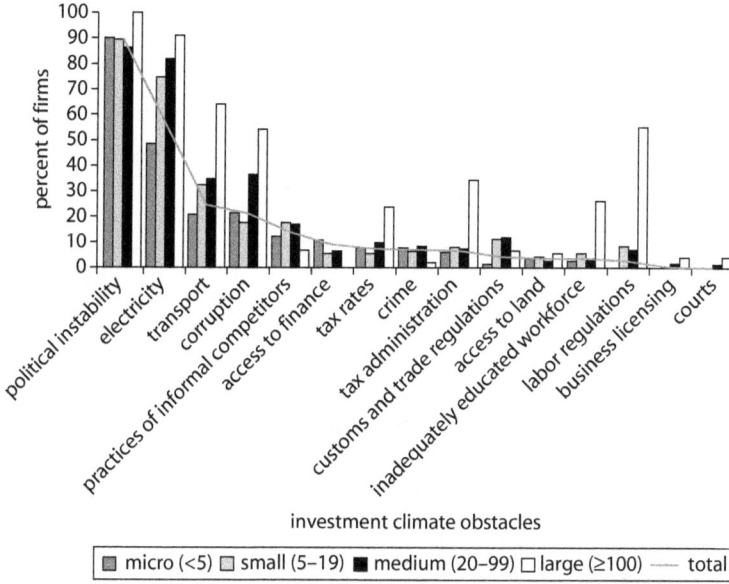

investment climate obstacles

micro (<5) □ small (5–19) ■ medium (20–99) □ large (≥100) ──── total

Source: Nepal Enterprise Survey 2009.

very severe obstacle. Data on number and duration of outages, however, are not significantly worse for these industries than for others.

Quality of infrastructure for transport is also poor. Firms in the manufacturing sector lose 1.4 percent of shipments to domestic markets as a result of breakage and spoilage. There are significant differences across regions: average losses are highest in the West (2.8 percent of shipments) and lowest in the East (0.36 percent). Firms in the Eastern region, and especially in large firms, have the worse perception of transportation as an obstacle to their business activity; 33.6 percent and 64.1 percent, respectively, rate transportation as a major or very severe obstacle (vis à vis the overall average of 24.5 percent).

Certain problems in transportation seem to be linked to political instability. Strikes are the main obstacle to transportation by road. Less than 5 percent of the firms report quality of roads, petrol availability, or distance to market to be the main problem in transportation.

Nepal's infrastructure is in poorer condition than in comparator countries (Figure 2.7). Chapter 4 provides a more detailed analysis of infrastructure in Nepal.

Figure 2.6   Exporting and Size of Firms in Nepal

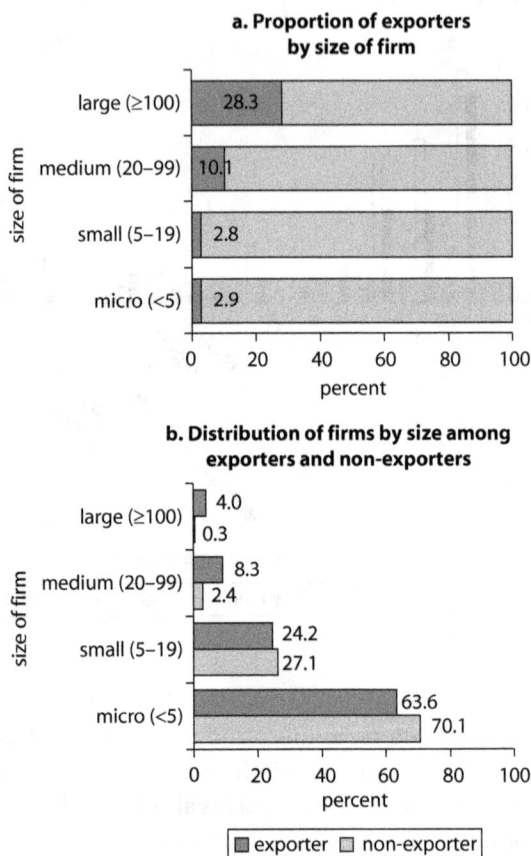

a. Proportion of exporters by size of firm

b. Distribution of firms by size among exporters and non-exporters

Source: Nepal Enterprise Survey 2009.

Table 2.1   Power Outages

Indicator	Value
% firms that experienced losses due to power outages	99.6
Average number of outages per month	57.3
Average duration of outage (hrs)	4.9
Average losses due to outages (% annual sales)	22.1
% firms that own or share a generator*	11.2
% electricity from generator*	25.8

Source: Nepal Enterprise Survey 2009.
Note: * indicates sample restricted to manufacturing sector.

Figure 2.7   Electricity and Transportation Infrastructure in Nepal and Comparator Countries

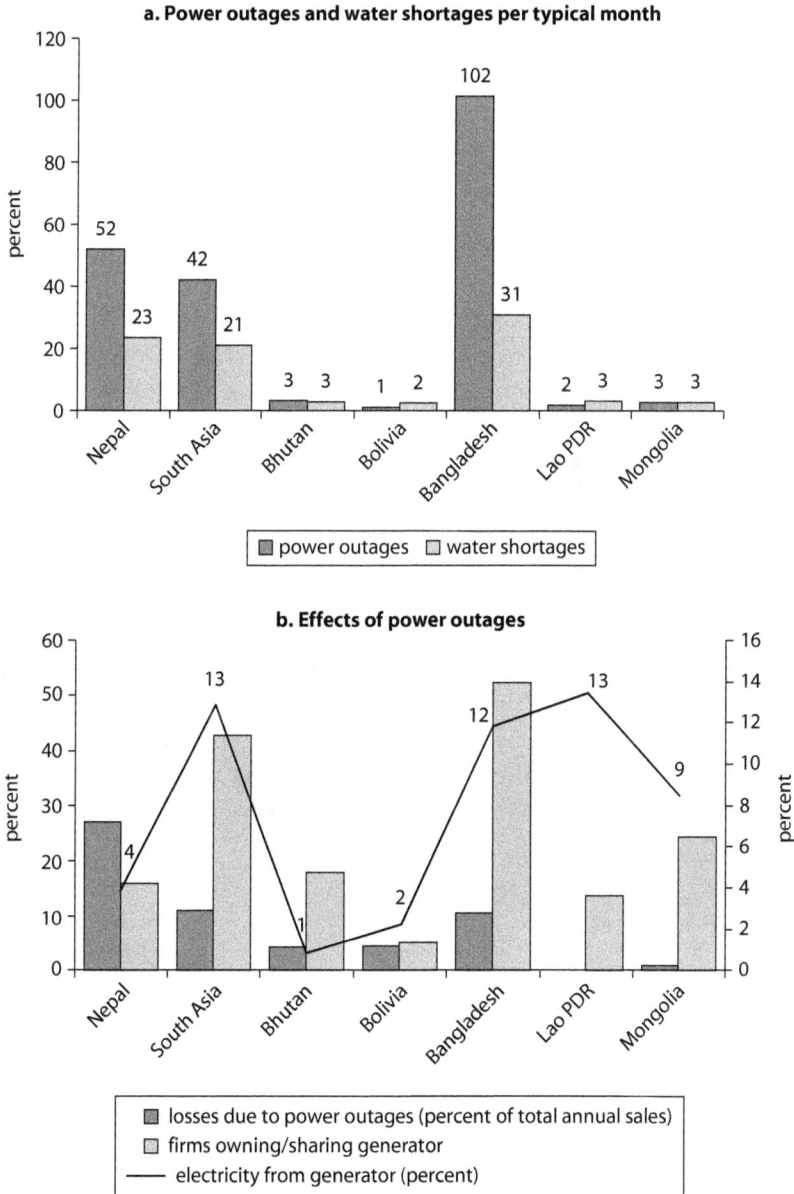

a. Power outages and water shortages per typical month

power outages   water shortages

b. Effects of power outages

losses due to power outages (percent of total annual sales)
firms owning/sharing generator
electricity from generator (percent)

Source: World Bank Enterprise Surveys, latest available year.
Note: Comparison restricted to firms with 5+ employees in sectors surveyed in most countries in the comparator group, i.e., manufacturing, retail, wholesale, hotels and restaurants, transport, and travel agencies.

Finance

Access to finance is the third most important obstacle for registered firms. Firms make little use of financial services: less than half of the enterprises have a checking or a savings account, only one out of three firms has a line of credit or a loan from a financial institution, and one out of ten has an overdraft facility. Firms also make little use of loans from banks to finance their current expenditure or their investments, as firms usually resort to internal funds. Bank borrowing finances less than 10 percent of firm current expenditures or investments (Table 2.2).

Access to finance is not perceived as an obstacle by large firms. Large firms have good access but still often choose not to resort to banks to finance their investments and operational expenses (Table 2.2). Micro firms are instead more constrained in accessing finance and, as a result, 10.8 percent of them perceive this dimension of the investment climate to be the most important. None of the large firms perceive access to finance as the most important problem. This could be a reflection of the lack of dynamism of these enterprises. They do not perceive access to finance as a major obstacle because they are not growing their operations or employment.

Access to finance in Nepal is low by regional and international standards. The proportion of firms that have a bank account and those that are financing fixed assets with bank loans are the second lowest in the comparator group (Figure 2.8).

Lack of appropriate financial products and services for small and medium enterprises (SMEs) is an important barrier to access to financial services. Collateral on loans are also part of the access to finance problem.

Table 2.2   Access to Finance

	All	Size			
		Micro (<5)	Small (5–19)	Medium (20–99)	Large (>=100)
% firms with checking or savings account	44.9	32.5	71.7	90.3	100.0
% firms with overdraft facility	10.2	4.3	21.2	45.9	78.5
% firms with line of credit or loan	29.0	24.7	38.1	46.5	61.9
% funds borrowed from banks, working capital	9.4	6.4	15.3	24.2	32.8
% funds borrowed from banks, fixed assets	6.4	0.2	11.7	11.9	35.7

Source: Nepal Enterprise Survey 2009.

Figure 2.8   Access to Finance in Nepal and Comparator Countries

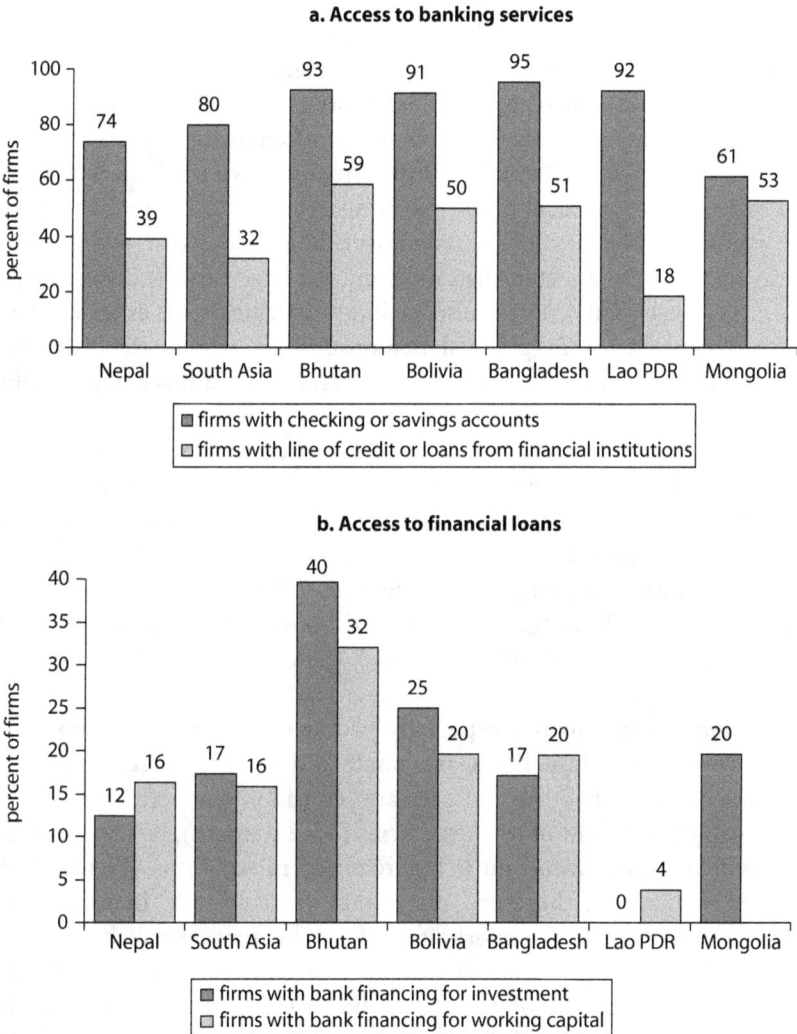

a. Access to banking services

firms with checking or savings accounts
firms with line of credit or loans from financial institutions

b. Access to financial loans

firms with bank financing for investment
firms with bank financing for working capital

Source: World Bank Enterprise Surveys, latest available year.
Note: Comparison restricted to firms with 5+ employees in sectors surveyed in most countries in the comparator group, i.e., manufacturing, retail, wholesale, hotels and restaurants, transport, and travel agencies.

The value of collateral required on average is one of the highest when compared to similar countries; furthermore, there is a large discrepancy between the type of collateral firms used and the assets they bought. Chapter 6 provides an in-depth analysis of access to finance for private enterprises in Nepal.

Labor

Labor regulations and an inadequately educated workforce are seen as major or very severe obstacles for 2.8 percent and 3.7 percent of the firms, respectively. Labor regulations are a bigger obstacle for large firms, for the manufacturing sector, and for exporters (55.2 percent, 17 percent, and 9.9 percent, respectively). Civil unrest often disrupts business activities and, as shown in Table 2.3, firms often perceive labor market issues to be related to political problems. Firms reported losing to civil unrest an average of 44.1 days of operation over the previous year—with micro firms being more affected than medium and large firms (50 days vs. 28 days per year). Civil unrest also includes activities such as strikes and direct involvement in political demonstrations, which are often not directed against the state but are rather against or in favor of a specific party or leader.

Nepal has one of the most rigid labor market regulatory frameworks in South Asia. Nepal ranks 150 out of 181 countries in the world according to Doing Business data in terms of the flexibility of labor regulations. Labor regulations in Nepal are especially rigid when it comes to dismissing employees, which is difficult and expensive; furthermore, firms have to pay substantial bonuses to workers on top of their salary, which ultimately increases the cost of labor for firms and discourages hiring.

Labor regulations are especially problematic for large firms and, as a result, Nepalese firms are small and show limited growth in employment. Labor regulations are considered a major business obstacle by over half of the large firms (55.2 percent), but by only 8.7 percent of small firms and 0.1 percent of micro firms (Figure 2.9). Labor regulations, therefore, discourage firm growth. In fact, firms employ on average 6.4 workers, and in the three years before the survey, the average annual growth rate in employment was 3.9 percent; but 75 percent of the firms did not increase the number of permanent workers at all.[3]

Table 2.3   Main Issues with Job and Main Labor Market Issues (% Respondents)

	Salary	Political problems	Benefits	Leave	Working conditions	Working hours	Skills development	Hiring and firing conditions
Workers	31.9	16.6	14.5	11.2	10.2	8.7	5.1	1.8
Firms	31.8	57.6	7.6	1.5	0.0	0.0	0.0	1.5

Source: Nepal Employee Survey 2009.

Figure 2.9   Rating Labor Regulations in Nepal as a Major or Very Severe Obstacle According to Size of Firm

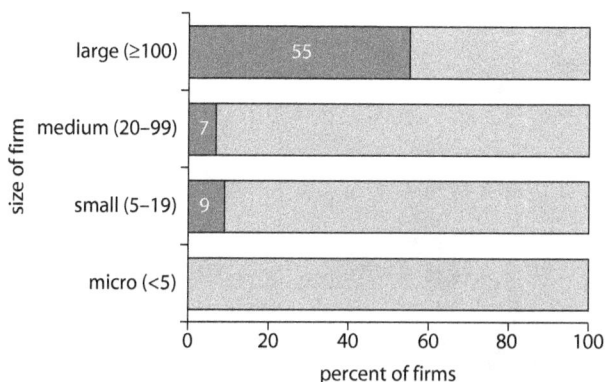

Source: Nepal Enterprise Surveys 2009.

Workers have inadequate skills. The employee survey reveals that in firms with five employees or more, one-fourth of the workers have a primary school level education or less and another 38 percent have a general secondary school degree.[4] Less than one-fourth of the surveyed workers (24 percent) have at least a university first degree.

A low share of skilled workers employed in the production process characterizes many manufacturing firms in Nepal. Restricting the sample to enterprises with 5 or more employees reveals that the share of skilled workers among production workers in Nepal is the lowest among the comparator countries for which data is available (58 percent) (Figure 2.10).

Manufacturing firms do not usually offer training to their employees. Compared to comparator countries, very few manufacturing firms (6.7 percent) in Nepal offer formal training to permanent full-time employees to improve their skills. The larger the firm, the greater the incidence of training; 26.3 percent of medium firms and 44.7 percent of large firms offer training programs.

Trade unions are mainly present in medium and especially in large firms, but the participation rate tends to be high in all firms where trade unions are active (Table 2.4). In the firms where unions are present, most workers (71 percent) belong to them and 64.7 percent of the firms lost working days due to trade union actions, with an average loss of 15.8 days.

Figure 2.10   Total Skilled and Unskilled Production Workers in Nepal and Comparator Countries and Skilled Workers' Share

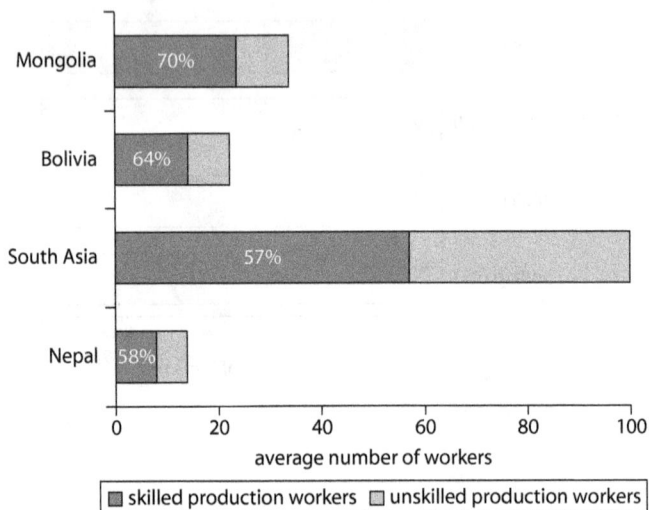

Source: World Bank Enterprise Surveys, latest available year.
Note: Percentages of the average share of skilled production workers. Comparison restricted to firms with 5+ employees in sectors surveyed in most countries in the comparator group, i.e., manufacturing, retail, wholesale, hotels and restaurants, transport, and travel agencies.

Table 2.4   Trade Union Participation

	% firms with trade unions	% workers affiliated with trade union[a]
Micro (<5)	0.1	100.0
Small (5–19)	14.3	69.4
Medium (20–99)	45.7	72.3
Large (>=100)	96.4	76.8
Total	5.4	71.0

Source: Nepal Enterprise Survey 2009.
Note: a. restricted to firms where unions are present.

Innovation and Technology

Little innovation takes place in manufacturing firms and there is limited use of technology imported from abroad (**Figure 2.11**). 0.5 percent of manufacturing firms have patents registered abroad and 9.3 percent have patents registered in Nepal. Among large firms, the proportion increases to 4.3 percent and 9.3 percent, respectively.

Figure 2.11 Indicators of Innovation and Technology for Nepal and Comparator Countries

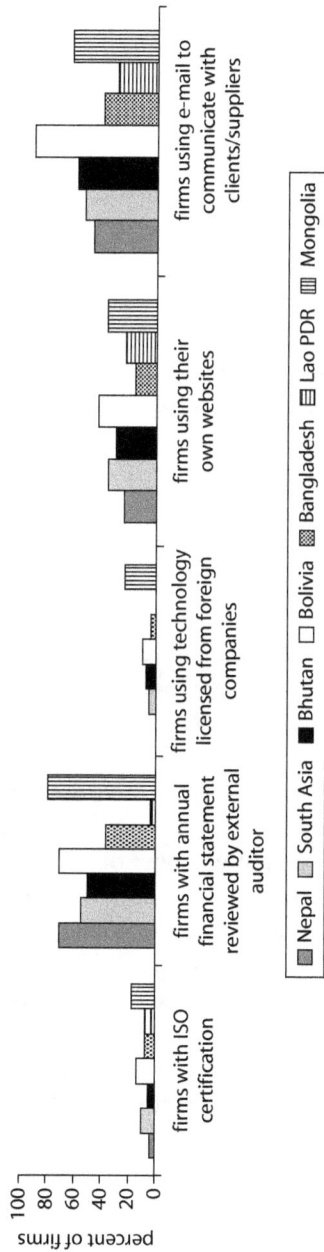

Source: World Bank Enterprise Surveys, latest available year.

Note: Comparison restricted to firms with 5+ employees in sectors surveyed in most countries in the comparator group, i.e., manufacturing, retail, wholesale, hotels and restaurants, transport, and travel agencies.

Fewer firms use email and websites than in any of the comparator countries except for Bangladesh and the Lao People's Democratic Republic (PDR). Also, incidence of ISO certification and use of foreign technology is lower than average (Figure 2.11).

Governance

The single aspect of the investment climate that most severely affects firms in Nepal is political instability. When asked whether their business operations were affected by political changes and instability during the year prior to the survey, 88.5 percent of the firms responded affirmatively. Ninety percent of the firms perceive political instability to be a major or very severe obstacle to their activity and 69.6 percent ranked it as the most important obstacle. Political instability is an equally severe problem across industries, regions, and firm size. In fact, in a ranking provided by the Economist Intelligence Unit (2009–10), Nepal has the 19th highest index of political instability.[5] Political instability includes many aspects beyond just civil unrest, such as unstable governments, regime change, and frequent government changes. Political instability also exacerbates other investment climate issues because it hinders the government's ability to implement and enforce existing policies. Furthermore, frequent changes of government and politicization open up opportunities for corruption, extortion, and crime.

In other aspects of governance, conversely, Nepal performs better than most comparator countries. The Nepal Enterprise Survey 2009 reveals that the amount of time spent dealing with regulations, dealing with tax officials, and obtaining permits is often lower than in comparator countries.

Nepal ranks fairly well in measures of how well minority shareholders are protected against misuse of corporate assets by directors, as measured by the Doing Business Report. It places in the top half of 183 countries measured on this dimension (World Bank 2009a). Nepal's above average rank is driven by the ease of shareholder suits and by the extent of disclosure index. On the contrary, the country appears to be quite weak in terms of extent of directors' liability.

Corruption and Crime

Corruption is seen as a major obstacle by one in five firms, which is low in comparison to comparator countries: the proportion is, for example, one in three for the South Asia region. Sixty-three percent of the firms perceive the court system to be fair and uncorrupted.

Results on perception of corruption are overall confirmed by moderate incidence of requests for informal payments during business interactions. According to the Graft Index,[6] firms are less likely to be asked for bribes in Nepal than in the South Asia region and some of the comparator countries. The most problematic transactions are requests for construction-related permits (17.8 percent of the firms were asked for gifts), requests for telephone connections (15.5 percent of the firms were asked for gifts), and tax inspections and dealing with government officials (15 percent each).[7] Among comparator countries, only Bhutan performs better than Nepal along these measures of corruption (Figure 2.12).

On the other hand, Nepal scores poorly in Transparency International's Corruption Perceptions Index. In 2009, Nepal ranked 143 out of 180 countries and scored second to last among its comparator countries (Table 2.5). According to Transparency International (2009), "political instability, lawlessness, nepotism, and lack of accountability prevail in the society and corruption is perceived to be a major concern. An anti-corruption agenda has not become a political priority." On the whole,

Figure 2.12   Indicators of Corruption in Nepal and Comparator Countries

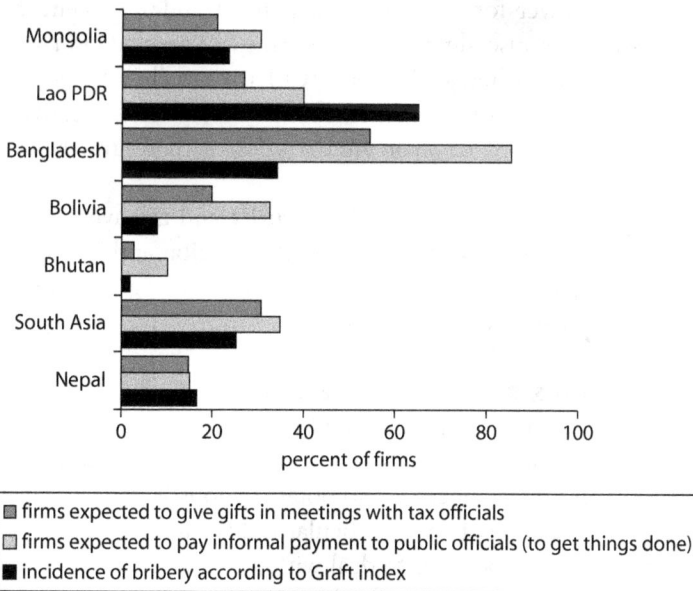

percent of firms

☐ firms expected to give gifts in meetings with tax officials
☐ firms expected to pay informal payment to public officials (to get things done)
■ incidence of bribery according to Graft index

Source: World Bank Enterprise Surveys, latest available year.
Note: Comparison restricted to firms with 5+ employees in sectors surveyed in most countries in the comparator group, i.e., manufacturing, retail, wholesale, hotels and restaurants, transport, and travel agencies.

Table 2.5   Corruption Perception Index (2009)

Country/territory	Rank	CPI 2009 score	Surveys used	Confidence range
Bhutan	49	5.0	4	4.3–5.6
Bolivia	120	2.7	6	2.4–3.1
Mongolia	120	2.7	7	2.4–3.0
Bangladesh	139	2.4	7	2.0–2.8
Nepal	143	2.3	6	2.0–2.6
Lao PDR	158	2.0	4	1.6–2.6

Source: Transparency International 2009.

then, corruption is likely to be widespread, but the costs associated with it are modest and are likely to be perceived by business owners as a petty expense.

For over two-thirds of the firms in Nepal, crime presents no obstacle at all. 7.3 percent of the firms rate crime as a major obstacle and only 1 percent identify it as the main investment climate problem. Thirteen percent of the firms suffered losses as a result of theft, robbery, vandalism, or arson, and the average loss amounted to 6.3 percent of annual sales. The incidence of losses due to crime and the average amount of such losses is much lower for large firms (2 percent and 1 percent, respectively), possibly because almost all large firms (99 percent) in Nepal pay for private security whereas 40 percent of the small firms and only 3 percent of the micro firms do. Firms that pay for private security spend on average 2.2 percent of their annual sales, without much variation across firm size.

The proportion of firms paying for security and the average security costs are about the same as in the South Asia region and in comparator countries. Comparator countries, however, experience greater losses as a result of criminal activity (Figure 2.13).

Regulations, Taxes, and Business Licensing

Excessive bureaucracy, poorly designed rules, and insufficient resources can make dealing with regulations difficult. Judging by the number of days that are on average necessary to obtain various licenses and permits, dealing with regulations is not particularly difficult in Nepal. Also, the time spent by senior managers to deal with bureaucracy and the number of required meetings with tax officials in a year are below average compared to comparator countries—even though Bangladesh performs consistently better along these dimensions (Figure 2.14).

Figure 2.13   Cost of Crime and Security in Nepal and Comparator Countries

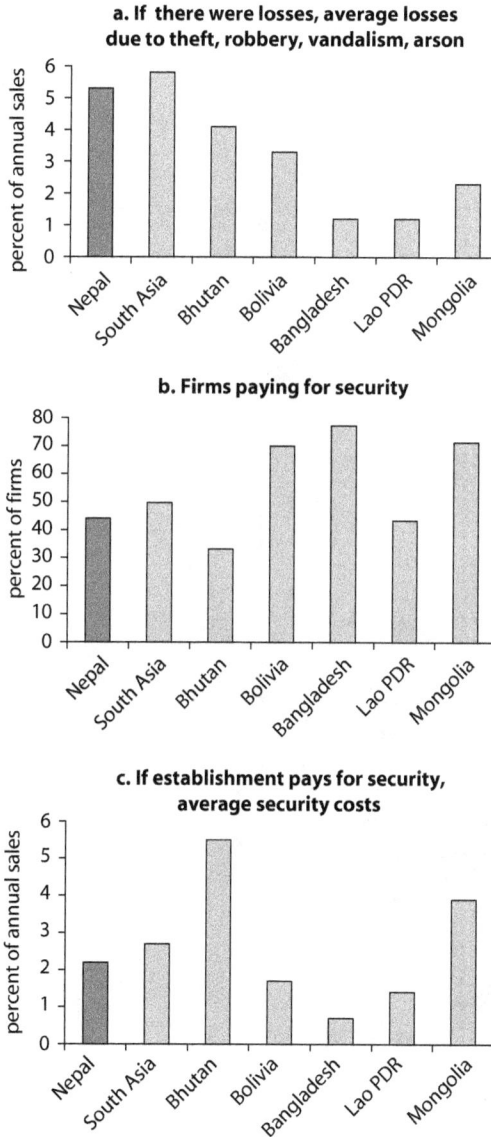

a. If there were losses, average losses
due to theft, robbery, vandalism, arson

percent of annual sales

Nepal, South Asia, Bhutan, Bolivia, Bangladesh, Lao PDR, Mongolia

b. Firms paying for security

percent of firms

Nepal, South Asia, Bhutan, Bolivia, Bangladesh, Lao PDR, Mongolia

c. If establishment pays for security,
average security costs

percent of annual sales

Nepal, South Asia, Bhutan, Bolivia, Bangladesh, Lao PDR, Mongolia

Source: World Bank Enterprise Surveys, latest available year.
Note: Comparison restricted to firms with 5+ employees in sectors surveyed in most countries in the comparator group, i.e., manufacturing, retail, wholesale, hotels and restaurants, transport, and travel agencies.

Figure 2.14   Time Spent Obtaining Licenses and Dealing with Regulations in Nepal and Comparator Countries

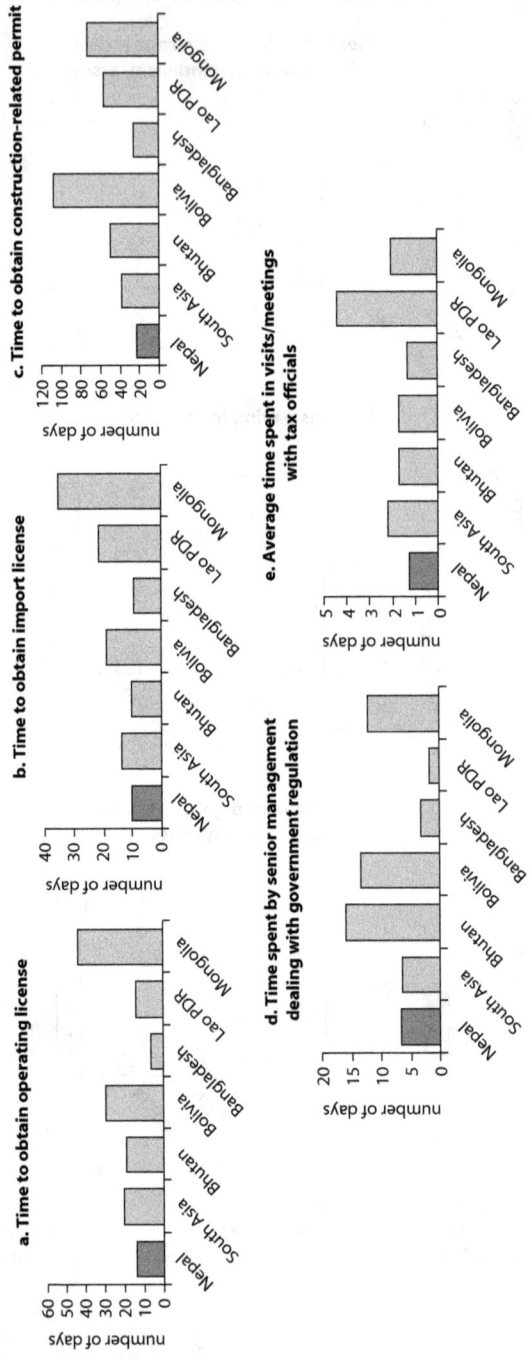

a. Time to obtain operating license

b. Time to obtain import license

c. Time to obtain construction-related permit

d. Time spent by senior management dealing with government regulation

e. Average time spent in visits/meetings with tax officials

Source: World Bank Enterprise Surveys, latest available year.

Note: Comparison restricted to firms with 5+ employees in sectors surveyed in most countries in the comparator group, i.e., manufacturing, retail, wholesale, hotels and restaurants, transport, and travel agencies.

Dealing with regulations is more difficult for large firms. While, on average, only 7 percent of the firms perceive tax rates and tax administration to be a major obstacle, the proportion is significantly higher among large firms (24 percent and 35 percent, respectively). In fact the "paying taxes" component of the Doing Business Index finds Nepal to have a high number of payments and time requirements, even though tax rates are, overall, lower than in many comparator countries (World Bank 2010a).

Government officials' interpretations of laws and regulations are not always consistent. 60.6 percent of the firms disagree with the statement that interpretation of laws and regulations is always consistent and predictable. Discontent with governance is once again stronger among medium and large firms and in the Eastern region.

Nepal was ranked 123 out of 183 economies in the overall ease of doing business (Table 2.6) (World Bank 2009a, 2010e, 2010f). Nepal appears to be doing well in terms of "Registering Property" whereas it performs below average in: 1) Trading Across Borders, 2) Employing Workers, 3) Dealing with Construction Permits, 4) Paying Taxes, 5) Enforcing Contracts, 6) Getting Credit, 7) Closing a Business, 8) Starting a Business, and 9) Protecting Investors. In particular, Nepal performs poorly with respect to trading across borders, employing workers, and dealing with construction permits (Table 2.7).

Starting and closing a business is relatively simpler in Nepal than in some of the comparator countries. Starting a business in Nepal involves a low number of procedures and low capital requirements, whereas the

Table 2.6   Doing Business Index

Ease of	Rank	World ranking	Comparator countries ranking
Doing business	**123**	Bottom third	Top half
Trading	161	Bottom third	Bottom half
Employing	148		
Licenses	131		
Taxes	124		
Contracts	122	Middle third	Bottom half
Credit	113	Middle third	Top half
Closing	105		
Starting	87		
Investors	73		
Property	26	Upper third	Top half

Source: World Bank 2009a.
Note: Columns 3 and 4 indicate, respectively, in which part of the world distribution and of the comparator countries distribution Nepal ranks—with respect to the overall Doing Business Index and to each component. Comparator countries are Bhutan, Mongolia, Lao PDR, and Bolivia.

Table 2.7   Doing Business Ranking 2010, Nepal and Comparator Countries

	Nepal	Bangladesh	Bhutan	Bolivia	Lao PDR	Mongolia
Doing business	**123**	**119**	**126**	**161**	**167**	**60**
Starting a business	87	98	80	167	89	78
Dealing with construction permits	131	118	126	101	115	103
Employing workers	148	124	12	183	107	44
Registering property	26	176	41	135	161	25
Getting credit	113	71	177	113	150	71
Protecting investors	73	20	132	132	182	27
Paying taxes	124	89	90	177	113	69
Trading across borders	161	107	153	121	168	155
Enforcing contracts	122	180	33	136	111	36
Closing a business	105	108	183	62	183	110

Source: World Bank 2009a.

time involved and especially the initial start-up costs are relatively high. Procedures for closing a business are instead made simple by the low cost of bankruptcy and a good recovery rate (Table 2.7).

Nepal performs well in terms of property registration due to a modest number of procedures and the short time necessary to complete the registration. The costs of registration, on the other hand, are relatively high. As for protection of minority shareholders, Nepal ranks in the top half in this dimension thanks to the ease with which shareholders can sue corporate directors.

Dealing with construction permits, paying taxes, and enforcing contracts is instead difficult because of the high number of procedures and length of time needed to complete them. Despite low overall tax rates, the country ranks poorly for paying taxes due to the high number of payments and time requirements. Finally, enforcing contracts is relatively difficult because of the number of calendar days needed to resolve disputes, which is higher than in comparator countries.

Notes

1. Political instability as defined in the survey included many aspects of Nepal's political problems such as: the armed conflict and the insurgency, civil unrest, frequent changes in government and regime, politically-motivated labor disruptions, strikes, *bhands*, and closures.

2. Indeed, the study team observed that some of the firms that were enumerated a couple of months earlier, were shut down when the enumerators went to

conduct the interview. Especially the manufacturing enterprises located in the industrial area of Kathmandu were closed or were in the process of being shut down due to excessive load shedding (power outages) and political problems.

3. The number of employees is computed on the basis of the number of full-time workers, both permanent and temporary (the latter weighted by the number of months they were employed in the firm). Employment growth only takes into consideration full-time permanent workers, due to lack of data on the number of temporary workers in the past.

4. These data are taken from the employee survey and therefore refer to firms with 5 or more employees.

5. The Political Instability Index represents the level of threat posed to governments by social protest. The index scores are derived by combining measures of economic distress and underlying vulnerability to unrest.

6. The Graft Index is measured as the proportion of instances in which firms were either expected or requested to pay a gift or informal payment in six different transactions: requests for an electrical connection, a water connection, telephone service, an import license, a construction-related permit, or an operating license.

7. Quantitative statistics on corruption are based on few observations, as few firms were involved in such transactions. The relevant sample size, including the statistic on government contracts, varies between six (applications for water connections) and 44 (applications for telephone connections).

CHAPTER 3

Performance of Private Sector Enterprises in Nepal

Private firms in Nepal are small both in terms of sales and employment. Performance is also poor, with labor productivity lower than in most comparator countries. Nepalese manufacturing firms have an advantage in terms of labor cost competitiveness (but not in labor competitiveness). Labor productivity and total sales are shown to be significantly higher in older firms, in firms that have more assets, among exporters, and in firms that are at least partly owned by foreigners. The investment climate dimensions that are found to have a significant correlation with performance are electricity, access to finance, and labor market characteristics. Therefore, in order to improve firm performance, besides improving the investment climate, policies should be put in place to encourage private investments, attract foreign capital, and facilitate trade.

Firm Performance and Costs of Poor Investment Climate

Unless political stability returns and economy-wide bottlenecks are well managed, it is difficult to envisage the private sector becoming an engine of growth or of Nepal emerging as a favorable investment destination. An analysis of the factors that can constrain investments, productivity, and growth is provided to help identify the dimensions of the investment climate that (most) need reforms.

Real Costs of Poor Investment Climate

A poor investment climate negatively affects firm performance by increasing costs and slashing labor and capital productivity. An initial assessment of the impact of the investment climate on firm performance can be made by looking at objective measures of some of the real costs related to the investment climate that are born by firms. Costs are higher in Nepal than in comparator countries for the dimensions directly relating to infrastructure (losses due to power outages, losses due to breakage or spoilage, and losses due to vandalism) (Table 3.1 and Figure 3.1).

The aggregate of such costs is also much larger in Nepal than in any comparator country when looking at costs measured as a percentage of total annual sales.

While Nepal compares well with comparator countries in terms of the number of days required to obtain permits, licenses, clearances, and utility connections (except for telephone connections) (Table 3.2), these favorable aspects are offset by conflict and the poor investment climate. Once the number of days lost to civil unrest and trade union

Table 3.1   Losses Due to Investment Climate Weaknesses

	Nepal	Bhutan	Bolivia	Bangladesh	Mongolia
Losses due to power outages (% total annual sales)	27.0	5.0	8.5	11.8	1.1
Losses due to theft, robbery, vandalism, or arson (% total annual sales)	6.1	4.2	3.6	1.4	2.3
Informal payments or gifts to public officials (% total annual sales)	0.5	0.4	2.2	1.09	1.4
Total annual cost of security (% total annual sales)	2.2	6.2	1.7	0.8	3.9
% total senior management spent on dealing with government regulations	8.7	16.2	14.9	3.73	12.0
% of consignment value lost in transit because of theft	0.0	1.9	0.1	0.0	2.6*
% of consignment value lost in transit because of breakage or spoilage	1.9	1.4	0.4	0.4	

Source: World Bank Enterprise Surveys, latest available year.
Note: Comparison restricted to firms with 5+ employees in sectors surveyed in most countries in the comparator group, i.e., manufacturing, retail, wholesale, hotels and restaurants, transport, and travel agencies. (*) For Mongolia this number is the percentage of consignment value lost in transit because of theft, breakage, or spoilage.

Figure 3.1   Costs Associated with Investment Climate Weaknesses in Nepal and Comparator Countries

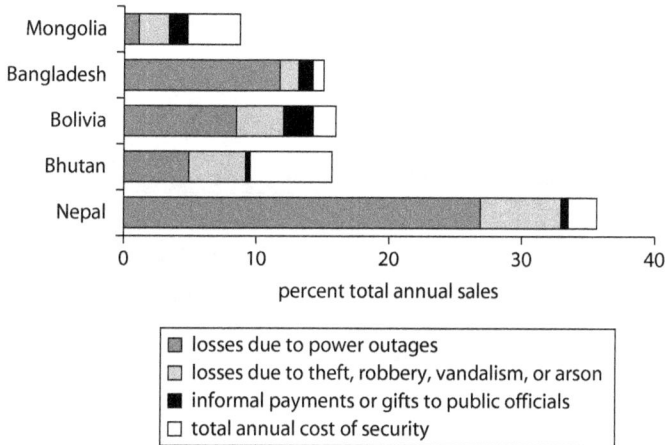

percent total annual sales

- ▨ losses due to power outages
- ☐ losses due to theft, robbery, vandalism, or arson
- ■ informal payments or gifts to public officials
- ☐ total annual cost of security

Source: World Bank Enterprise Surveys, latest available year.
Note: Comparison restricted to firms with 5+ employees in sectors surveyed in most countries in the comparator group, i.e., manufacturing, retail, wholesale, hotels and restaurants, transport, and travel agencies. Losses due to civil unrest and trade union actions are not included in this chart as enterprises were not asked to report them as a proportion of annual sales but rather as the number of days lost.

Table 3.2   Average Number of Days to Obtain Permits and Connections to Utilities

	Nepal	Bhutan	Bolivia	Bangladesh	Lao PDR	Mongolia
Electrical connection	9	16	15	50	16	18
Water connection	11	16	44	36	44	83
Telephone connection	35	5	13	94	3	8
Clear customs for exports	6	2	13	8	8	19
Clear customs for imports	14	5	26	10	11	8
Construction-related permit	23	46	101	28	44	47
Import license	10	10	18	10	21	30
Operating license	15	15	28	6	14	40

Source: World Bank Enterprise Surveys, latest available year.
Note: Comparison restricted to firms with 5+ employees in sectors surveyed in most countries in the comparator group, i.e., manufacturing, retail, wholesale, hotels and restaurants, transport, and travel agencies.

actions are added (where Nepalese firms lose a total of 50 working days), the real cost of conflict and the poor investment climate in Nepal becomes evident (Figure 3.2). This added burden on the private sector is daunting, especially when coupled with losses due to power outages and crime.

Figure 3.2   Average Number of Days Lost in Nepalese Firms Due to Labor Issues

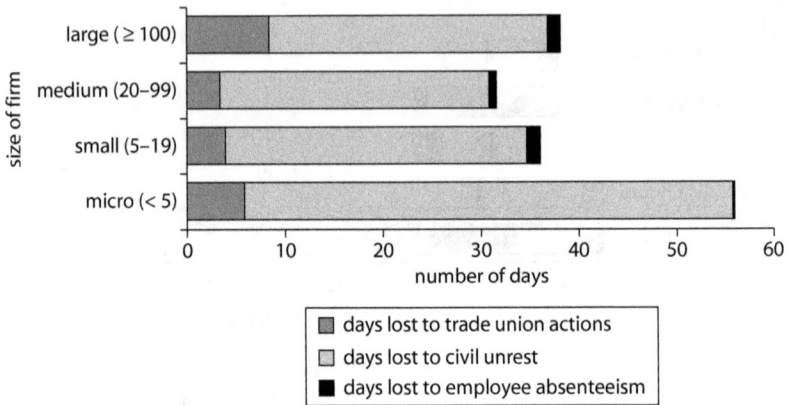

Source: Nepal Enterprise Survey 2009.

Firm Performance

Poor performance both in terms of sales and employment characterized enterprises in Nepal. The average firm's total sales amounted to US$415 thousand (in 2005 prices)—the lowest within the comparator countries group (Table 3.3). Over the three years before the survey, sales grew at an average annual rate of 9 percent, lower than in Bhutan and Mongolia, but higher than in Bangladesh and Lao PDR. The average number of full-time permanent employees is far smaller than in the comparator countries, and firms have been able to increase employment by 7 percent per year on average.

Employment growth in Nepal has been driven by the services sector. Between 2005/06 and 2007/08 the average growth rate in the number of employees among enterprises was 3.9 percent; the growth rate, however, was much lower in the manufacturing sector (1 percent) and negative in the tourism industry (Figure 3.3).

Capacity utilization for manufacturing firms with five or more employees, on the other hand, was on average 80.8 percent, which is quite high. Utilization was 77.1 percent in South Asia, 61.8 percent in Bolivia, 79.7 percent in Bangladesh, and 65.7 percent in Mongolia; the average level of utilization for the comparator countries covered by the Enterprise Survey is 72.5 percent.[1] This might indicate that limited capacity and investments rather than lack of demand constrains productivity in Nepal.

Table 3.3   Firm Performance in Nepal and Comparator Countries

	Sales		Workers	
	Average (thousand 2005 US$)	Average growth rate (%)	Average number	Average growth rate (%)
Nepal	415	8.7	14	6.5
Bhutan	1,804	26.8	25	15.0
Bangladesh	1,780	3.8	179	6.2
Lao PDR	494	3.7	23	1.2
Mongolia	1,367	35.9	40	15.6

Source: World Bank Enterprise Surveys, latest available year.
Note: Comparison restricted to firms with 5+ employees in sectors surveyed in most countries in the comparator group, i.e., manufacturing, retail, wholesale, hotels and restaurants, transport, and travel agencies. Growth rates are computed for the three years before the survey.

Figure 3.3   Average Employment Annual Growth Rate in Nepal, FY2005/06 to FY2007/08
(% points)

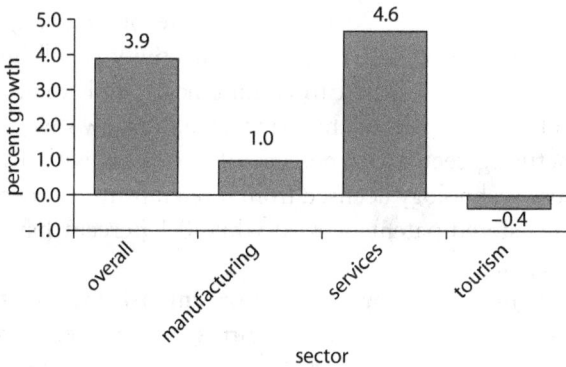

Source: Nepal Enterprise Survey 2009.

Reflecting poor integration in the global market, very few Nepalese firms export their products abroad. Overall, only 3.1 percent of the firms export their products either directly or indirectly; among firms with five or more employees, 3.8 percent of the firms are exporters (Table 3.4). Among large firms, the incidence of exporting firms rises to 28.3 percent, which is still low by international standards. Firms are twice as likely to be exporters in the manufacturing sector as in other sectors.

Table 3.4   Exporting in Nepal and Comparator Countries

	% exporter firms
Nepal	3.8
South Asia	20.0
Bhutan	8.6
Bolivia	19.2
Bangladesh	6.1
Lao PDR	9.4
Mongolia	7.6

Source: World Bank Enterprise Surveys, latest available year.
Note: Comparison restricted to firms with 5+ employees in sectors surveyed in most countries in the comparator group, i.e., manufacturing, retail, wholesale, hotels and restaurants, transport, and travel agencies.

Little innovation occurs in the private sector in Nepal. Nepalese firms with 5 or more employees perform poorly against most of the indicators in the survey associated with innovation and technology adoption (Figure 3.4). Only 3 percent of the firms have an internationally recognized quality certification; 70 percent, on the other hand, have their financial statements certified. Internet connectivity is still limited; 46.2 percent of the firms use email to communicate with their clients and suppliers and 23.3 percent of the firms have their own website. Within the manufacturing sector, 0.7 percent of the firms with five or more employees use technology licensed from foreign firms, 0.6 percent of the firms have registered patents abroad while 0.1 percent have registered patents in Nepal.

Large firms use technology much more intensively, but still little by international standards. Among large firms, 27.1 percent have international quality certification and 99.1 percent have their financial statements audited; 99.1 percent of them use email to communicate with clients and suppliers; and 75.2 percent have a website. Within the manufacturing sector, 8.6 percent of the large firms use foreign technology, 4.3 percent registered patents abroad, and 67.3 percent registered patents inside the country.

Firms that innovate and adopt technology tend to perform better. Firms that adopt innovating behavior, such as using international quality certification, using technology licensed from foreign companies, and registering patents abroad and domestically, have on average significantly higher labor productivity (Table 3.5).

Figure 3.4   Innovation and Technology Adoption in Nepal and Comparator Countries

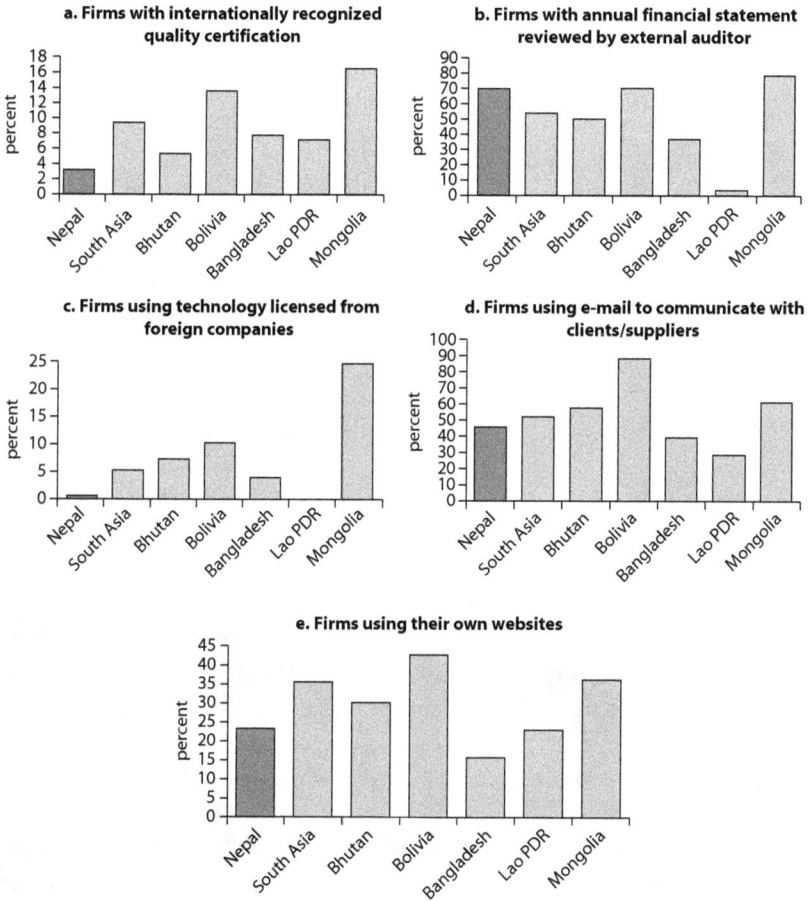

a. Firms with internationally recognized quality certification

b. Firms with annual financial statement reviewed by external auditor

c. Firms using technology licensed from foreign companies

d. Firms using e-mail to communicate with clients/suppliers

e. Firms using their own websites

Source: World Bank Enterprise Surveys, latest available year.
Note: Comparison restricted to firms with 5+ employees in sectors surveyed in most countries in the comparator group, i.e., manufacturing, retail, wholesale, hotels and restaurants, transport, and travel agencies.

Labor Productivity and Other Indicators of Firm Performance in the Nepalese Private Sector

Limitations of the data constrain the analysis of firm performance: First, the survey only has two years of data on sales and labor, and many firms fail to report materials and investment; as a consequence, total

Table 3.5   Firms' Performance and Innovation Adoption

Firm has...	Average sales per worker (Nr)	Average value added per worker (Nr)
International quality certification		
Yes	6,981,825	522,966
No	922,051	201,881
Technology licensed from foreign company		
Yes	4,506,468	1,200,497
No	498,272	138,442
Patents registered abroad		
Yes	2,854,928	1,345,884
No	500,746	136,045
Patents registered in Nepal		
Yes	1,735,687	407,950
No	385,397	114,936

Source: Nepal Enterprise Survey 2009.

factor productivity cannot be properly measured and firm performance will be represented through total sales, employment, and labor productivity. Second, the broad industry coverage makes it harder to justify a single production function to fit all the different industries; as a result, the performance of firms will not be compared across industries. Third, while it would be very important to differentiate quality among firms in the services industry, this is not possible in the current dataset due to lack of information on prices. Finally, the analysis is adjusted for sampling weights to account for the over sampling of large firms in the survey.

The industrial composition of the sample, which consists of a cross-section of 486 firms, is rather diverse. In terms of industry coverage, 38 percent of the sample is in the manufacturing industry and 30 percent in retail (Table 3.6). The telecommunications industry has the least number of firms, only 3; the other two small industries are the automobile services industry and the computing industry. Within the manufacturing sector, the main product mix of firms consists of apparel, furniture, plastic, and basic metals. *In the following paragraphs, the performance analysis will only be carried out for sectors with the largest sample size, i.e., hotel and restaurants, manufacturing, and retail.*

The largest of the industries under analysis is manufacturing. Overall, average firm sales in 2007/08 were Nrs 7.9 million, and Nrs 7 million in 2005/06, with an average growth rate of 3.7 percent. The average sales per firm in the manufacturing industry were Nrs 20 million in 2007/08.

Table 3.6   Distribution of Sample by Industry and Region

Industry	Region West	Central	East	Nepal	% of total
Overall	**98**	**328**	**60**	**486**	**100**
Automobile services	0	5	3	8	1.7
Computing	2	3	2	7	1.4
Hotel and restaurants	18	61	5	84	17.3
Manufacturing	46	120	21	187	38.5
Retail	25	103	18	146	30.0
Telecommunications	0	2	1	3	0.6
Transportation and travel agencies	5	26	4	35	7.2
Wholesale	2	8	6	16	3.3

Source: Nepal Enterprise Survey 2009.

The hotel and restaurant industry grew the fastest with an average annual growth rate of 8.5 percent, followed by manufacturing with an average annual growth rate of 4.8 percent (Table 3.7).

The manufacturing industry is also the largest in terms of job creation. On average, a manufacturing firm employed about 14 workers in 2007/08; the fastest expanding industry in terms of employment is, however, hotels and restaurants (8 percent) (Table 3.7). Overall, firms in Nepal are quite small, with an average firm size of 6 workers.

Table 3.8 compares the average sales and employment of all the industries across the three regions: East, Central, and West. While firms in the Central region are larger in terms of average sales and the number of workers, both sales and employment are expanding faster in the Western region.

Table 3.9 presents average labor productivity by industry for the two periods, as well as the implied average annual growth rates. Labor productivity is computed both as the value of sales per worker employed by the firm and as the value added per worker employed. Value added is defined as the difference between sales and the cost of materials. Value added per worker is a more precise measure of labor productivity than sales per worker because it is net of the cost of intermediate inputs; however, in this dataset it is only measurable for a sufficient number of firms in the manufacturing and retail industries.

The most productive industry in terms of sales per worker is retail, but in all the three industries analyzed average labor productivity is lower than in the best performing sectors and therefore lower than the overall

Table 3.7   Enterprise Sales and Employment Growth by Industry

	Sales		Number of workers	
	Average 2007/08 (thousand Nrs)	Avg annual growth rate since 2005/06 (%)	Average 2007/08	Avg annual growth rate since 2005/06 (%)
Overall	**7,941**	**3.7**	**6.0**	**3.9**
Automobile services	154,084	8.4	14.8	25.9
Computing	9,990	18.1	6.4	−4.4
Hotel and restaurants	4,453	8.5	9.6	8.0
Manufacturing	20,042	4.8	14.1	1.0
Retail	2,620	1.0	3.3	3.5
Telecommunications	447	−21.0	11.3	2.9
Transportation and travel agencies	10,338	9.8	5.3	4.1
Wholesale	7,876	10.4	5.2	0.7

Source: Nepal Enterprise Survey 2009.

Table 3.8   Enterprise Sales and Employment Growth Rates by Region

	Average 2007/08 (thousand Nrs)			Average annual growth rate since 2005/06 (%)		
	West	Central	East	West	Central	East
Sales	4,951	10,704	3,864	10.7	2.6	0.0
Employment	4.6	6.6	5.4	5.1	3.8	2.4

Source: Nepal Enterprise Survey 2009.

Table 3.9   Labor Productivity by Industry

	Sales per worker		Value added per worker
	Average 2007/08 (thousand Nrs)	Avg annual growth rate since 2005/06 (%)	Average 2007/08 (thousand Nrs)
Overall	**979**	**−0.3**	**200**
Automobile services	13,542	−17.5	
Computing	1,465	22.5	
Hotel and restaurants	200	0.6	
Manufacturing	577	3.3	157
Retail	877	−2.7	209
Telecommunications	47	−23.9	
Transportation and travel agencies	1,710	7.0	
Wholesale	1,124	9.8	

Source: Nepal Enterprise Survey 2009.

average for the whole country (Table 3.9). On the other hand, manufacturing outperforms the overall average in terms of labor productivity growth with a 3.3 percent increase in the past three years. The value added produced by the average worker in the manufacturing sector was Nrs 157 thousand, less than the in the retail sector (Nrs 209 thousand).

Sales per worker are highest in the Central region but firms are growing faster in the West. Looking at value added per worker, we find that labor productivity in the manufacturing and retail industries is actually higher in the West (Table 3.10).

The average level of labor productivity increases with size (Table 3.11); labor productivity growth, on the other hand, shows the same trend overall but not necessarily within sectors.

Average labor productivity is also much larger for exporters than for non-exporters, both in levels and in growth rates (Table 3.12). While this is certainly linked to the fact that exporters are on average larger, the correlation between exporting and labor productivity seems to be strong.

Table 3.10   Average Labor Productivity by Region

	Sales per worker						Value added per worker		
	Average 2007/08 (thousand Nrs.)			Avg annual growth rate since 2005/06 (%)			Average 2007/08 (thousand Nrs.)		
	West	Central	East	West	Central	East	West	Central	East
Overall	615	1,142	820	5.36	−1.42	−2.53	281	185	162

Source: Nepal Enterprise Survey 2009.

Table 3.11   Average Labor Productivity by Size

	Average 2007/08 (thousand Nrs)				Avg annual growth rate since 2005/06 (%)			
	Micro	Small	Medium	Large	Micro	Small	Medium	Large
Overall	796	1,430	1,026	1,652	−1.38	1.91	6.04	7.16

Source: Nepal Enterprise Survey 2009.

Table 3.12   Average Labor Productivity for Exporters and Nonexporters

	Average 2007/08 (thousand Nrs)	Avg annual growth rate since 2005/06 (%)
Overall	**979**	**−0.29**
Non-exporter	969	−0.44
Exporter	2,122	15.40

Source: Nepal Enterprise Survey 2009.

In the next section of this chapter, the causal relationship between being an exporter and productivity will be explored.

The labor productivity of most firms is concentrated around its low average value. The distribution of value added per worker is very concentrated around its mean and there are very few examples of good performers that could lead the way for others. Performance is even more concentrated in services (where small firms prevail) than in manufacturing (Figure 3.5).

Nepal performs poorly by all indicators of firm performance, especially in terms of growth in labor productivity and exporting. In order to better assess the performance of Nepalese firms, we compare some of the indicators of firm performance with comparator countries. Cross-country comparisons by industry reveal that Nepal performs worse than the comparator countries in most categories, both in levels and in growth rates (Table 3.13).

Nepalese manufacturing firms have low unit labor costs. Nepal's manufacturing firms have low labor costs, which result in very low unit labor costs (Table 3.14).[2] However, while unit labor costs are low due to low nominal wages, the combination of low and stagnating or declining productivity and real exchange rate appreciation over the past two years means that unit labor costs are rising, albeit from a low point.

Figure 3.5   Distribution of Value Added per Worker by Sector

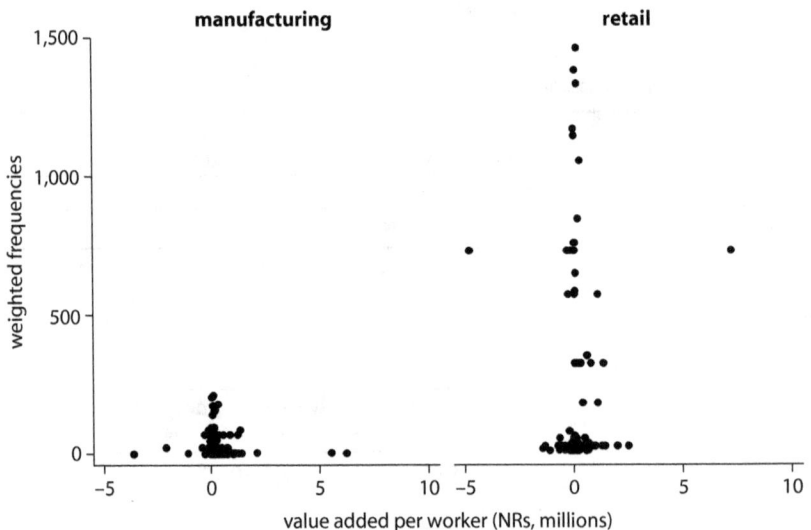

Source: Nepal Enterprise Survey 2009.

Table 3.13 Cross-Country Comparisons of Firm Performance by Industry

	Sales		Labor productivity		Employment		Exporter
	Average (thousand 2005 US$)	Avg annual growth rate (%)	Average (thousand 2005 US$)	Avg annual growth rate (%)	Average number	Avg annual growth rate (%)	% firms
Overall							
Nepal	415	8.7	22	2.4	14	6.5	3.8
Bhutan	1,804	26.8	106	12.4	25	15.0	8.4
Bangladesh	1,780	3.8	12	4.8	179	6.2	27.8
Lao PDR	494	3.7	29	4.4	23	1.2	9.5
Mongolia	1,367	35.9	23	22.3	40	15.6	7.6
Manufacturing							
Nepal	623	6.0	20	4.8	17	0.8	7.6
Bhutan	2,676	8.3	89	−8.8	41	17.4	34.3
Bangladesh	2,113	8.4	13	3.8	228	7.4	34.9
Lao PDR	524	6.6	19	4.4	40	3.2	21.2
Mongolia	1,208	34.2	18	27.8	44	7.0	22.3
Retail							
Nepal	285	5.3	25	−7.6	10	12.6	4.8
Bhutan	624	16.8	89	6.6	11	10.7	1.4
Bangladesh	785	−7.5	9	9.3	30	1.0	6.1
Lao PDR	557	11.4	51	7.0	8	2.0	12.7
Mongolia	697	24.5	21	14.9	22	9.7	1.6

(continued next page)

Table 3.13 (continued)

	Sales		Labor productivity		Employment		Exporter
	Average (thousand 2005 US$)	Avg annual growth rate (%)	Average (thousand 2005 US$)	Avg annual growth rate (%)	Average number	Avg annual growth rate (%)	% firms
Wholesale							
Nepal	530	19.7	54	21.4	10	-1.7	3.2
Bhutan	1,695	35.3	198	19.4	9	15.9	7.8
Lao PDR	1,851	20.2	70	21.8	35	-2.0	22.0
Mongolia	3,906	32.0	30	15.3	87	16.2	4.6
Hotels & Restaurants							
Nepal	276	12.3	6	3.1	17	9.3	0.0
Bhutan	470	35.2	16	33.0	23	2.2	0.0
Lao PDR	282	-0.4	21	-0.1	16	-0.3	0.0
Mongolia	271	35.9	11	22.3	19	13.6	0.0
Transport & travel agencies							
Nepal	230	7.5	25	3.3	8	8.9	2.9
Bhutan	773	45.7	60	23.8	11	21.9	0.0
Lao PDR	524	-5.9	13	-7.0	32	1.0	0.0
Mongolia	5,190	32.3	23	30.3	40	3.4	19.7

Source: World Bank Enterprise Surveys, latest available year.

Note: Comparison restricted to firms with 5+ employees in sectors surveyed in most countries in the comparator group, i.e. manufacturing, retail, wholesale, hotels and restaurants, transport, and travel agencies.

Table 3.14   Cross-Country Comparisons of Manufacturing Unit Labor Costs

	Value added per worker (thousand 2005 US$)	Unit labor cost (index)
Nepal	6,233.6	20.3%
Bangladesh	4,822.5	49.2%
Lao PDR	14,166.9	26.7%
Mongolia	8,471.3	65.0%

Source: World Bank Enterprise Surveys, latest available year.
Note: Comparison restricted to firms with 5+ employees.

Labor Productivity and the Investment Climate

This section analyzes the factors that can affect sales and labor productivity of firms within an industry. Empirical evidence shows that, among other things, materials and capital inputs, age, ownership, and export status can drive firm sales and labor productivity. In addition to materials and capital inputs, firm age and ownership status have been shown in the past to be relevant determinants of firm performance. Older firms are likely to be large, but may not be more productive, while firms with foreign ownership (FDI firms) could be more productive if foreigners brought in not just capital, but management knowhow and superior technology (Kee and Krishna 2008). There is also a robust relationship between exporter status and firm performance. Exporters tend to be larger and more productive. Typically, more productive firms become exporters (Fernandes 2008), but there is also some empirical evidence suggesting that exporters learn from their exporting experience and become more productive (De Loecker 2007). It is also possible that the more innovative a firm is, the better is its performance, given that innovation is the key driver for firm productivity.

In order to explore the role of various firm characteristics in explaining differences in labor productivity, we carry out a regression of sales per worker on such firm characteristics. The regression analysis consists of a simple ordinary least squares (OLS) regression model to correlate measures of firm performance (total sales, sales per worker, and value added per worker) to a number of inputs (correlates) that the literature has proven significant. We do not attempt to estimate a firm production function, which would require a much more detailed dataset than the one effectively available from the Nepal Enterprise Survey 2009 where firms outside the manufacturing sector do not report fuel costs, electricity costs, or materials. The regression results only identify significant correlations and not causation because of the well-known problem of possible endogeneity of input choice.

The OLS regression analysis uses robust standard errors to control for the usual *heteroskedasticity* of firm level data. Moreover, given that the survey oversampled large firms, weighted least squares are applied. Industry and region fixed effects are included in the regression to make sure that all of the comparisons are not influenced by industry and region specific factors.

The results show that having more fixed assets and being older are associated with larger sales (Table 3.15). Most interestingly, being an exporter or a firm that has attracted FDI is also associated with larger sales. For manufacturing and retail firms, the regression results show that firms that use more material inputs tend to have larger sales.

Larger fixed assets are not necessarily associated with higher labor productivity, but the firm's age is. Moreover, exporters and FDI firms are all shown to be statistically significantly more productive, as shown in Column 1 of Table 3.16—where labor productivity is related to firms' fixed assets, materials, age, exporter status, and FDI firm status.[3] In Column 2 the sample is restricted to manufacturing and retail; here the

Table 3.15   Correlates of Total Sales

	Dependent variable: log of sales		
	(1)	(2)	(3)
Materials		0.786***	0.795***
		(0.061)	(0.073)
Fixed assets	0.222**		0.151**
	(0.097)		(0.059)
Age	0.075***	0.002	0.004
	(0.023)	(0.009)	(0.015)
Exporters	2.077***	0.405*	0.16
	(0.593)	(0.213)	(0.278)
FDI firms	1.253*	0.377	0.078
	(0.718)	(0.273)	(0.349)
Industry fixed effects	Yes	Yes	Yes
Region fixed effects	Yes	Yes	Yes
Number of firms	174	320	98

Source: Nepal Enterprise Survey 2009.
Notes: Regressions are adjusted to reflect sampling weights. Estimation (2)–(3) limited to manufacturing and retail due to availability of information on cost of materials.
White robust standard errors in parentheses. *, **, and *** denote statistical significance at 90, 95, and 99 percent respectively.

result is weak: productivity is higher among firms that have large material inputs but it is lower among older firms. Column 3 further controls for firm fixed assets showing that they are an important control, as productivity is now higher among exporters and FDI firms.

Overall, regression results suggest that firms with larger fixed assets and older firms are larger in terms of sales, so are exporters and FDI firms. The latter also have higher labor productivity.

An assessment of the relationship between investment climate and firm productivity helps shed further light on firm performance. Historical data would be necessary to determine a causal relationship between measures of the investment climate and firm productivity. Since such data is not available for Nepal, the analysis below will be restricted to adding objective measures of the investment climate to the above regression to determine their correlation with a firm's output and labor productivity.[4]

Firms with higher average productivity find that political instability is a major or very severe obstacle compared with other firms, indicating that political instability is possibly hindering the performance of the most productive firms (Table 3.17).[5]

Access to finance and electricity supply show consistent correlations with firm performance. Higher reliance on banks—as opposed to internal

Table 3.16   Correlates of Labor Productivity

	Dependent variable: log sales per worker			Dependent variable: log value added per worker	
	(1)	(2)	(3)	(4)	(5)
Materials		0.563***	0.417***		
		(0.066)	(0.081)		
Fixed assets	−0.001		0.011		0.114
	(0.078)		(0.062)		(0.076)
Age	0.031*	−0.022***	−0.015	−0.033	−0.006
	(0.017)	(0.008)	(0.013)	(0.023)	(0.022)
Exporters	2.116***	0.113	1.153***	1.870***	1.402**
	(0.455)	(0.385)	(0.412)	(0.374)	(0.623)
FDI firms	0.837**	−0.208	0.377*	0.41	0.877
	(0.387)	(0.264)	(0.217)	(0.531)	(0.834)
Industry fixed effects	Yes	Yes	Yes	Yes	Yes
Region fixed effects	Yes	Yes	Yes	Yes	Yes
Number of firms	174	320	98	263	87

Source: Nepal Enterprise Survey 2009.
Notes: Regressions are adjusted to reflect sampling weights. Estimation (2)–(5) limited to manufacturing and retail due to availability of information on cost of materials.
White robust standard errors in parentheses. *, **, and *** denote statistical significance at 90, 95, and 99 percent respectively.

funds or informal sources—for borrowing working capital is linked to better performance (Table 3.18).[6] At the same time, a higher number of outages are associated with lower sales and lower sales per worker. Results are instead weak with respect to costs of security and crime.

Other dimensions of the investment climate have not been found to be significantly associated with sales or labor productivity. The size of the dataset does not allow us to determine whether this effectively

Table 3.17   Perception of Political Instability and Firm Performance

Political instability is...	Average sales per worker	Average value added per worker
a major or very severe obstacle	1,043,853	217,405
not a major obstacle	404,033	79,903

Source: Nepal Enterprise Survey 2009.

Table 3.18   Investment Climate Variables and Firm Performance

	Dependent variable			
	(1)	(2)	(3)	(4)
	Total sales	Sales per worker	Value added	Value added per worker
Investments (log)	0.222*	0.022	0.271**	0.027
	(0.120)	(0.096)	(0.126)	(0.091)
Age	0.063**	0.024	0	−0.026
	(0.024)	(0.018)	(0.026)	(0.017)
Exporter	1.627***	1.924***	0.312	0.857*
	(0.396)	(0.362)	(0.587)	(0.502)
FDI	1.399**	0.912**	1.734	1.514**
	(0.703)	(0.408)	(1.325)	(0.751)
N. outages per month[a]	−0.084*	−0.069*	−0.123***	−0.125***
	(0.049)	(0.039)	(0.043)	(0.036)
Cost of security	0.053	−0.002	0.112	0.067
(% of total annual sales)	(0.078)	(0.051)	(0.115)	(0.079)
Losses due to crime	0.038	0.025	0.244	0.216
(% of total annual sales)	(0.088)	(0.066)	(0.187)	(0.161)
Working capital borrowed	0.017**	0.01	0.043***	0.029***
from banks (%)	(0.007)	(0.007)	(0.009)	(0.007)
Industry fixed effects	Yes	Yes	Yes	Yes
Region fixed effects	Yes	Yes	Yes	Yes
N	170	170	83	83

Source: Nepal Enterprise Survey 2009.
Notes: Regressions are adjusted to reflect sampling weights. Estimation (2)–(3) limited to manufacturing and retail due to availability of information on cost of materials.
a. indicates variables instrumented with region/ industry average
White robust standard errors in parentheses. *, **, and *** denote statistical significance at 90, 95 and 99 percent respectively.

implies that such dimensions are not relevant or that—rather—some dimensions are measured more poorly and the relationship is therefore not captured by the regression analysis.

Concluding Remarks

The analysis of the performance of the private sector in Nepal, based on the Nepal Enterprise Survey 2009, sheds light on the reasons behind the low investment rate and growth in the country.

Sales and employment have increased over the past two years but labor productivity has contracted. Performance in terms of labor productivity varies across industries, but is declining in the Central region.

Labor productivity and sales are low compared to comparator countries. Compared to comparator countries, the private sector in Nepal has lower sales and lower labor productivity, measured as sales per worker. Growth rates are also lower. Furthermore, firms are on average smaller in size and the incidence of exporters is much lower. However, given low nominal wages, Nepal has low unit labor costs (an advantage that is undermined by low and declining productivity).

An analysis of firms' sales as measured against inputs suggests that higher investments are associated with a higher average productivity, *ceteris paribus*, but the direction of causality could go both ways. Productivity is also higher among older firms that are exporters, and firms that receive FDI.

In terms of the impact of a number of investment climate dimensions, better access to finance is associated with higher sales and higher labor productivity, while electricity outages are associated with poorer performance.

The empirical analysis suggests that having larger fixed assets, more FDI, and being an exporter are associated with greater labor productivity, especially among firms with good access to finance and decent power supply. Therefore, policies that promote investment, trade, FDI, and access to finance, while ensuring better energy supply should be put in place in order to help improve the performance of the private sector in Nepal.

Notes

1. Information on capacity utilization is not available in the Bhutan and Lao PDR surveys.

2. Unit labor cost is measured as labor cost per worker over value added per worker.

3. Similar to the previous specification, we control for full sets of industry and region fixed effects and apply weighted least squares to correct for sampling bias.

4. The main problem with an OLS estimate is the possible endogeneity of certain investment climate variables with respect to firm productivity.

5. However, given that around 90 percent of firms reported political instability as a major or severe constraint, this result should be interpreted cautiously.

6. It is important to keep in mind that there is no clear causality direction in the association between access to bank credit and performance: bank credit can improve performance and, at the same time, banks may be more willing to lend to well-performing firms.

CHAPTER 4

Infrastructure: A Major Constraint to Private Sector Development

Partly due to difficult geographic characteristics, Nepal's infrastructure is underdeveloped and poorly maintained, especially with regard to power generation and transportation. This chapter explains that although the country is operating at much below its hydropower generation potential, electricity supply is insufficient, unreliable, and expensive, leaving 99 percent of the firms subject to frequent power outages that cost firms 22 percent of annual sales. Transport infrastructure is also insufficient and unreliable, especially in road transport; 2 percent of consignment value is lost on average due to breakage and spoilage during transport resulting from lack of alternate routes and frequent strikes. Investments for infrastructure need to be increased, focusing on transport and power. For the former, it is essential that all districts are connected by all-season roads while for the latter; investments to advance the electrification rate and to increase water storage are needed.

Nepal's Infrastructure Conditions

Extensive and effective infrastructure is key to an economy's competitiveness and growth. Without proper infrastructure, firms cannot use modern production technologies and cannot connect to their input and output markets; production costs increase and competitiveness declines. Poor infrastructure also affects the business environment and discourages foreign investments, hampering the mix of economic activities that can develop.

Three key dimensions of infrastructure are critical for competitiveness: transport, electricity, and telecommunications (World Economic Forum 2009). An effective transport infrastructure enables entrepreneurs to access input and output markets and facilitates the movement of workers. An adequate and reliable electricity supply is essential for enterprises to be able to produce without interruptions, in a timely fashion, and without excessive expenditure on electricity. Finally, telecommunications infrastructure increases productivity by making relevant information available for decision making by all economic actors.

The state of Nepal's infrastructure is generally poor, especially with regard to electricity generation and transport. The limited infrastructure in the country and its poor quality have long acted as constraints to investments and growth (Table 4.1).

While the government's spending for infrastructure development is similar to other South Asian countries as a portion of GDP, in absolute terms, such investments are insufficient and have been decreasing over

Table 4.1   Comparative Infrastructure Indicators

	Bangladesh	Bhutan	India	Nepal	Sri Lanka
Electricity consumption	136	—	480	70	378
per capita (kWh)	(2005)		(2007)	(2007)	(2007)
Household electrification	46.5	41.1	67.9	61.2	80.7
rate	(2007)	(2003)	(2005)	(2006)	(2002)
Road density	2079	93	2226	121	1422
(km/km² of land)	(2007)	(2007)	(2007)	(2007)	(2007)
Paved roads (% total)	9.5	62.0	47.4	56.9	81.0
	(2007)	(2007)	(2007)	(2007)	(2007)
Telephone lines	0.83	4.5	3.2	2.8	17.8
(per 100 population)	(2008)	(2007)	(2008)	(2008)	(2008)
Cellular subscription	27.67	22.73	29.24	11.59	57.14
(per 100 population)	(2008)	(2007)	(2008)	(2007)	(2008)
Internet users	0.32	6.08	6.93	1.41	5.92
(per 1,000 people)	(2007)	(2007)	(2007)	(2007)	(2008)
GDP per unit of energy use	7	—	4.7	2.9	8
(constant 2005 PPP $)	(2006)		(2006)	(2006)	(2006)

Source: World Development Indicators (World Bank 2009d); World Bank Demographic and Health Surveys 2009; UN Millennium Indicators Database 2009; ICT Indicators Database (International Telecommunication Union 2009).
Note: Year of latest available data in parenthesis.
— = not available.
PPP = purchasing power parity.

time. Between 1990 and 2007, expenditure on electricity, gas, and water contracted by 32 percent in real terms; only expenditure for transport and communications increased in real terms over the same period (MOF 2007). The conflict has made infrastructure much worse by the combination of physical destruction and discouraging investments.

Low levels of investment also damaged the overall quality of infrastructure, as reflected in the poor ranking of Nepal in overall infrastructure quality (Table 4.2).

Electricity and Power Supply

Electricity supply in Nepal is inadequate, unreliable, and expensive. Over the years, Nepal's demand for electricity has increased but per capita consumption is the lowest in the region (Figure 4.1). Low consumption is due to low coverage—i.e., insufficient access—and insufficient availability for those that do have access to electricity. Coverage is about 48 percent of the population (including grid and off-grid access), with wide regional variations (MOF 2007), which translates into about 15 million people—mostly living in rural areas and remote districts—without access to electricity. Even the portion of the population with access to electricity does not have sufficient supply to meet its requirements. Because of the chronic supply-demand gap, the Nepal Electricity Authority is not able to provide an uninterrupted supply of electricity to grid-connected consumers, especially during the dry season when river flows, on which the country's generation capacity is based, are naturally low.

Moreover, Nepal's regulated electricity tariff is one of the highest in the region and one of the highest among Nepal's comparator countries (Figure 4.2).

Table 4.2   Global Competitiveness Index—Rank in Infrastructure (Out of 133)

	Nepal	Mongolia	Bolivia	Bangladesh
Quality of overall infrastructure	130	133	124	125
Quality of roads	126	133	123	95
Quality of railroad infrastructure	109	77	93	65
Quality of port infrastructure	119	116	115	113
Quality of air transport infrastructure	107	128	112	116
Available seat kilometers	85	116	86	61
Quality of electricity supply	133	112	90	128
Telephone lines	105	98	96	117

Source: World Economic Forum 2009.

Figure 4.1   Electric Power Consumption per Capita in Nepal and Comparator Countries

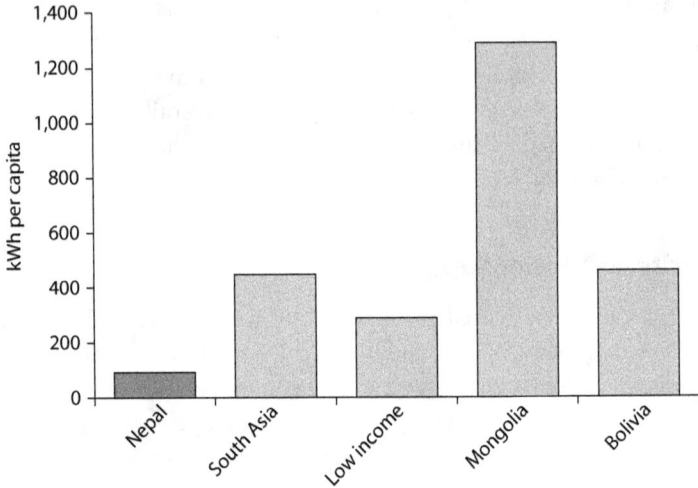

Source: World Bank 2010a.
Note: Low-income economies are those in which 2009 GNI per capita was $995 or less, as per the World Bank's definition (World Development Indicators).

Figure 4.2   Consumer Cost of Getting Electricity in Nepal and Comparator Countries

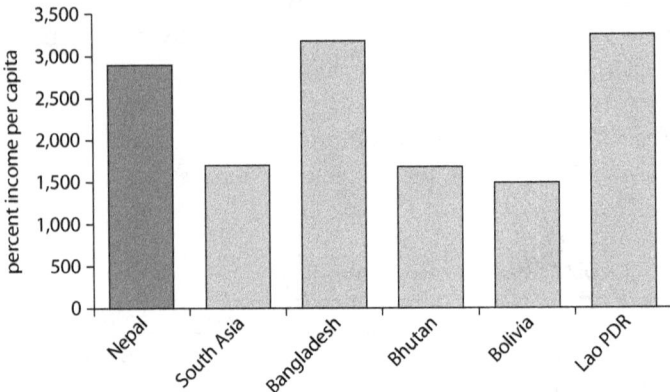

Source: World Bank 2010c.

Nepal's installed generation capacity is much lower than its hydro-power generation potential and existing capacity is under-utilized. It is estimated that Nepal has a potential of about 80,000 megawatts (MW) in hydroelectric power and could even export energy to India and Bangladesh (if its interconnection with India improves) where energy demand exceeds supply. Of the theoretical potential 80,000 MW, about 42,000 MW are technically and economically viable; however, a capacity of only 564 MW has been developed (NEA 2008; Majagaiya 2009). In addition, existing capacity is under-utilized, as it is estimated that over the past two or three years only two-thirds of the power generation capacity was utilized. The main reason for under-utilization is absence of water storage, which exposes power generation to seasonal fluctuations in river levels.

Roads and Transport

Transport infrastructure is also inadequate and unreliable. Of Nepal's 75 districts, five do not have connections to the country's road network and 17 district headquarters have only seasonal road connections. Out of a total road network of around 35,000 km (including some 1,300 bridges) only 4,242 km are black topped. More than half of the population does not have year-round ready access to roads. Most of the roads are concentrated in the lowland Terai and hill areas. Some villages in remote areas are over 10 days' walk from the nearest road. Nepal's road density, at 0.6 km of road per 1,000 people, is the lowest in the region; Bhutan, a country with similar topographic characteristics, has a much higher road density (Table 4.3).[1] The transport system is also inefficient due to the poor condition of the roads and obsolete transport services. More than one-third of the road network is not in trafficable condition and most of the vehicles are old and obsolete. There are also problems of syndicates and lack of competition in the transport operators sector. Indeed, operators/owners have syndicates that restrict competition on various public transport routes, while workers are unionized and active.

Table 4.3   Comparison of Access to Roads in Selected South Asian Countries (2007)

	Bangladesh	Bhutan	India	Nepal	Sri Lanka
Road density in terms of land (km/1000 km² of land)	2,079	93	2,226	121	1,422
Road density in terms of population (km/1,000 people)	1.9	6.5	3.0	0.6	4.7
Paved roads (% total)	9.5	62.0	47.4	56.9	81.0
Access to all-season roads (% population)	39	47	61	43	65

Source: World Bank 2009d.

The lack of alternate routes as well as frequent strikes are factors behind the unreliability of the transport network. The East-West Highway is the main route linking the eastern and western borders; the roads from the main entry points and dry ports all connect to this highway. Due to lack of alternate routes, disruptions in traffic on the East-West Highway or connected roads can lead to losses in trade and shortages of essential commodities. Such disruptions are rather common and mostly due to slides and washouts caused by monsoons or due to transport strikes or protests.

Logistic services are also in poor shape. There are a negligible number of privately owned and managed container depots for efficient cargo handling and no operators with large prime movers to handle 40 foot containers. Cross-border infrastructure and customs facilities are in poor condition, increasing processing and transportation time.

As a result, transport costs are high in Nepal. According to the Doing Business Report, the cost of exporting and importing a container is much higher in Nepal than in Bangladesh, India, and Pakistan (World Bank 2010e). Pre-shipment transport costs are estimated to be twice those of regional competitors.

Air transport, on the other hand, is thriving and attracts significant private sector participation. As in other countries with many mountainous areas, air transport has become a major mode of transport for both people and goods. Nepal has 51 airports, including one international airport in Kathmandu, three regional hubs, 43 domestic airports, and others. Four additional airports are being constructed and private airlines have entered the market. While passenger traffic is thriving, air cargo traffic has been fluctuating, suggesting fluctuations in comparative advantage vis-à-vis land transport. The railway network in Nepal is almost non-existent. The network consists of two railways; one connects Nepal's inland container depot with India and the other is a 51-km spur of the line connecting Janakpur with Jayanagar in Bihar (which is a narrow gage train line of which only 35 km are in operation).

Telecoms

While the telecommunications infrastructure is still below regional standards, it has improved constantly over the years. The density of fixed and mobile telephone lines in Nepal is still lower than in the region and in comparator countries (except for fixed telephone lines in Bangladesh), but it has grown rapidly in the past decade. Growth has been driven primarily by private investments. Cost of access to telecommunication services, on the other hand, is lower than in comparator countries (Table 4.4).

Infrastructure as a Constraint to the Business Climate

The Enterprise Survey 2009 provides data on access to infrastructure relating to electricity, transportation, telecommunications, and water for registered and unregistered firms in the manufacturing and services sectors. The survey instrument has two sets of infrastructure indicators. The first set measures the quality of infrastructure by collecting data on the number of outages and losses connected to it. The second set of indicators evaluates the efficiency of infrastructure services by quantifying delays and corruption encountered in obtaining connections.

More firms in Nepal perceive both electricity and transportation as major or very severe obstacles to business than in comparator countries. In Nepal, 75.6 percent of the non-micro formal enterprises perceive electricity to be a major or very severe obstacle to their business and 33.2 percent of these firms perceive transportation to be a major or very severe constraint (Figure 4.3).[2] Indeed, electricity is rated the second most important obstacle, after political instability: 15.7 percent of the enterprises[3] indicated it as the most important constraint to their activity. Access to land, on the other hand, was rated as a major or very severe obstacle by only 4 percent of all formal enterprises.

Telecommunications are not perceived to be a major investment climate constraint. Perception on telecommunications was only surveyed among retailers and was rated as a major or very severe obstacle to business by only 4 percent of retailers overall.

Table 4.4   Telecommunications Services: Comparison of Access and Costs

	Telephone lines (per 100 people)[a]	Mobile cellular subscriptions (per 100 people)[a]	Internet users (per 100 people)[a]	Residential fixed line telephone tariff (US$ per month)[b]	Mobile cellular prepaid tariff (US$ per month)[b]
Nepal	2.5	11.6	1.4	3.4	2.9
South Asia	3.2	22.8	6.6	3.5	1.9
Low income	4.4	16.5	3.7	9.0	10.0
Bhutan	4.4	22.1	5.9	3.5	3.0
Bolivia	7.1	34.2	10.5	22.7	5.9
Bangladesh	0.8	21.8	0.3	—	—
Mongolia	6.2	35.1	12.3	—	—

Source: World Bank 2010a.
Note: a. data refer to 2007; b. data refer to 2008. — = not available.

Figure 4.3   Percent of Firms Rating Electricty and Transportation as Major or Very Severe Investment Climate Obstacles in Nepal and Comparator Countries

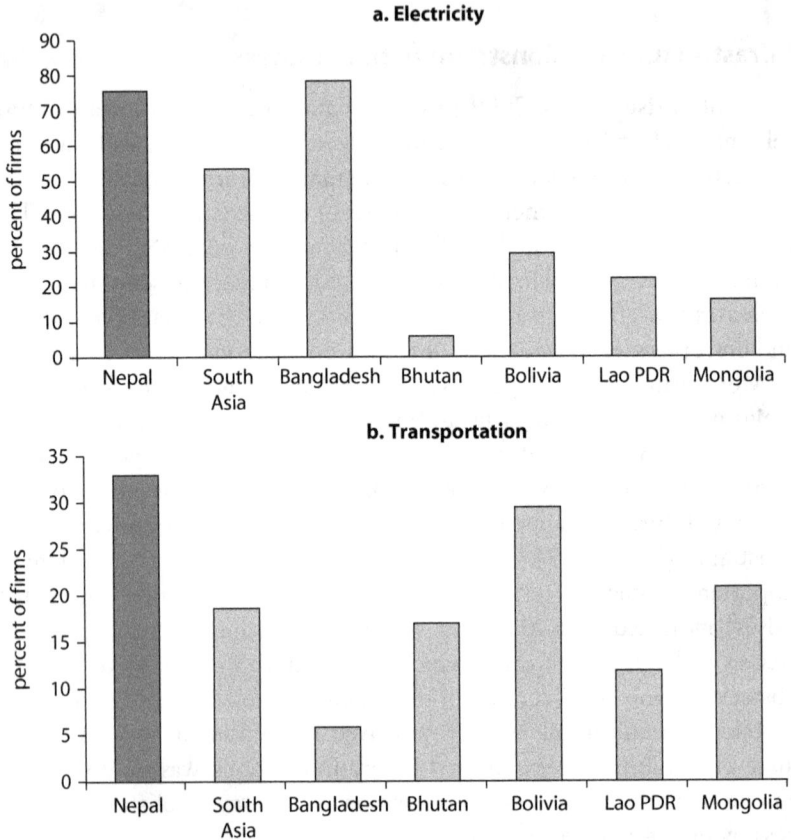

Source: World Bank Enterprise Surveys, latest available year.
Note: Comparison restricted to firms with 5+ employees in sectors surveyed in most countries in the comparator group, i.e., manufacturing, retail, wholesale, hotels and restaurants, transport, and travel agencies.

The main problems faced by firms with regard to transport infrastructure are strikes in transportation by road and airfreight capacity in transportation by air. Manufacturing and retail firms were asked about the main obstacle faced in transportation. For transportation by road, 96 percent of the firms indicated strikes as the main obstacle; for transportation by air, the main obstacle was airfreight capacity for 37 percent of the firms and customs at the airport for 35.3 percent of the firms. Losses during transport are also common and relatively high (Table 4.5).

Table 4.5   Losses during Transport as Percentage of Sales

	Due to theft, shipments to domestic markets	Due to breakage or spoilage, direct exports
Nepal	0.4	1.9
South Asia	0.4	2.0
Bhutan	—	2.2
Bolivia	2.0	0.4
Bangladesh	0.02	0.44
Lao PDR	—	0.0
Mongolia	—	—

Source: World Bank Enterprise Surveys, latest available year.
Note: Comparison restricted to firms with 5+ employees in sectors surveyed in most countries in the comparator group, i.e., manufacturing, retail, wholesale, hotels and restaurants, transport, and travel agencies.
— = not available.

Enterprises operating in the tourism sector report that 69.5 percent of tourists face transport difficulties while trying to reach the operator's premises and 97 percent of the tourism enterprises suffered losses that could be attributed to transportation difficulties.

The Nepal Enterprise Survey 2009 does not provide information on access to electricity for formal enterprises, but it is safe to assume that most of them have access to the power grid since the survey was conducted in urban areas. On the other hand, access is not increasing as only 1.9 percent of the firms in the survey applied for an electrical connection over the previous year.

While access to electricity is good in urban areas, the reliability of the service is very poor. All of the firms in the Eastern and Western regions and 99 percent of the firms in the Central region report having suffered power outages. On average, establishments are left without power twice a day, as the average number of outages in a month is 57.3. Outages last on average 4.9 hours.[4]

Outages cost firms a consistent portion of their revenues. Formal firms estimate that losses due to power outages amount to about 22 percent of their sales. Losses appear to be higher for manufacturing and tourism than for other services and retail (Figure 4.4). On average, manufacturing firms spend 5.3 percent of their total annual sales on electricity.

In order to cope with irregularity of power availability, some firms use generators. The proportion of firms that own or share generators, however, is not particularly high in Nepal when judged against comparator countries, especially considering that the average number of power outages in Nepal is much higher than in comparator countries (Table 4.6). On average,

Figure 4.4   Revenue Losses among Informal and Formal Firms in Nepal Due to Power Outages

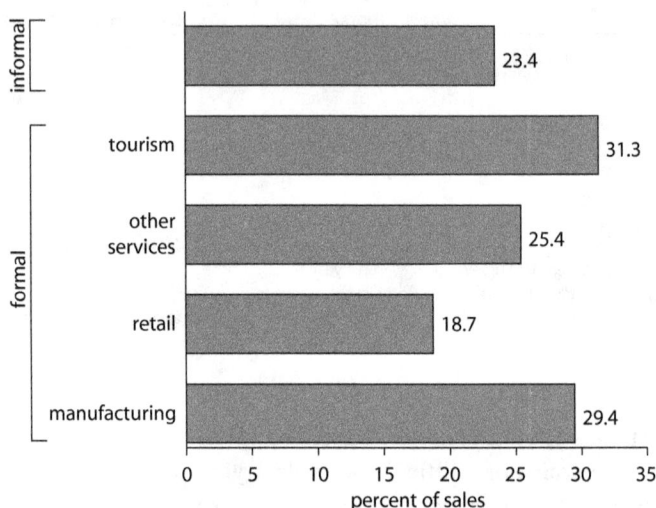

Source: Nepal Enterprise Survey 2009.

Table 4.6   Power Outages and Ownership of Generators in Nepal and Comparator Countries

	% firms owning or sharing a generator	Number of outages in a typical month
Nepal	15.7	52.0
South Asia	42.8	42.2
Bhutan	17.8	3.1
Bolivia	5.2	1.0
Bangladesh	52.3	101.6
Lao PDR	13.5	1.7
Mongolia	24.2	3.0

Source: World Bank Enterprise Surveys, latest available year.
Note: Comparison restricted to firms with 5+ employees in sectors surveyed in most countries in the comparator group, i.e., manufacturing, retail, wholesale, hotels and restaurants, transport, and travel agencies.

26 percent of the electricity used by the establishments comes from generators; electricity produced by generators is, however, generally more expensive than electricity from the grid and firms that own or share generators sustain higher costs for fuel (4.7 percent of their annual sales as opposed to 4 percent for firms that do not own generators).

Access to electricity infrastructure services is, on the other hand, rather efficient in Nepal. Data from the Enterprise Survey show that the

Table 4.7   Obtaining Access to Infrastructure Services: Time and Corruption Encountered

	Delay in obtaining a connection (days)			% firms expected to give gifts to get the connection		
	Electricity	Water	Telephone main line	Electricity	Water	Telephone main line
Nepal	9.0	10.5	7.8	11.0	0.0	8.8
South Asia	49.1	64.5	31.6	31.9	26.6	22.7
Bhutan	19.4	22.1	6.1	8.5	0.0	14.3
Bolivia	15.2	50.5	11.6	3.2	0.0	1.3
Bangladesh	50.3	36.3	75.0	42.4	76.1	52.7
Lao PDR	—	44.4	3.3	—	0.0	0.0
Mongolia	20.0	81.5	10.1	15.6	14.3	12.6

Source: World Bank Enterprise Surveys, latest available year.
Note: Comparison restricted to firms with 5+ employees in sectors surveyed in most countries in the comparator group, i.e., manufacturing, retail, wholesale, hotels and restaurants, transport, and travel agencies. Delay in obtaining connections is only based on 9 observations as the question was restricted to the very few firms that applied for a connection in the past year.
— = not available.

number of days necessary to obtain a connection to the power grid is lower in Nepal than in comparator countries (Table 4.7). The incidence of requests for gifts or informal payments during the application process is also lower than in the region.

The set of pilot indicators on accessing electricity from the Doing Business Indicators project[5] provide further insights on the procedures, time, and cost required for a business to obtain an electricity connection (World Bank 2010c). According to the findings of this report, the time necessary to obtain a connection to the power grid in Nepal is lower than in most comparator countries while the number of procedures required for the application process is higher (Figure 4.5).

Water supply is also sometimes subject to shortages. 8.8 percent of the formal firms in manufacturing and retail and 33.3 percent of the informal firms experienced insufficient water supply; on average, firms experienced 15 to 20 shortage episodes in a month that lasted for a day. Obtaining a water connection and a telephone line takes less time in Nepal than in the rest of the South Asia region, but longer than in some of the comparator countries, especially for the telephone line. On average, 10 days were necessary to obtain a water connection and 8 days to obtain a telephone line. When applying for a telephone line, 9 percent of the firms were asked for gifts and informal payments; none of the firms were asked for gifts and informal payments when applying for a water connection (see Table 4.7).

Figure 4.5   Indicators (Time and Procedures) for Acquiring Electricity by Firms in Nepal and Comparator Countries

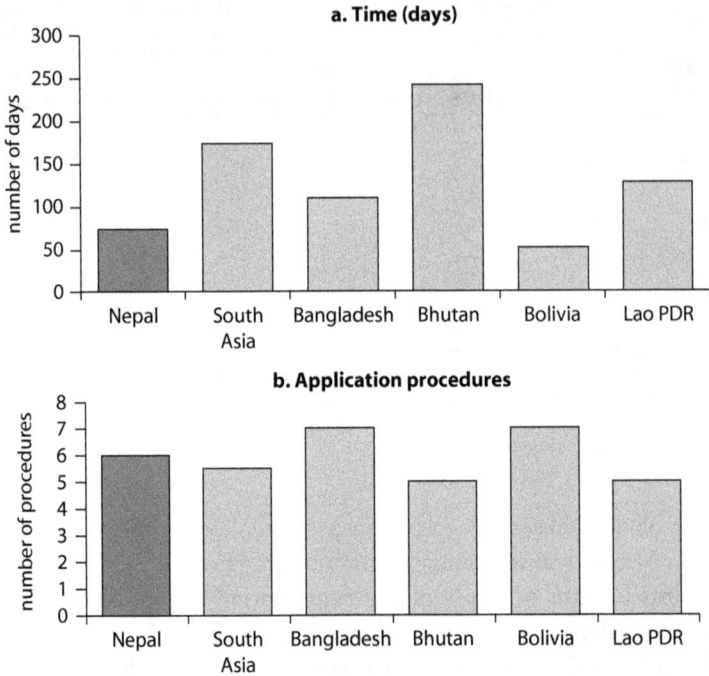

a. Time (days)

b. Application procedures

Source: World Bank 2010c.

The proportion of firms that use Internet services in Nepal is also lower than in most comparator countries, especially in terms of using email to communicate with clients and suppliers (Figure 4.6). Furthermore, 56 percent of the enterprises have less than three hours of Internet access per day; only 22 percent of the enterprises have more than 6 hours of access per day. Finally, 10 percent of the registered retailers have a high-speed connection on their premises and 29 percent of them were afflicted by shortages in the connection that occurred on average 8 times per month for a few minutes.

Conclusions

Nepal needs to increase the electrification rate and to increase water storage capacity. Nepal has an abundant hydropower potential; in order

Figure 4.6   Business Use of Internet by Firms in Nepal and Comparator Countries

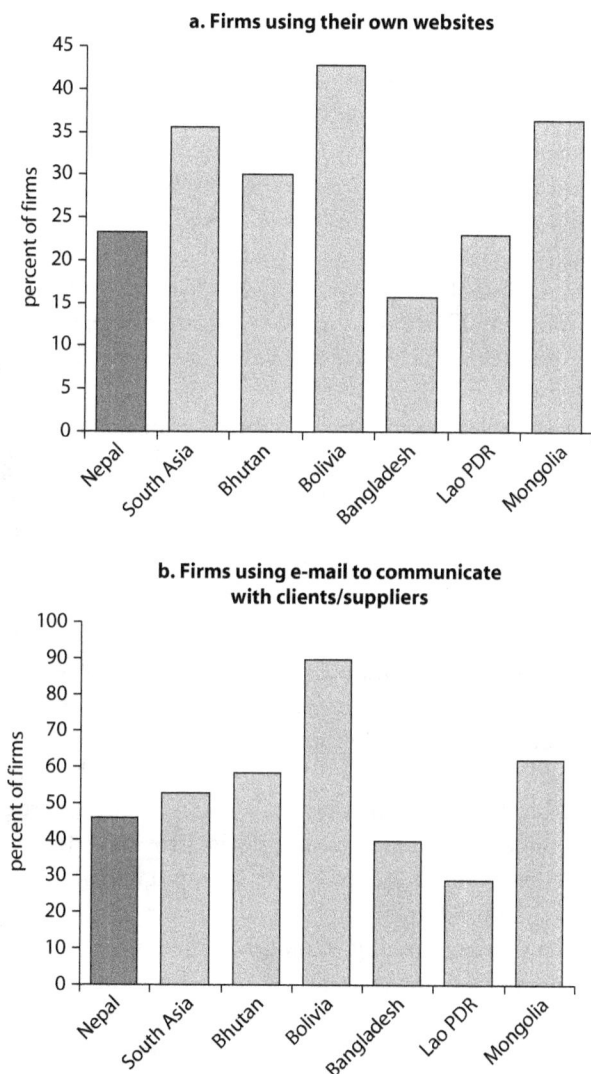

a. Firms using their own websites

b. Firms using e-mail to communicate with clients/suppliers

Source: World Bank Enterprise Surveys, latest available year.
Note: Comparison restricted to firms with 5+ employees in sectors surveyed in most countries in the comparator group, i.e., manufacturing, retail, wholesale, hotels and restaurants, transport, and travel agencies.

to exploit it and raise electricity consumption, investment in the electricity sector has to increase substantially—especially investments to upgrade the grid and to increase water storage capacity. The existing generation capacity is in fact under-utilized because of inadequate storage capacity, which exposes hydropower plants to fluctuations of water levels in the rivers. Expansion of cross-border transmission capacity with India needs to be accelerated, as this is the fastest way to end load-shedding. Electricity tariffs should also be reformed in a manner that does not hurt businesses already suffering from poor supply.

While solving these problems is a long-term endeavor that needs to start now and requires a broad program of public support and funding (including Viability Gap funding) for enhanced power supply, the investment climate for private hydropower developers can be improved sooner by, for example, establishing a "one-window" agency to facilitate hydropower development. Currently, Nepalese private hydropower developers suffer many obstacles (such as in obtaining licenses and getting permissions, etc.).

Development of transport infrastructure is critical in Nepal. With one-third of the country accessible only on a limited basis—it is difficult to access markets and to capitalize on the country's comparative advantages in tourism opportunities and hydropower development. Nepal needs to increase funding to strategically expand, maintain, and rehabilitate its road network. A focused approach on connecting the major urban centers and improving the road links to India, which are essential for trade, should be coupled by a medium-term strategy to connect all districts by all-season roads. These roads are low volume roads requiring low investment for an affordable and safe transport system. Bringing existing roads into a trafficable condition is itself a daunting task. Highways and feeder roads should have adequate maintenance for better transport efficiency.

The private sector could have a role in providing better transport services. Current volumes of trade traffic do not seem to demand high volume roads, limiting their investment appeal to the private sector. Therefore, viability gap funding should be explored and a Viability Gap Fund (VGF) set-up with government and donor resources. The VGF (similar to the one set up in India) would provide funding for those private-sector infrastructure projects that would not be able to break even and make a profit (i.e., would not become viable) without additional support. This effort should be complemented by an attempt to identify commercial corridors with potentially high traffic for private sector investment and PPPs. In addition, a detailed analysis and study of PPP options and funding modalities suitable for Nepal should be undertaken given the low turnover, country risks, and capacity constraints of local investors. This should be coupled with a review and improvement of the PPP framework as well as more education on PPP options and funding modalities.

Notes

1. This data is based on the road inventory published by the Department of Roads and does not include many rural roads. If rural roads are included, total road length would amount to around 35,000 km, and the density would rise to about 1.4 (still lower than regional comparator countries).

2. When including the microenterprises, these ratios become 90 percent and 25 percent, respectively.

3. Micro and non-micro, in this case.

4. The average number of outages is 57.3 outages per month for all formal firms (including microenterprises, i.e., firms with less than 5 employees). The average number of outages per month for all formal non-micro enterprises is 52 outages per month. This is the number used in comparisons with other countries. The average number of outages per month for informal enterprises is 59.2 outages per month as per the informal survey.

5. The report provides data for 140 economies covered by the Doing Business report, collected through a case study presented to respondents.

CHAPTER 5

Investment Climate in the Informal Sector

The informal sector in Nepal accounts for about 70 percent of employment and encompasses a wide variety of activities and sub-sectors. Most informal firms are very small and mostly employ unpaid workers. The main reason for not registering is that entrepreneurs do not see benefits from registration; on the other hand, access to finance is the main benefit associated with registering. The main investment climate obstacles for informal firms are lack of demand and lack of access to finance. Improving productivity and working conditions of informal firms is an important component of private sector development and of the growth and poverty reduction agenda. While measures to bring informal firms into the formal sector are important, they should be coupled with increasing links to the formal sector, promoting human capital development, simplifying regulations in the formal sector, and reducing entry costs.

Concept and Definition

According to the International Labour Organization (ILO), the informal economy is that part of the market economy that covers informal employment both in formal and informal enterprises, which are small, unregistered, or unincorporated enterprises.[1] The informal sector covers a wide range of activities and is usually dominated by the services sector. Most informal sector workers are not registered and are not covered by labor laws and basic labor standards. Non-wage employment is the norm. Informal businesses are also often unable to access formal financial services and business development services—typically having access only to micro finance.

Therefore, the informal sector is characterized by low productivity, a limited scope of activities, and limited prospects for expansion. Informal enterprises usually operate on a small scale, with capital goods being used for both business and household purposes. Informal businesses usually have limited access to output and input markets and use simple technology. Their investments are scant, working conditions are poor, and their incentive to seek knowledge is weak.[2]

Still, in developing countries, the informal sector is an important source of employment for the poor, the unskilled, and women—thereby playing an important role in reducing the incidence of poverty.

The Informal Sector in Nepal

Nepal's inability to pursue rapid, sustained, and broad-based economic growth limits the scope for creating productive jobs in the formal sector and reducing poverty. The majority of poor people are still outside of the formal economy, dependent overwhelmingly on agriculture for their livelihoods. They lack access to productive assets and gainful employment, which limit their participation in the growth process.

The informal sector is estimated to account for a significant proportion of production, consumption, and employment in the Nepalese economy. However, as is the case in many other countries, it is hard to measure the size of the informal sector in Nepal. The two rounds of the Nepal Living Standards Survey (NLSS) (in 1995/96 and 2003/04; CBS 1996, 2004) and the two rounds of the Nepal Labour Force Survey (NLFS) (1998/99 and 2007/08; CBS 1999, 2008) measured only non-agricultural informal activities because of the difficulty of defining informal sector activities in the agricultural sector (Table 5.1).[3]

According to the 2008 round of the NLFS, 70 percent of total non-agricultural employment is informal. During the last nine years, the population employed in the non-agricultural informal sector grew by 29.3 percent. Nepal's informal sector is highly heterogeneous in terms of the types of activities and sub-sectors it encompasses, with the largest group of informal sector workers being shop salespersons, followed by

Table 5.1   Estimates of Informal Sector in Nepal

NLFS and NLSS surveys	Definition	Share of total
1995/96	Unregistered non-farm enterprises	88%
1998/99	Informal non-agricultural employment	73%
2003/04	Unregistered non-farm enterprises	81%
2008	Informal non-agricultural employment	70%

Source: CBS 1996, 1999, 2004, and 2008.

mining and construction laborers, bricklayers, carpenters, housekeeping and restaurant service workers (Table 5.2).

Characteristics of Non-Agricultural Informal Enterprises in Nepal

The data collected through the Nepal Informal Enterprise Survey 2009 offer an opportunity to assess the main characteristics of non-agricultural informal firms and the investment climate they face. The survey focuses exclusively on informal enterprises, defined as those enterprises that are not registered with the Inland Revenue Department.

Most informal firms are very small, micro enterprises employing four or fewer workers. The largest number of informal firms are located in the Central region (66.2 percent), 20 percent are located in the Eastern region, and 13 percent in the Western region. Most informal firms (47.5 percent) produce or sell food and beverages. Another 21 percent are in the apparel industry, including tailors, embroiderers, and apparel producers (Figure 5.1).

Informal enterprises are predominantly micro firms. In the sample, 64 percent of the firms employ less than five workers and 35 percent employ 5 to 19 workers.[4] **There is also little variation in firm size over time.** Overall, 52.5 percent of the firms currently employ the same number of workers as at their establishment, while 8 percent employ fewer workers and 39.5 percent employ more. With an **average age of 8.4 years**, informal firms have a shorter average life cycle than formal firms, whose average age is 9.6 years. Three quarters of the informal firms do not keep the business financial accounts separate from household accounts. The proportion is even higher for micro firms (85.7 percent).

Informal businesses are predominantly owned by a single owner (90 percent). In 31.7 percent of the firms, the owners are women, compared to 28.3 percent in formal firms. **Most entrepreneurs in the informal sector have low educational attainment and little training.** For 44 percent of

Table 5.2 Persons Aged 15 Years and Over Currently Employed in Non-Agricultural Sectors (Thousand Workers and %)

Occupation	Both sexes			Male			Female		
	Non-agricultural sector	Informal sector jobs	Percent informal	Non-agricultural sector	Informal sector jobs	Percent informal	Non-agricultural sector	Informal sector jobs	Percent informal
Total	**3074**	**2142**	**69.7**	**2090**	**1379**	**66**	**985**	**763**	**77.5**
1. Legislators, senior officials	70	59	83.6	57	47	83.3	13	11	85
2. Professionals	203	22	10.9	155	19	12.2	48	3	7
3. Technicians	228	48	21	147	38	25.9	82	10	12.2
4. Clerks	117	10	8.3	96	7	7.4	21	3	12.4
5. Service workers	854	775	90.7	512	448	87.5	343	328	95.6
6. Agricultural workers	10	7	74.2	8	6	75.1	2	1	70.4
7. Craft & related trade workers	915	793	86.7	626	530	84.7	289	263	91
8. Plant & machine operators	150	78	52.1	140	73	52	10	5	53.5
9. Elementary occupations	519	350	67.5	342	211	61.8	177	139	78.5
10. Armed forces	8	0	2.2	7	0	2.3	0	0	0

Source: CBS 2008.

Figure 5.1   Distribution of Non-Agricultural Informal Enterprises in Nepal by Region, Size, Age, and Business Type
percent

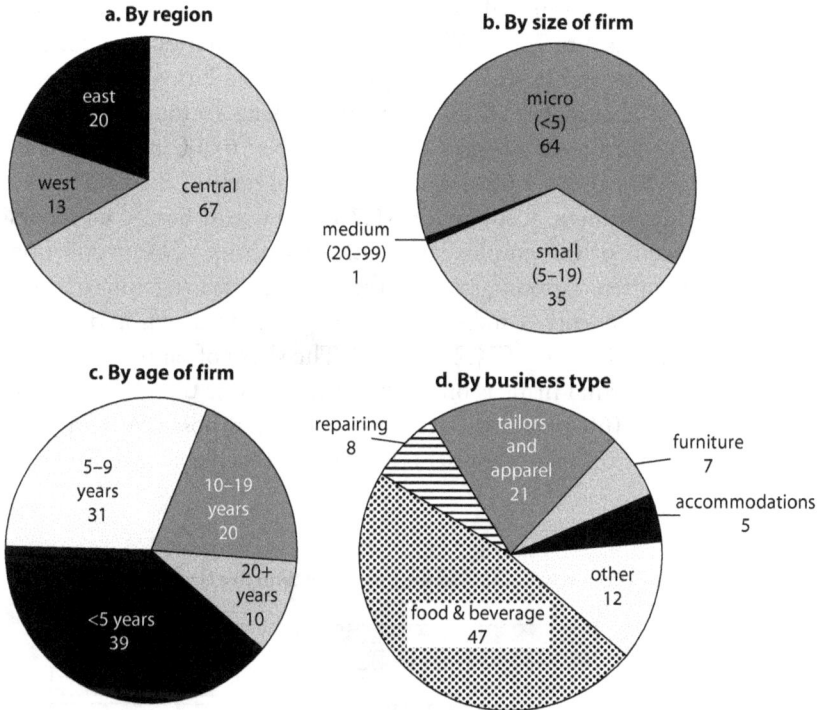

a. By region

b. By size of firm

c. By age of firm

d. By business type

Source: Nepal Informal Survey 2009.

informal entrepreneurs, the highest attained degree is from secondary school, while 39.2 percent of the owners have completed primary school; only 10 percent have some university-level training. **Informal entrepreneurs are often self-taught and may lack business skills.** Twenty-five percent of the owners were unemployed before starting their current business, while 50 percent were already self-employed in the same or different activity.

On average, informal firms in the sample employed 4.1 people, including both paid and unpaid workers, compared with six employees in all formal firms (including micro). Seventeen percent of the firms report that the number of paid workers in the busiest months of the year is larger than the number of workers in the slowest months.

Most workers employed in informal businesses are unpaid. On average, unpaid workers account for 60 percent of the employees but micro firms as well as firms in the accommodations industry tend to have a much larger share (Figure 5.2).

Informal firms pay on average lower salaries than registered firms. The approximate monthly salary of paid workers in this sample of informal businesses was Nrs 3,944 (Table 5.3).[5] Average salaries are higher in the Central region and in small firms (Nrs 4,354 and Nrs 4,624, respectively) and are also higher in the furniture making sector. The average salary paid by formal enterprises is just over Nrs 6,500 in the overall sample—which is about 1.65 times the informal sample average.

On average, women account for 31.7 percent and family members for 35.5 percent of the employees in informal firms.[6] The proportion of family members working in the firm is larger among micro firms (40.4 percent), recently established firms (43.3 percent), and in the accommodations industry (74.2 percent). The share of family members employed in informal firms is on average much lower than the share of unpaid workers (60 percent), with the difference possibly being the proportion of non-family members that do not receive a wage for their

Figure 5.2   Proportion of Informal Workers in Nepal Who Are Unpaid

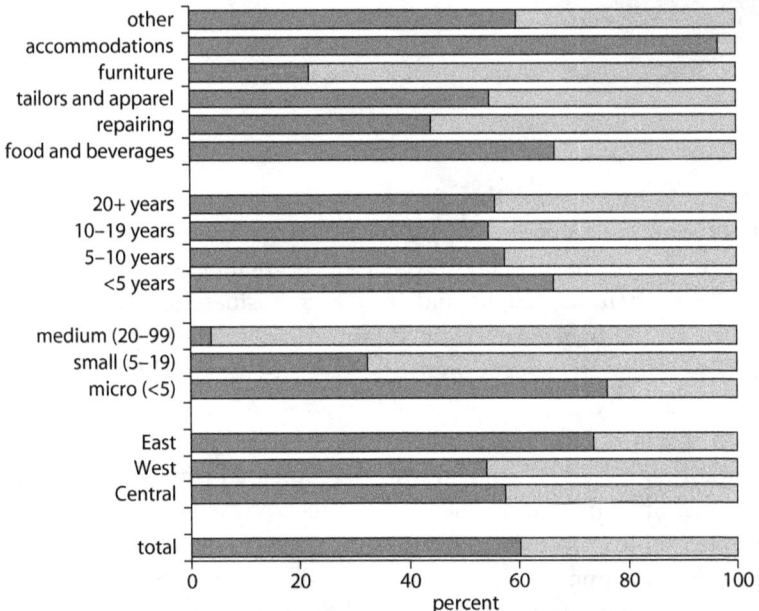

Source: Nepal Informal Survey 2009.

Table 5.3   Average Monthly Salary Paid by Firms in Selected Industries: Formal vs. Informal Firms (Nrs)

Informal		Formal manufacturing	
Sector	Average salary	Sector	Average salary
Total	**3,944**	**Total**	**6,510**
Food and beverages	3,185	Food, beverages, tobacco	5,384
Tailors and apparel	3,906	Textiles	5,409
		Garments	5,660
Furniture	8,121	Furniture	12,906

Source: Nepal Enterprise and Informal Survey 2009.
Note: Firms reported the average monthly salary paid to their workers. Formal manufacturing firms were asked to restrict the information to production workers.

work. These workers most likely receive other forms of compensation, such as food or shelter, or work as apprentices.[7]

Downstream linkages to other firms (formal or informal) are limited, hindering the sector's ability to play a role in the supply chain for the formal sector. Slightly more than half of the surveyed informal firms (53.2 percent) manufacture their main product themselves (Table 5.4). In addition, only four firms in the sample sold part of their output to other firms or businesses; the rest sold all of their output to final consumers. A few more firms (12.5 percent) produced under contract—for either other businesses or persons.

Monthly sales per worker in the informal sample averaged Nrs 14,760 in the month previous to the interview; for most firms, sales per worker are, however, less than Nrs 9,000 (Table 5.5). Labor productivity is on average slightly higher in the Western region, among small firms, and among older firms. Labor productivity in the informal sector is, therefore, much lower than in the formal one, where sales per worker are Nrs 81,500 a month on average.

Informal businesses' revenues are not diversified, as an average of 87.5 percent of their sales depended on the firm's main product. For half of the sample, the main product actually accounted for all of the firm's sales. Industries with relatively more differentiation are food and beverages, accommodations, and other industries.

Informal firms report wide variations in sales between the slowest and the busiest month. The average percentage variation, in terms of sales per worker, is 252 percent and the median variation is 186 percent. Seasonal variations in average sales are shown in Figure 5.3. The bottom of each line represents average sales in the slowest month; the top of the line

Table 5.4   Informal Firms Manufacturing Their Main Product (% Firms)

Total	53.2
Food and beverages	53.6
Repairing	16.7
Tailors and apparel	57.1
Furniture	100.0
Accommodations	80.0
Other	23.1

Source: Nepal Informal Survey 2009.

Table 5.5   Total Sales per Worker, the Past Month (Nrs)

	Mean	Median	25th percentile	75th percentile
Total	14,760	8,571	5,000	18,000
Size				
Micro (<5)	13,838	10,000	5,000	15,000
Small (5–19)	16,407	6,750	4,000	25,000
Industry				
Food and beverages	17,978	12,679	7,500	24,500
Repairing	6,615	5,500	4,000	7,500
Tailors and apparel	6,686	4,083	2,750	8,036
Furniture	13,987	9,375	4,786	25,833
Accommodations	4,792	4,875	3,000	6,000

Source: Nepal Informal Survey 2009.

represents average sales in the busiest month, while the cross represents average sales in a normal month. For the overall sample, average sales per worker in the busiest months were 2.7 times the average sales of the lowest month. Variations are largest among firms established 20 or more years ago and are smallest in the Eastern region.

Working hours are on average considerably longer in the informal sector. The average number of hours per week is 71.4; and one-fourth of informal businesses operate 87.5 hours per week or more. The long operating hours are attributed to the fact that many informal firms operate in the restaurant and hotel industry where business hours tend to be long.

Registration

Roughly half of the informal firms would like to be registered with the Inland Revenue Department while the other half would not. Preference for registration is stronger among small firms in the Central region.

Figure 5.3   Seasonal Variations among Informal Firms in Nepal: Sales per Worker in Slowest, Normal, and Busiest Month, Nrs

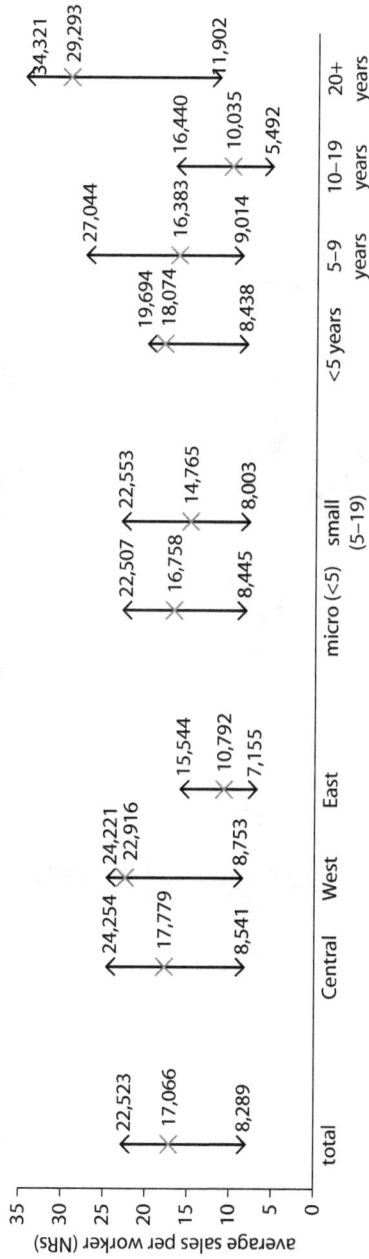

Source: Nepal Informal Survey 2009.
Note: Bottom of each line represents average sales in the slowest month; top of each line represents average sales in the busiest month; cross represents average sales in a normal month.

For 46 percent of the firms, the main reason why they are not registered is because they see no benefit from registration. Among the rest, the most common reasons for not registering are the difficulties involved in obtaining information on the registration procedures and the fees involved in the registration process. Interestingly, the time involved in the registration process and the taxes on registered businesses were rated as the main reason for not registering by only 6 percent of the firms (Figure 5.4).

Figure 5.4   Main Reason an Informal Firm in Nepal Is Not Registered

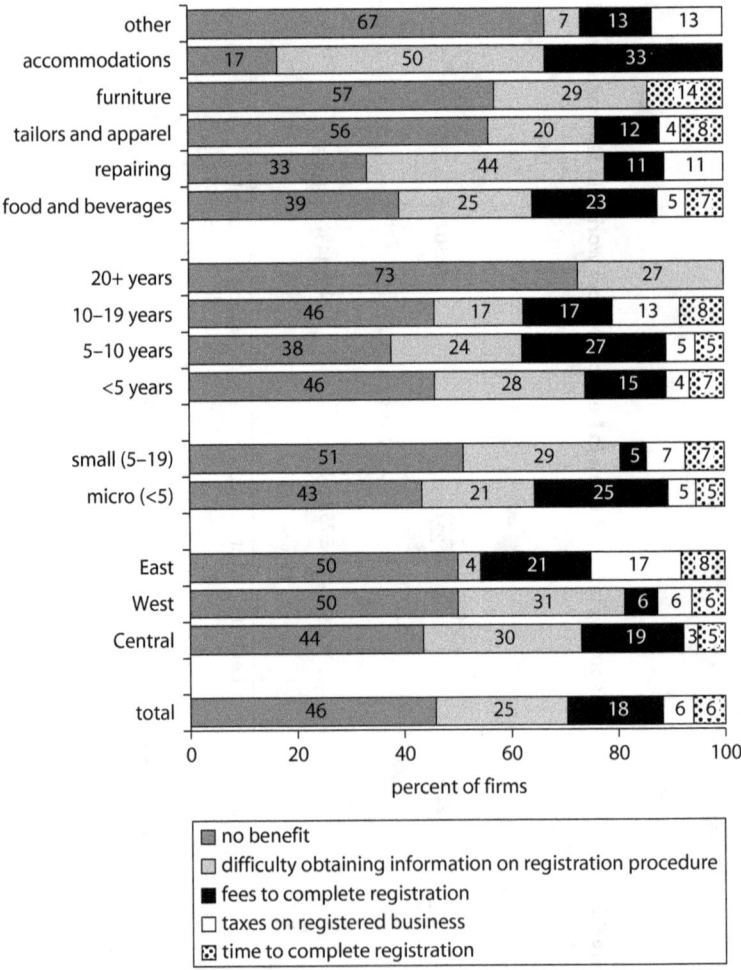

Legend:
- ▓ no benefit
- ▢ difficulty obtaining information on registration procedure
- ■ fees to complete registration
- □ taxes on registered business
- ⊠ time to complete registration

Source: Nepal Informal Survey 2009.

None of the firms in the sample report having to make informal payments in order to remain unregistered. On average, firms expect registration to take 10 days.

Access to finance is the main advantage that informal firms associate with formal registration. Forty-six percent of the firms see improved access to finance as one of the benefits their business activity could obtain by registering. Two other commonly perceived advantages (about 20 percent of the firms) are better opportunities for negotiation with formal firms and better access to government programs and services (Figure 5.5). Better access to markets and stronger legal foundations on property rights are viewed as an advantage by about 10 percent of the firms, while improved access to raw materials or to infrastructure, improved access to workers, and less bribes to pay are perceived as possible advantages of registration by 5 percent of the firms or less.

Main Investment Climate Obstacles for Informal Firms

The main investment climate obstacles for informal firms are, in order, lack of demand, access to finance, and political instability. For 40.7 percent of the firms, the most important obstacle faced by the business is lack of demand. Access to finance and political instability are the closely ranked second and third obstacles, having being chosen by 25.4 percent and 23.7 percent of the firms, respectively (Table 5.6).

Political instability and access to finance are also two of the most commonly reported major or very severe obstacles in the formal sector. Firms

Figure 5.5   Improvements Nepalese Firms Believe Could Be Obtained by Registering

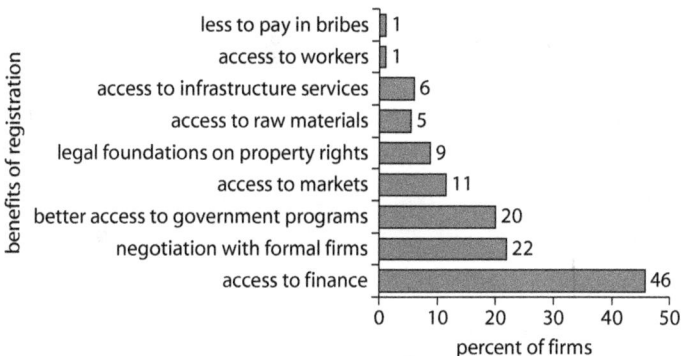

Source: Nepal Informal Survey 2009.

Table 5.6 Most Important Perceived Obstacle Faced by the Business (% Firms)

	Limited demand for products	Access to finance	Political instability	Public infrastructure	Access to land	Crime, theft, and disorder	Workforce education
Total	**40.7**	**25.4**	**23.7**	**4.2**	**4.2**	**0.8**	**0.8**
Region							
West	42.3	21.8	21.8	6.4	5.1	1.3	1.3
Central	37.5	12.5	50.0	0.0	0.0	0.0	0.0
East	37.5	45.8	12.5	0.0	4.2	0.0	0.0
Size							
Micro (<5)	43.4	27.6	23.7	2.6	1.3	1.3	0.0
Small (5–19)	36.6	22.0	22.0	7.3	9.8	0.0	2.4
Age							
<5 yrs	43.5	28.3	21.7	6.5	0.0	0.0	0.0
5–9 yrs	45.9	24.3	21.6	0.0	8.1	0.0	0.0
10–19 yrs	34.8	30.4	21.7	0.0	4.3	4.3	4.3
20+ yrs	25.0	8.3	41.7	16.7	8.3	0.0	0.0
Industry							
Food and beverages	37.5	35.7	21.4	3.6	1.8	0.0	0.0
Repairing	44.4	11.1	22.2	0.0	22.2	0.0	0.0
Tailors and apparel	52.0	12.0	24.0	4.0	4.0	0.0	4.0
Furniture	37.5	50.0	0.0	0.0	12.5	0.0	0.0
Accommodations	0.0	16.7	50.0	16.7	0.0	16.7	0.0

Source: Nepal Informal Survey 2009.

in the Central region and older firms perceive political instability as the most important obstacle relatively more often. The obstacle ranking is the same in the informal and the formal sectors, considering that "lack of demand" was not listed as one of the possible obstacles to be ranked in the formal survey instrument, whereas electricity was not listed as one of the possible obstacles to be ranked in the informal survey. Practices of the informal businesses, on the other hand, are a major to very severe obstacle to 14 percent of the formal businesses. The next two sections provide insights on the investment climate dimensions that are most often problematic for informal firms.

Access to Finance for Informal Firms

One of the most common constraints faced by informal and small enterprises is access to finance. The capital needed to start and sustain informal businesses is often borrowed from relatives, friends, and informal lenders that usually charge very high interest rates. Micro finance programs, on the other hand, offer financial services to informal firms but have limited funds and their scope is often inadequate as business size increases.

Twenty-seven percent of all informal firms perceive access to finance as the top potential benefit to becoming formal by registering with the Inland Revenue Department (Figure 5.6). Access to finance is especially important for informal firms that are older (42 percent), in the West region (50 percent) and East region (33 percent), and small firms (34 percent).

Only 23.3 percent of the informal firms have a bank account and 34 percent have a loan. Of the firms that have a bank account, only 18 percent have an account for the business that is separate from the household's account. Access to bank accounts for informal firms is about half of access for formal firms (44.9 percent).

Eighty percent of the firms report not having applied for a loan in the past year. Aside from not needing a loan (quoted by 50 percent of the firms that did not apply), the most commonly reported reasons for not applying are the complexity of the application procedures (19.8 percent) and high interest rates (11.5 percent).

Loans to informal firms are often provided by microfinance institutions and by moneylenders rather than by commercial banks.[8] The most common sources of financing for the most recently approved loans were by far microcredit institutions (43.9 percent of firms) followed by banks

Figure 5.6   Most Important Benefit to Registering Expected by Informal Firms in Nepal

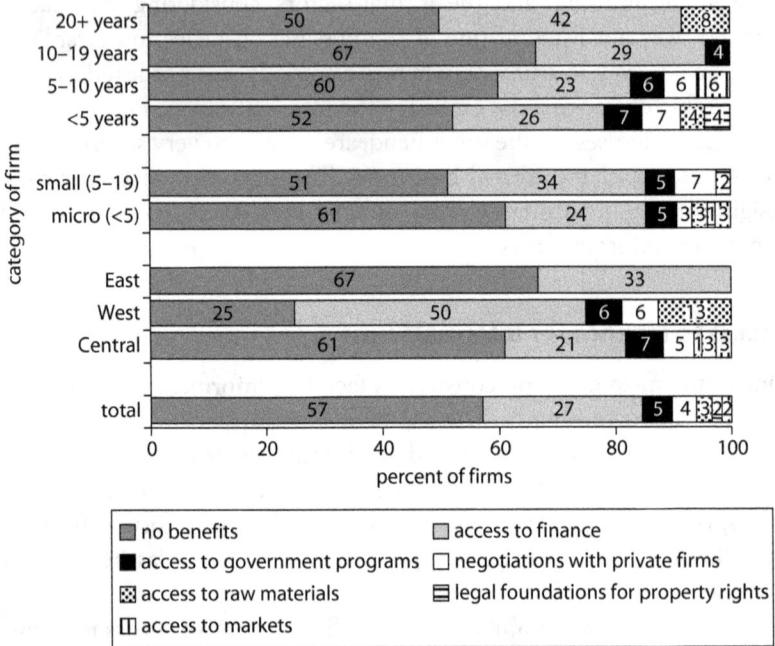

Source: Nepal Informal Survey 2009.

(26.8 percent). Almost 10 percent of the informal firms resort to money-lenders—more than the proportion of firms that obtained a loan from suppliers or customers (7.3 percent). Other sources of credit used by informal businesses are relatives (Table 5.7). Few informal firms are able to borrow from commercial banks and other formal credit institutions because i) collateral requirements are usually stringent and do not meet the characteristics of the asset owned by informal entrepreneurs; ii) procedures for loan applications are often cumbersome and lengthy; and iii) high transaction costs make small loans—such as those typically needed by informal firms–unprofitable.

A relatively high proportion of loans were granted without formal guarantees: 39 percent of the firms report not being asked for a guarantee. Banks and micro-credit institutions generally ask for guarantees in more than three-quarters of the cases, whereas only 25 percent of moneylenders ask for them.

Nepalese informal firms often buy supplies on credit. At least half of the firms buy on credit (with the exception of furniture makers). Resorting

Table 5.7   Source of Financing for the Most Recently Approved Loan (% Firms)

	Bank	Moneylenders	Microcredit institutions	Input suppliers or customers	Other
Total	26.8	9.8	43.9	7.3	12.2
Region					
West	23.3	10.0	50.0	6.7	10.0
Central	50.0	16.7	16.7	0.0	16.7
East	20.0	0.0	40.0	20.0	20.0
Size					
Micro (<5)	26.9	11.5	34.6	11.5	15.4
Small (5–19)	28.6	7.1	57.1	0.0	7.1
Medium (20–99)	0.0	0.0	100.0	0.0	0.0
Age					
<5 yrs	33.3	11.1	33.3	0.0	22.2
5–9 yrs	8.3	8.3	58.3	25.0	0.0
10–19 yrs	25.0	12.5	50.0	0.0	12.5
20+ yrs	66.7	0.0	33.3	0.0	0.0

Source: Nepal Informal Survey 2009.

to this source of financing is more common for informal firms than it is for formal ones; the proportion of formal firms buying on credit in the formal survey is 35.2 percent.

Purchases of fixed assets and working capital are mostly financed through internal funds. Fifteen percent of the firms purchased fixed assets in the past year and most of them purchased machinery and equipment. Ninety-four percent of the informal firms financed purchases of fixed assets through internal funds (as opposed to 72 percent of formal firms) while 22.2 percent of the firms used microfinance (Figure 5.7).

Infrastructure and Access to Land

Poor infrastructure seems to be less constraining for informal firms than for formal ones. Poor public infrastructure is the most critical obstacle for only 4.2 percent of the informal enterprises, compared to limited demand, which is the most critical obstacle for 40.7 percent of them. Almost all informal firms are vulnerable to interruptions in municipal services such as electricity and water, but many informal business operations benefit from access to modern technologies such as cell phones.

While access to electricity is widespread, (98 percent are connected to the electricity grid), **the quality of service is very poor and imposes considerable losses on informal firms.** Ninety-nine percent of the

Figure 5.7   Source of Financing for Fixed Assets by Informal Firms in Nepal

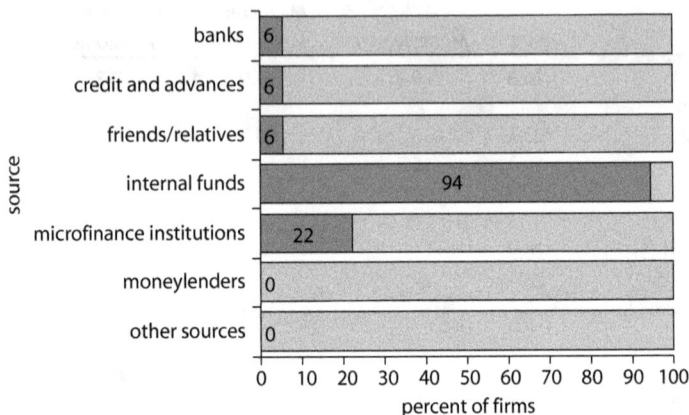

Source: Nepal Informal Survey 2009.

informal firms in the sample experienced at least one power outage in the month previous to the survey; the average informal firm experienced 59.2 outages in the last month, with each outage lasting on average eight hours. Such disruptions impose considerable losses on firms: on average, firms declare to have lost 23 percent of their sales, but small firms and firms established over 10 years ago lose between 27 and 31 percent of their sales.

Provision of water is also subject to outages. Of the firms that make use of water for their business activity (45 percent of the sample), one-third experienced insufficient water supply in the month previous to the interview.

One-third of the informal businesses operate on household premises. The likelihood of operating within the premises of the household is higher for younger firms and for micro firms. Among the businesses that conduct their business outside the house, most (57.5 percent) have semi-fixed premises, which means that they have fixed premises but the structure is temporary (e.g., stalls) (Table 5.8). Only two firms in the sample operate without fixed premises (5 percent of the firms operating outside the household); these firms are typically micro street food vendors. This might have a bearing on performance.[9]

Most of the informal firms (92.4 percent) do not own the land or the premises they occupy. The only exception is the informal accommodations industry, where about half of the firms own their premises (which is likely

Table 5.8   Premises for Informal Businesses Operations (% Firms)

	Business location		Type of location for businesses operating outside household premises		
	Within household premises	Outside household premises	Fixed premises and permanent structure	Fixed premises and temporary structure	Without fixed premises
Total	**66.7**	**33.3**	**37.5**	**57.5**	**5.0**
Region					
West	68.8	31.3	44.0	56.0	0.0
Central	68.8	31.3	40.0	60.0	0.0
East	58.3	41.7	20.0	60.0	20.0
Size					
Micro (<5)	70.1	29.9	47.8	43.5	8.7
Small (5–19)	61.9	38.1	25.0	75.0	0.0
Age					
<5 yrs	70.2	29.8	64.3	35.7	0.0
5–9 yrs	70.3	29.7	18.2	72.7	9.1
10–19 yrs	58.3	41.7	20.0	80.0	0.0
20+ yrs	58.3	41.7	40.0	40.0	20.0
Industry					
Food and beverages	70.2	29.8	47.1	41.2	11.8
Repairing	44.4	55.6	20.0	80.0	0.0
Tailors and apparel	84.0	16.0	50.0	50.0	0.0
Furniture	0.0	100.0	25.0	75.0	0.0
Accommodation	100.0	0.0	—	—	—
Other	60.0	40.0	33.3	66.7	0.0

Source: Nepal Informal Survey 2009.
Note: The last three columns report the distribution by type of premises of the firms in the second column.
— = not available.

to be the household's house). Virtually all firms that do not own their premises have to pay rent, meaning that only a few firms in the sample occupy their premises without any right to do so. The average monthly rent is over Nrs 5,000, which is on average 18 percent of total sales.

Insecurity in land ownership hinders firms' productivity because it increases the riskiness of the firm and discourages entrepreneurs from making improvements to the premises. Lack of secure property rights also increases business riskiness and makes it more difficult to access infrastructural services.

Policy Implications and Recommendations

Given its pervasiveness and contribution to poverty reduction, policy makers need to acknowledge that improving productivity, incomes, and working conditions in the informal sector is an important component of the growth and poverty reduction agendas in Nepal. For this reason, measures related to the informal sector cannot be merely aimed at formalizing these activities or making it more difficult for informal actors to carry out their activities. Measures to support the informal sector should include:

Strengthening linkages to the formal sector. The survey reveals that the informal sector has limited linkages with the formal sector and that low-income households constitute the main market for most informal enterprises. By strengthening these linkages, informal firms can gain more scope for expansion both by improving their access to inputs and especially by expanding markets for their products. Additionally, informal firms can obtain more credit and access to more advanced technologies by interacting with formal enterprises. These linkages can be strengthened through technical assistance (provided by small business development agencies and non-governmental organizations (NGOs)) focusing on small and micro-businesses) focused on marketing and business planning, as well as through strengthened and simplified contract enforcement. The latter would support the spread of subcontracting and franchising, which can be prime avenues for such linkages. At the same time, it is important that subcontracting does not become simply a way to reduce costs and that formal firms do not gain excessive power in fixing prices. Therefore, initiatives are necessary to provide informal firms with information on prices and market conditions. The creation of business associations for informal entrepreneurs could also be promoted in order to strengthen their bargaining power.

Promoting human capital development. Human capital development is key to increasing the productivity of the informal sector and, at the same time, improving the opportunities of informal workers to find employment in the formal sector. Besides increasing literacy rates and educational attainment, especially among the most disadvantaged groups in the population, active labor market policies—such as training and skill-development programs—are recommended. Many entrepreneurs are self-taught and lack business skills; entrepreneurship training could help develop their management capabilities allowing them to expand the potential of their business. Finally, access to technical knowledge should be provided to workers involved in informal artisan activities, who often possess substantial human capital usually acquired through several years of intensive apprenticeships. Apart from allocating more of its own resources, the government could encourage NGOs and the private sector to provide skills training.

Simplifying regulations and enhancing their transparency. The Enterprise Survey reveals that lack of information about complicated registration procedures is the second most common reason why firms choose not to register (after seeing no benefits in registering). The mismatch between most regulatory requirements—usually designed for medium and large firms—and the needs of smaller firms needs to be addressed.

Establishing a one-stop shop for registration, which would decrease registration procedures, facilitate the provision of information, and avoid overlapping and contradictory regulation. In particular, the number of licenses and other documents for which a Tax Clearance Certificate is required should be reduced (World Bank 2007a).

Promoting better access to finance. Better access to finance is the major benefit that informal firms associated with being formally registered. Informal sector operators usually borrow the capital necessary to start and run their business from relatives, friends, and informal lenders. Few of them are able to borrow from commercial banks and other formal credit institutions. Financing for informal firms has expanded in the last years through savings cooperatives and microfinance. These should be encouraged as well as financial infrastructure improvements, such as the establishment of a movable assets registry that small informal firms can use to secure their borrowings.

Notes

1. Informality is not easily defined and measured, in part because there is a "continuum of degrees of informality in terms of different characteristics such as nature of registration, payment of taxes, contractual arrangements, etc." Some informal activities may even be registered with local authorities that collect taxes or that allocate market stalls and charge for their use.

2. Though the majority of workers are low-skilled or unskilled, the informal sector also includes highly-skilled workers involved in artisan activities where workers often possess unique skills acquired through years of intensive work.

3. The NLFS defined employment in the informal sector as: i) paid employees in private unregistered company or other with less than 10 employees; ii) persons operating own account enterprises with no employees; iii) persons operating own enterprise with regular paid employees or family members without pay, or other with less than 10 employees.

4. Only one firm in the informal sample belongs to the medium size group (i.e., employs 20 workers or more); this firm has been excluded from the rest of the sample description.

5. Statistics about average salary in informal firms have been computed excluding those firms that reported a zero average salary.

6. This number only refers to employees and does not account for the owner. As a consequence this statistic is not fully representative and does not concern one-person firms.

7. It could also be the case that the respondents, usually the owners, counted themselves among the number of workers not receiving a wage, but did not count themselves as family members, counting only members other than themselves.

8. The proportion of firms resorting to moneylenders among firms that currently have a loan is significantly larger than the proportion of firms that declared resorting to moneylenders for financing either working capital or fixed assets. This could be a reflection of an increase in financing from moneylenders because the first question specifically refers to the most recent loan, while the second refers to the past year. The discrepancy could, however, also result from the limited subsample on which the question on the source of the latest loan is based.

9. Agarwal and Dhakal (2009), in their study of the Chitwan district, find that being mobile and semi-mobile enterprises, rather than having fixed premises, is negatively correlated with an enterprise's earnings.

CHAPTER 6

Expanding Firm Access to Finance in Nepal

Over the past 20 years, Nepal's financial sector has broadened as the number and type of financial intermediaries have expanded. Access to finance is correlated strongly with firm performance in Nepal; however, access to financial services for firms remains limited. This chapter looks at Nepal's financial system, examines supply-side constraints, and highlights the demand for credit and other financial products by Nepalese firms, particularly the micro, small, and medium enterprises (MSMEs). The results highlight that the first order priority is to address weaknesses in the banking sector and that financial access is a key constraint for many enterprises in Nepal that limits their productivity. The reasons for limited access are complex, but include weak financial infrastructure, which does not relay adequate and timely information, inability of banks to provide profitable lending to MSMEs at acceptable costs, and more subtle barriers such as eligibility criteria and lack of appropriate financial products. MSMEs (the majority of firms in Nepal) are instead burdened by high collateral requirements and resort to internal sources of funding (which are invariably limited). The result is a suboptimal equilibrium of supply of and demand for financial services. Inter alia, the aim should be to improve the financial infrastructure for credit, as well as the ability of banks to downscale profitably.

Financial development is an important component of a country's ability to grow, and access to finance at the firm level is important for firm-level productivity and survival (Banerjee and Duflo 2008; Levine 2005; Rajan and Zingales 1998; Beck, Demirgüç-Kunt, and Maksimovic 2005). Indeed, as the analysis of the performance of Nepalese enterprises shows (see Chapter 3), access to finance is consistently correlated with better firm performance in terms of labor productivity and total sales. Higher reliance on banks—as opposed to internal funds or informal sources—for borrowing working capital is linked to better performance.

Nepal's Financial Sector

Nepal's financial sector is broad and expanding. From four licensed financial institutions in 1980, the number of licensed financial institutions monitored and supervised by the NRB increased to 180 in 2005 and 263 in 2010. They include: 27 commercial banks, 78 development banks, 79 finance companies, 18 microfinance development banks, 16 credit cooperatives, and 45 financial NGOs. Alongside these financial institutions, more than 12,000 cooperatives, registered with the Department of Cooperatives, are actively engaged in accepting deposits from and making loans to their members and remain largely unregulated. In terms of size, the total assets and liabilities of the financial sector in Nepal expanded to 103 percent of GDP in July 2009 from 86.3 percent of GDP in July 2008 (NRB 2009, 2010).[1]

The depth of Nepal's financial sector has overtaken the South Asia average over the past few years. Financial sector depth, measured as the level of domestic credit provided to the private sector as a share of GDP, increased in Nepal from around 28 percent in 2005 to 56 percent in 2010 (Figure 6.1) (World Bank 2009d). Similarly, the overall private credit to deposit (C/D) ratio increased to more than 73 percent as of July 2010 (the C/D ratio shoots up to 82 percent when foreign exchange deposits are excluded) (NRB 2009, 2010).[2] This growth is due to several reasons including expansion of lending for real estate and consumption, coupled with very low (near zero) real interest rates between 2007 and 2009 (real interest rates only increased to around 1.5 percent in FY2009/10 (NRB 2009, 2010).

Despite the increase in the number of financial institutions and the increase in credit flowing into the economy, the provision of banking facilities has not improved significantly over time. Demographic and geographic branch and automated teller machine (ATM) penetration over the last eight years has hovered around 2 branches and less than one ATM per 100,000 people, the lowest rate in South Asia.[3] Hence, only

Figure 6.1   Domestic Credit Provided to Private Sector in Nepal and Comparator Countries, Percent GDP

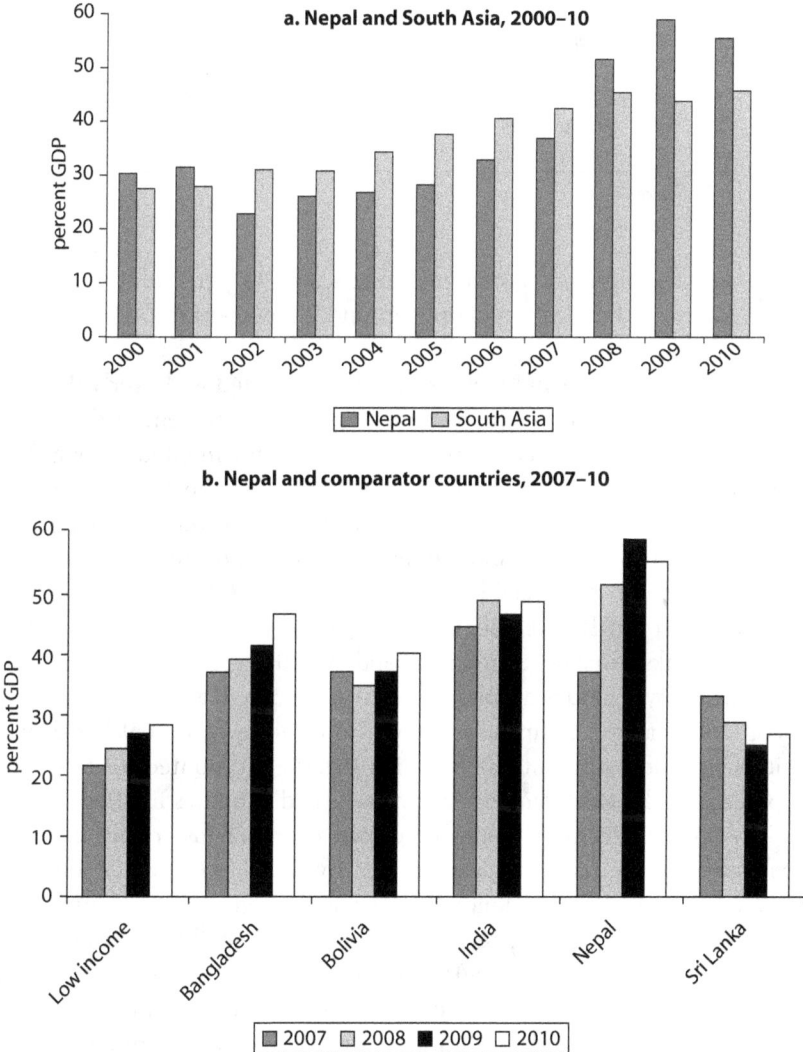

a. Nepal and South Asia, 2000–10

Nepal   South Asia

b. Nepal and comparator countries, 2007–10

2007   2008   2009   2010

Source: World Bank 2009d.

about 0.002 percent and 0.001 percent of the total population are served in terms of branch and ATM availability, respectively (Table 6.1). Usage of banking services also seems to be limited and declining in some cases. Deposits per 1,000 people decreased to 107 per 1,000 people in 2008 from an average of 111 over the previous five years. Use of commercial

Table 6.1   Provision of Banking Services in Nepal, 2008

Banking service	Number
Branches per 100,000 people	2
Branches per 1,000 km	3
ATMs per 100,000 people	Less than 1
ATMs per 1,000 km	Less than 1
Deposit accounts per 1,000 people	107
Loan accounts per 1,000 people	25

Source: World Bank 2010d.

bank facilities, therefore, is confined to less than 11 percent of the population in terms of deposits and only around 2.5 percent in terms of loans (World Bank 2010d).

The banking sector in Nepal is both concentrated and overly diffuse. The three largest commercial banks account for 25 percent of the banking sector's assets; the remaining 75 percent is fragmented among 260 financial institutions. Commercial banks dominate the financial sector. According to the NRB, the 27 commercial banks accounted for around 80 percent of total assets and liabilities of the entire financial sector in 2010 (together, commercial banks had an asset to GDP ratio of 69 percent in 2009) (NRB 2009, 2010). The remainder was split among development banks, finance companies, and microfinance institutions. The latter category includes around 78 institutions ranging from savings and credit cooperatives, to financial NGOs, to rural development banks and microcredit development banks, which together accounted for less than 3 percent of the total banking sector assets and liabilities in 2010.

The financial sector in Nepal has grown at a much faster pace than the real sector in the past few years, driven by excessive liquidity resulting from an accommodative monetary policy and burgeoning migrant remittance flows. Indeed commercial banks' assets and liabilities expanded by around 30 percent in FY2008/09 and around 10 percent in FY2009/10. This liquidity was channeled through the banking system into lending to the real estate sector and consumption. **In addition, persistent low capital adequacy in State-owned banks and high loan to deposit ratios in small financial institutions, continue to pose risks to the banking sector.** Nepal is the only country in South Asia whose banking system had negative capital adequacy until 2008 (Sophastienphong and Kulathunga 2010) (Figure 6.2). Although capital adequacy turned positive in 2008, at 4 percent, the ratio was well below the statutory requirement of 10 percent. Two of the three large State-owned banks **had negative capital up to 2008**

Figure 6.2   Capital Adequacy Ratio Levels in South Asian Countries, 2004–08

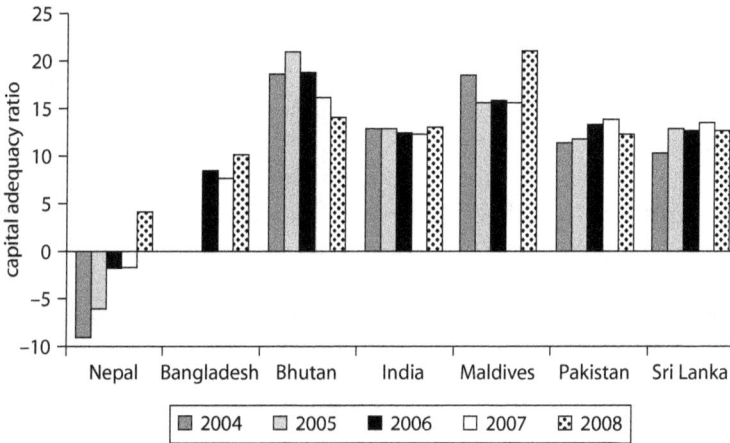

Source: Sophastienphong and Kulathunga 2010.

and continue to be inadequately capitalized due to large accumulated losses.[4] In addition, there are many small institutions that have both small capital and deposit bases with loan portfolios that typically reach up to 130 percent of their deposits.

Firm Access to Finance in Nepal

As discussed in Chapter 3, access to financial services correlates strongly with firm performance and productivity in Nepal. However, financial access declined during the conflict years and remains limited to a small segment of the population. The conflict forced many financial institutions to close down their rural and remote branches. On the other hand, as mentioned earlier, the number and type of financial intermediaries have grown rapidly in urban areas.

Despite forty years of government mandates to banks to increase access to finance for SMEs, progress has been limited. The "priority sector lending" program, requiring banks to make loans to small businesses, has not addressed the financial sustainability of such lending and is being phased-out. Its main failing was that banks saw it as an annual tax and did not use it to address the essential reasons banks and SMEs do not naturally enter into relationships, namely, the lack of products, procedures, lending technologies, and institutional/informational support systems to lend profitably to SMEs.

Access to finance is the third most important obstacle to registered firms, though only about 8 percent of firms see it as the most important constraint. It is especially a constraint for MSMEs, where 25, 4, and 16 percent of firms, respectively, view access to finance as a major or severe constraint (Figure 6.3). Large firms do not perceive access to finance as an obstacle. Although large firms have good access, they still often choose not to resort to banks to finance their investments and operational expenses. This could be a reflection of the lack of dynamism of these enterprises. They do not perceive access to finance as a major

Figure 6.3   Access to Finance Rated as Major or Severe Constraint by Size of Firm in Nepal and Comparator Countries

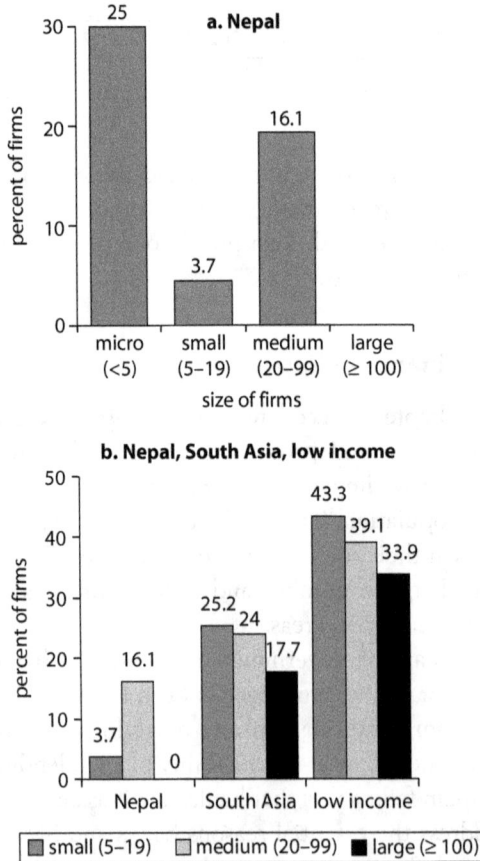

Source: World Bank Enterprise Surveys, latest available year.
Note: In panel b, comparison restricted to firms with 5+ employees in sectors surveyed in most countries in the comparator group, i.e., manufacturing, retail, wholesale, hotels and restaurants, transport, and travel agencies.

obstacle since they are not growing their operations enough to require expanded financial access.

Access to finance in Nepal, as measured by the proportion of firms that have a loan or a bank account, is one of the lowest among comparator countries. While the number of loans on which collateral is required is below the average, when collateral is required, the average value is very high as a proportion of the loan amount. For their most recent loan or line of credit, on average, firms reported that the collateral requirements were 260 percent of the loan value[5]; only Bhutan and Lao PDR have higher values among the comparator countries (Table 6.2).

Firm Use of Financial Services

Firms make little use of financial services: less than half of the enterprises have a checking or a savings account, only one out of three firms has a

Table 6.2   Nepal Enterprise Survey 2009: Access to Finance Indicators

	% firms using banks to finance investments	Bank finance for investment (%)	% firms using banks to finance expenses	Working capital bank financing (%)
Nepal	17.5	12.4	32.2	16.3
South Asia	27.2	17.4	32.9	15.9
Bhutan	64.2	39.7	59.5	32.1
Bolivia	22.2	24.9	39.4	19.6
Bangladesh	24.7	17.1	43.1	19.6
Lao PDR	0.0	0.0	10.9	3.8
Mongolia	26.5	19.6	—	—
	% firms with line of credit / loans	% firms with a checking or savings account	Loans requiring collateral (%)	Value of collateral required (% loan amount)
Nepal	39.1	73.7	80.9	259.7
South Asia	32.1	79.9	83.8	177.8
Bhutan	58.6	92.6	97.3	283.4
Bolivia	50.1	91.3	96.7	185.2
Bangladesh	50.8	95.3	91.4	147.1
Lao PDR	18.3	92.1	100.0	312.0
Mongolia	52.9	61.4	95.5	41.2

Source: World Bank Enterprise Surveys, latest available year.
Note: Comparison restricted to firms with 5+ employees in sectors surveyed in most countries in the comparator group, i.e., manufacturing, retail, wholesale, hotels and restaurants, transport, and travel agencies.
— = not available.

line of credit or a loan from a financial institution and one out of ten has an overdraft facility. Firms also make little use of loans from banks to finance their current expenditure or their investments because they usually resort to internal funds. Less than 10 percent of these expenditures are financed through borrowing from banks (Table 6.3).

Firm use of financial services in Nepal is quite low by regional and international standards. Only two out of five firms with five or more employees have a line of credit or a loan from a financial institution, compared to three out of five firms in Bhutan (Figure 6.4). On average, Nepalese firms use banks to finance only 12 percent of investments and 16 percent of their expenses. The proportion of firms that have a bank account is the second lowest in the comparator group.

Sources of Firm Finance in Nepal

On average, Nepalese firms finance 82 percent of their day-to-day working capital needs through internal funding and the rest through external financing (Figure 6.5). External financing is primarily through bank

Table 6.3   Use of Financial Services by Nepalese Firms

		Size			
	All	Micro (<5)	Small (5–19)	Medium (20–99)	Large (>=100)
% firms with checking or savings accounts	44.9	32.5	71.7	90.3	100.0
% firms with overdraft facility	10.2	4.3	21.2	45.9	78.5
% firms with line of credit or loan	29.0	24.7	38.1	46.5	61.9
% funds borrowed from banks, working capital	9.4	6.4	15.3	24.2	32.8
% funds borrowed from banks, fixed assets	6.4	0.2	11.7	11.9	35.7
			Region		
	All		West	Central	East
% firms with checking or savings accounts	44.9		48.3	44.4	42.8
% firms with overdraft facility	10.2		7.6	11.9	6.9
% firms with line of credit or loan	29.0		36.9	26.4	29.2
% funds borrowed from banks, working capital	9.4		9.4	7.7	16.0
% funds borrowed from banks, fixed assets	6.4		14.7	3.6	4.4

Source: Nepal Enterprise Survey 2009.

Figure 6.4   Access to Finance in Nepal and Comparator Countries

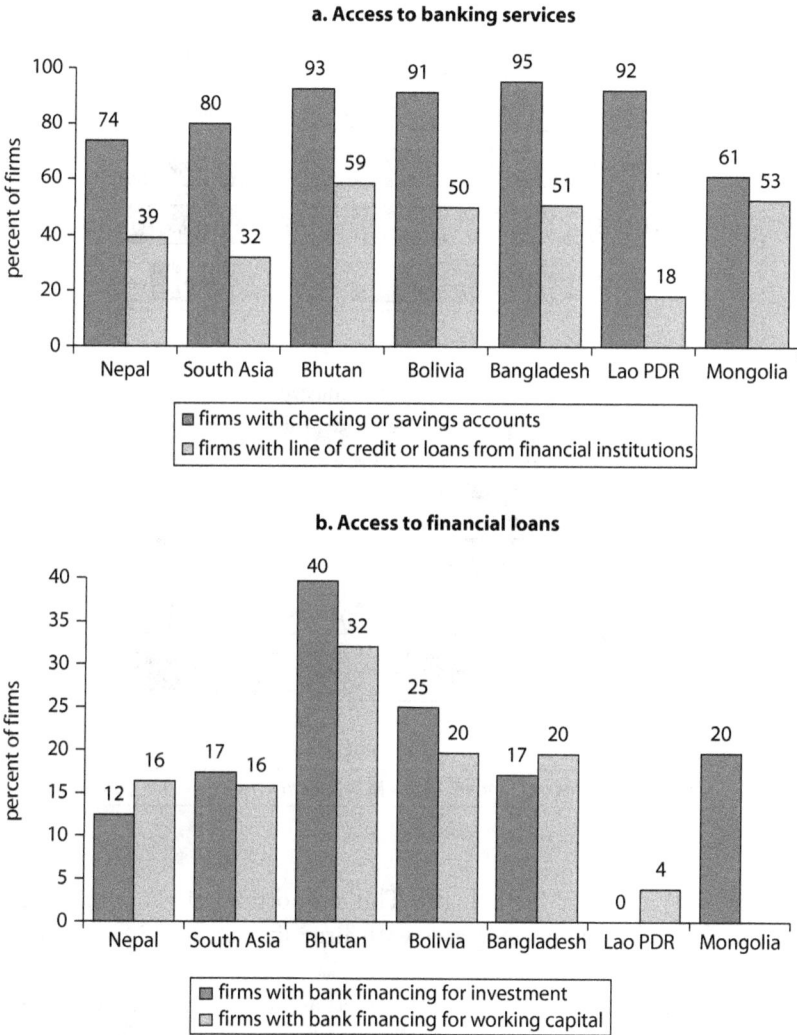

a. Access to banking services

firms with checking or savings accounts
firms with line of credit or loans from financial institutions

b. Access to financial loans

firms with bank financing for investment
firms with bank financing for working capital

Source: World Bank Enterprise Surveys, latest available year.
Note: Comparison restricted to firms with 5+ employees in sectors surveyed in most countries in the comparator group, i.e., manufacturing, retail, wholesale, hotels and restaurants, transport, and travel agencies. Sample restricted to firms with 5+ employees

loans (9.4 percent of overall financing) with very little coming from sup-
plier/customer credit (2.8 percent of the total). Manufacturing firms
finance three quarters of their day-to-day needs through internal funding and another 17.3 percent through bank loans. Services firms finance
83.4 percent of their day-to-day needs through internal funding but only

Figure 6.5   Sources of Working Capital Financing in Nepal

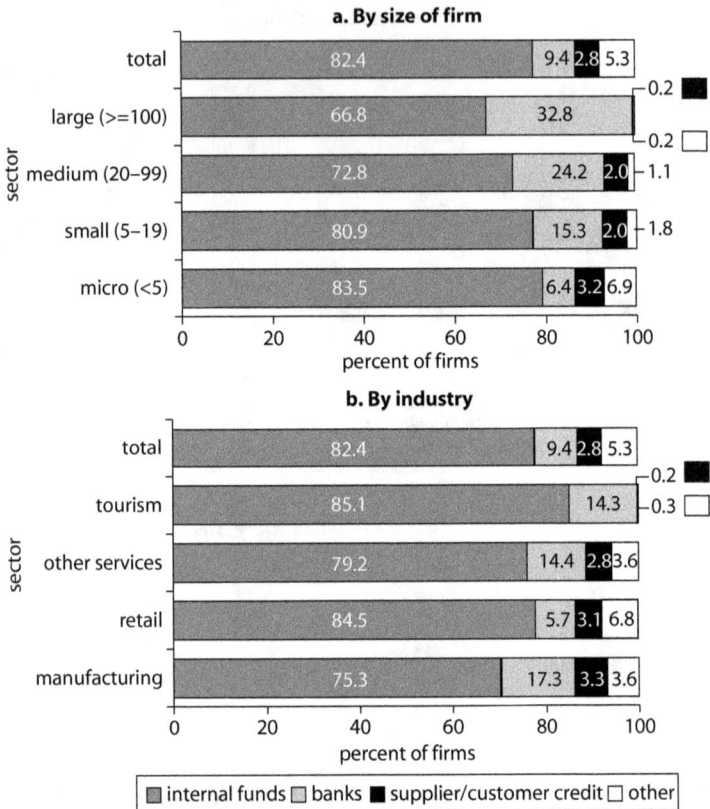

a. By size of firm

b. By industry

☐ internal funds ☐ banks ■ supplier/customer credit ☐ other

Source: Nepal Enterprise Survey 2009.

8.2 percent through bank loans. The proportion of working capital financed through banks increases with firm size, up to 32.8 percent in large firms.

Sources of investment finance (or fixed asset finance) follow a similar pattern to working capital finance. The majority of investment financing (72 percent) comes from internal resources, and only 6.4 percent comes from bank financing. Compared to comparator countries, Nepalese firms with more than five employees have the second lowest share of investments financed by banks (12.4 percent) (Figure 6.6).

Supply of Financial Services to Nepalese Firms

Eligibility requirements, processing times, and loan sizes affect the supply of financial services, and play a role in determining the extent to which

Figure 6.6   Sources of Investment Financing for Nepal and Comparator Countries: Retained Earnings, Bank Finance, Owner's Contribution, Other Financing

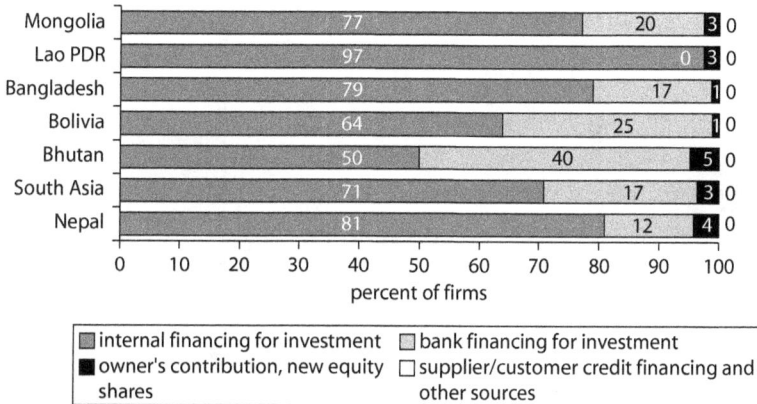

Source: World Bank Enterprise Surveys, latest available year.
Note: Comparison restricted to firms with 5+ employees in sectors surveyed in most countries in the comparator group, i.e., manufacturing, retail, wholesale, hotels and restaurants, transport, and travel agencies.

firms can and will access financial services. Nepal has the highest number of documents required to access financial services—four documents, compared to an average of two documents in 60 other countries. Given the high degree of informality in Nepal, only a small proportion of the population and small businesses can produce these documents (World Bank 2007c). Nepal, on the other hand, ranks average on the speed at which loans are processed; it takes 11 days to process an SME loan application and 10 days to process a business loan application (World Bank 2007c).

The smallest amount of loans banks in Nepal have made to business is about 200 times GDP per capita, while the minimum amount a consumer can borrow is 12 times GDP per capita.[6] Small firms tend to face greater access barriers than do large firms. The minimum SME loan amount is almost 30 times GDP per capita, casting doubt on whether banks in Nepal can meet the borrowing needs of small firms (World Bank 2007c) (Figure 6.7).

Obstacles to Increased Access to Financial Services for Nepalese Firms

Between FY2007/08 and FY2008/09, only 23 percent of Nepalese firms applied for a loan. Fifty-seven percent indicated that they had no need for a loan (in itself an indication that firms are not growing or investing

Figure 6.7   Affordability of Access to Loans in Nepal and Comparator Countries

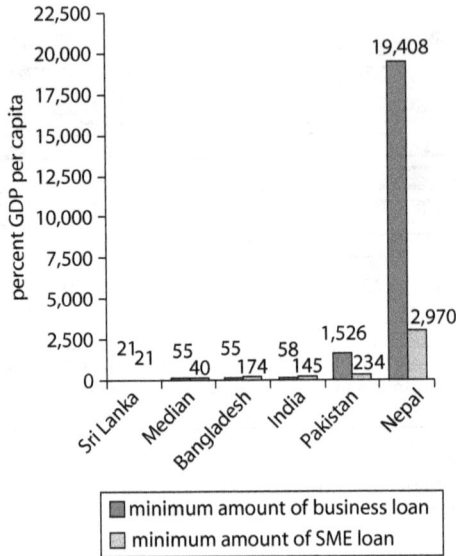

Source: World Bank 2007c.

beyond what their internal sources allow them to), 9.5 percent cited interest rates as being too high, another 9 percent cited high collateral requirements, 8 percent cited the application procedures as being too burdensome, and 15 percent cited other reasons (Figure 6.8).

The lack of appropriate financial products and services for businesses and SME's is an important barrier to access to financial services in Nepal. Collateral requirements on loans are also part of the problem of access to finance; 81 percent of all firms reported needing collateral to secure a loan (Figure 6.9). The value of collateral required on average is one of the highest when compared to comparator countries. The value of collateral required for a loan varies across firm size and age, though the value is very high for most firms.

However, it is not only the value of collateral required to secure a loan that reduces access, but rather the type of collateral that is acceptable to a bank. In Nepal, the most required type of collateral is personal assets of the owner (70.4 percent of firms have partially or fully collaterized this way, which are typically the land and/or buildings of the owner), followed by accounts receivable (25 percent), land and buildings (of the company) (14.8 percent) and machinery and equipment (10.6 percent). A firm

Figure 6.8   Reasons Nepalese Firms Did Not Apply for a Line of Credit
percent of firms

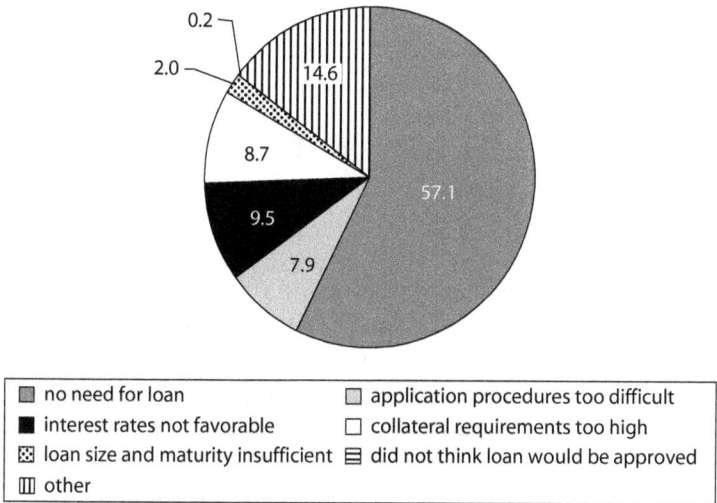

Legend:
- no need for loan
- interest rates not favorable
- loan size and maturity insufficient
- other
- application procedures too difficult
- collateral requirements too high
- did not think loan would be approved

Source: Nepal Enterprise Survey 2009.

Figure 6.9   Firms Needing Collateral and Value of Collateral Needed for a Loan in Nepal and Comparator Countries

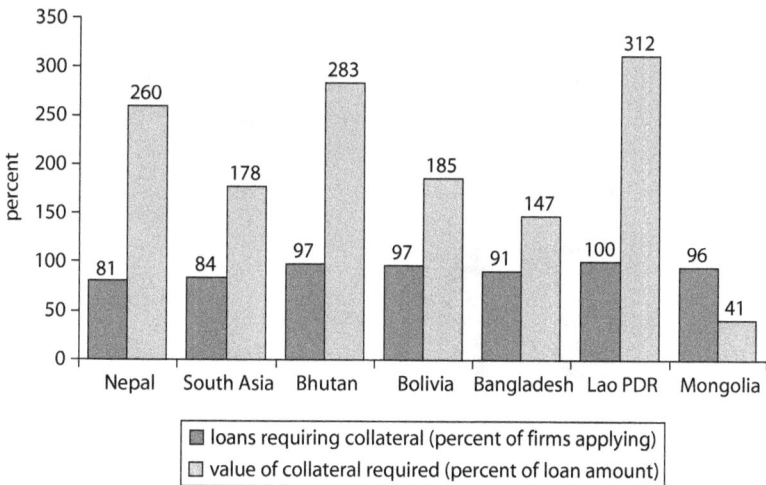

Legend:
- loans requiring collateral (percent of firms applying)
- value of collateral required (percent of loan amount)

Source: World Bank Enterprise Surveys, latest available year.
Note: Comparison restricted to firms with 5+ employees in sectors surveyed in most countries in the comparator group, i.e., manufacturing, retail, wholesale, hotels and restaurants, transport, and travel agencies.

owner in Nepal takes all the risk of a loan personally, indicating there is a need to create new classes of collateral. Banks usually require immovable property such as land or buildings or an owner's own assets to secure a loan, while most firms' property and assets are vested in movable property such as machinery, inventory, or accounts receivable

Further, there is a discrepancy between the type of collateral firms used and the assets they bought. In 2008, all the firms purchased equipment, and only 8 percent purchased land. However, only 10.6 percent of firms used their equipment for collateral, and 14.8 percent used personal assets (typically, land and buldings) (Figure 6.10). Expanding the class of collateral firms can use could expand access to finance for firms. Expanding the use of movable property as collateral would allow firms to better leverage their assets in a productive manner.

While collateral and lending terms matter to firms, the broader institutional environment also matters for creditors. When property rights are not clearly defined, firms cannot offer land, buildings, or movable property as collateral because of lack of clear titles (or the inability of banks to monitor whether the movable property has been pledged as collateral

Figure 6.10   Types of Collateral Required by Banks for Most Recent Line of Credit by Nepalese Firms

percent

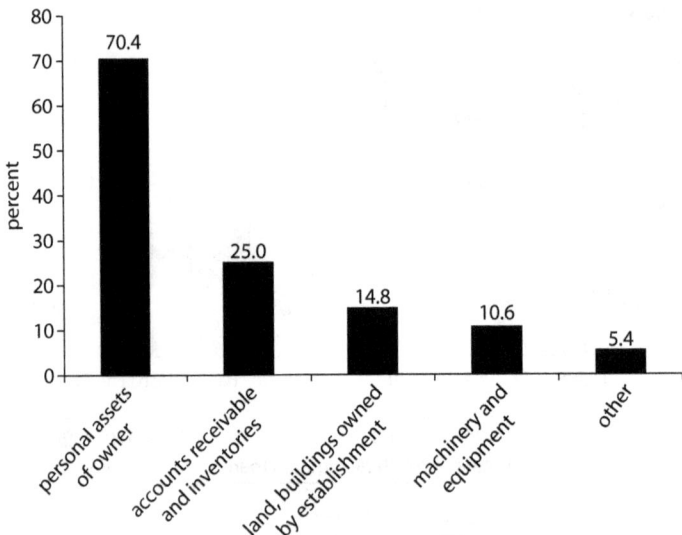

Source: Nepal Enterprise Survey 2009.

to other financial institutions). In addition, sharing credit information improves banks' knowledge of applicants, permitting more accurate prediction of repayment probability and increasing borrower repayment incentives.

Compared to comparator countries, Nepal ranks relatively poorly on "getting credit" because of the lack of coverage of public and private credit bureaus and its low score in the credit information index. The Doing Business indicator on "getting credit" measures both the legal rights of borrowers and lenders and the sharing of credit information. The credit information index measures the rules affecting the scope, access, and quality of credit information and the extent of public registry and private credit bureau coverage. Nepal performs poorly in all of these areas. In addition, there are no public credit bureaus in Nepal (Table 6.4 and Figure 6.11).

Nepal's credit information index has remained at two out of six over the past four years (World Bank Doing Business Historical Database). Data on firms and individuals are distributed only by private credit bureaus. Both positive and negative data are distributed by the private credit bureau; however, it provides very limited information on borrowers. The credit bureau requests information and keeps records only for borrowers with loans above Nrs 1 million; it is not useful for small business lending.

In summary, banks in Nepal find it difficult to serve small businesses profitably. Their procedures are too complex; their most popular bank product—overdrafts (lines of credit)—is inappropriate for many small businesses, which do not deposit their revenues in banks; their interest rates do not adequately reflect the costs of serving this segment; and they require high levels of immovable collateral. In addition, the absence of an

Table 6.4   Doing Business 2010: Getting Credit

	Rank	Strength of legal rights index (0–10)	Depth of credit information index (0–6)	Public registry coverage (% of adults)	Private bureau coverage (% of adults)
Mongolia	71	6	3	22.2	0
Bolivia	113	1	6	11.6	33.9
Nepal	113	5	2	0	0.3
Bangladesh	71	7	2	0.9	0
Lao PDR	150	4	0	0	0
Bhutan	177	2	0	0	0

Source: World Bank 2009a; World Bank Doing Business Historical Database, http://www.doingbusiness.org/CustomQuery.

Figure 6.11   Credit Information Index and Coverage in Nepal and Comparator Countries

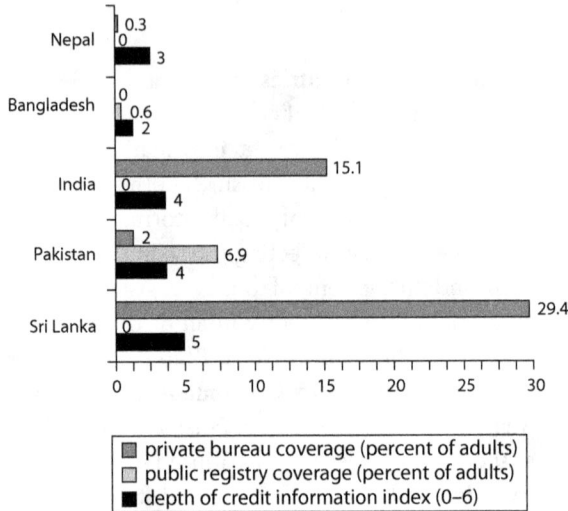

Source: World Bank 2009a.

operating registry to record liens on movable assets, and the fact that the credit bureau only covers loans larger than Nrs 1 million make lending to this sector more difficult.

Conclusions and Recommendations

The NRB is responsible for monitoring and supervising the growing banking sector in Nepal. To effectively fulfill this responsibility and to ensure the soundness and stability of the financial system, the NRB needs to put special emphasis on enhancing its supervisory and regulatory capacity. Priority should be given to addressing the issue of effective enforcement and supervisory forbearance.

To help lenders increase small business lending, the government could develop an enabling environment that makes small business lending safer, cheaper, and faster. This can be achieved through:

- **Broadening the range of assets acceptable as collateral through operationalizing a secured transactions registry.** In the absence of a secured transactions mechanism, lenders find it risky to accept movable property as collateral for loans. In 2006 the GoN enacted the Secured Transactions (ST) Act. The ST Act provides the legal framework for the establishment of a Secured Transaction Registration Office. Although the Credit Information Company Limited (CICL) has been designated to perform the function of the registry, the ST Act has still not been operationalized. It is recommended that the Act be put into practice by setting up the Registration Office and creating a registration database in which a public record of obligations secured by movable property can be stored. The Registration Office could be Internet-based and include features of good practice filing and archiving.

• **Deepening the reach of the Credit Information Bureau (CIB).** The CIB operates with a high level of autonomy, as 90 percent of its ownership is by commercial banks. However, the bureau has very limited coverage. The bureau coverage should be expanded through improved management information systems of both the CIB and participating banks so that it can better serve SMEs. Upgrading the system at the bureau alone is not adequate. Member/participating banks and FIs should also be adequately equipped and have the capacity to share/exchange information, especially given that many SMEs do not have audited (or even written) statements, and thus require the services of a credit bureau to help them access credit from banks more cheaply and speedily.

• **Commercial Bank Downscaling:** Commercial banks could scale down to smaller market segments by developing appropriate products and risk management systems that can serve MSMEs. These can be developed through technical assistance and capacity building programs that are provided by development partners. In addition, non-interest subsidized lines of credit by the NRB or development partners can be provided to those banks that take up the capacity building in order to on-lend to MSMEs. Typically, Nepalese commercial banks have used other intermediaries, such as microfinance institutions (MFIs) and microfinance development banks (MEDBs) to reach the unbanked population, and some have opened their own MFIs to downscale. However, the share of other financial institutions such as savings and credit cooperatives, NGOs, rural development banks, and MFDBs is still small in Nepal. Hence, commercial banks should lead the way to design strategies to ensure financial inclusion.

• **Providing technical assistance and financial literacy training to firms** (especially to SMEs) in order to enhance their capacity to develop and present bankable proposals, and provide support to SMEs to keep better accounts. This would ensure that SMEs have the capacity to successfully apply for a loan and effectively utilize loans for the growth of their businesses.

- **Designing and implementing partial risk guarantees and other financial products** aimed at reducing the risk associated with existing collateral and supporting the banking system in adopting better risk assessment measures (based more on cash flows rather than on fixed assets). Such schemes would address information asymmetries, the high costs of processing smaller credit transactions, and constraints in the enforcement of contracts. In Nepal, the existing government-supported credit guarantee scheme has been in existence for decades but has not been properly utilized, nor does it have the capacity, resources, or appropriate regulatory framework. Therefore, it needs to be revamped.

- **Addressing other constraints to access to finance, such as**
  - enhancing creditors rights so that banks/FIs are more comfortable lending to this sector with less fixed collateral;
  - strengthening the Land Registration Office for ease of registration and release of collateral, in addition to preventing duplication/fraud;
  - improving the skills level in the financial sector through supporting and enhancing the capabilities of the newly established National Banking Training Institute, and finally,
  - developing the appropriate regulatory framework for mobile banking.[7]

Notes

1. All GDP data are from the Nepal Rastra Bank. Data were compiled from the archive of Nepal Rastra Bank Recent Macroeconomic Situation Reports to create their own monthly time-series database, which was used for the analysis in this ICA. http://www.nrb.org.np/ofg/press.php?tp=recent_macroeconomic&&vw=15.

2. The three state-owned banks have lower C/D ratios. The C/D ratio (excluding foreign exchange deposits) shot up to 87 percent in April 2010, but the NRB intervened to lower it.

3. However, in FY2010, there was a marked expansion in bank branches from 752 to 966. In addition, there was a lot of expansion in ATM terminals.

4. The combined negative net worth of these two banks has actually been reduced from around Nrs 30 billion in 2003 to Nrs 16 billion as of 2010.

Without them, the capital adequacy ratio for the whole industry would be well over 12 percent.

5. Given that urban based land collateral is given to banks even for small borrowing requirements, the value of collateral may exceed the loan amount significantly.

6. These figures do not include MFI loans or loans by unregulated cooperatives.

7. A few banks, such as Bank of Kathmandu and Laxmi Bank, have already developed limited mobile banking applications, including sending and receiving money between customers of the same bank, and mobile phone-based payment services. However, the lack of proper NRB guidelines and unavailability of a USSD platform offered by the mobile phone operators (as opposed to the SMS-based platform, which has a higher security risk and is costlier) is slowing down further developments. The authorities could encourage operators to develop and/or acquire this technology.

CHAPTER 7

The Labor Market in Nepal

The labor market in Nepal is characterized by rigid regulations and unioniza-tion that reduce the incentives to hire workers through formal contracts, result-ing in insufficient job-creation and high levels of unpaid work and underemployment. This drives many Nepalese to migrate for work abroad. Therefore, the country finds itself in a situation where workers employed in the domestic market are generally well protected, while many job seekers have to go abroad and work in much worse conditions. Labor laws also provide for minimum wages with very little differentiation across skill levels; as a result, labor productivity and investments in human capital are low. Large firms are most constrained by labor regulations and are also often subject to trade union actions. Political issues and wage issues are the most common causes of such actions, and there is a fair amount of inter-play between labor and political issues. In order to encourage employment and labor productivity growth, ways should be explored to reduce non-wage labor costs, to pilot flex-ible labor regimes in special economic zones, and to create additional labor court branches to speed up the resolution of labor cases.

Composition of the Labor Market

Nepal's population has risen rapidly over the past thirty years and at the same time has become younger and more urbanized. Nepal's population of around 28 million is growing at 2 percent per year, and the ratio of population to arable land is one of the highest in the world. The urbanization rate is increasing rapidly: the urban population accounted for 17 percent of the total population in 2008, compared to 4.2 percent in 1971 (CBS 2008).

The youth bulge created by the demographic transition and the cessation of the armed conflict have increased the labor supply (mostly unskilled), putting pressure on the labor market. Indeed, people in the 15–64 age group in 2008 accounted for 56.5 percent of the population, increasing from 54.6 percent in 1998/99. On the other hand, the labor force participation rate (i.e., the proportion of the population aged 15 years and above who were currently economically active) decreased from 85.8 percent in 1998/99 to 83.4 percent in 2008 (CBS 2008).

Very high levels of unpaid work also characterize Nepal's labor market. Based on the 2008 NLFS, almost 90 percent of men and 80 percent of women are "economically active." Yet almost one-half (44 percent) of the workforce are unpaid family members, of whom the majority are women. More than three-fifths of women are unpaid family members, and those who do work for pay are more likely to be engaged in self/family agricultural work (21 percent). In contrast, more than one-quarter of men are in paid employment. The majority of 15–24 year olds (85 percent) are unpaid family workers. Therefore, it is important to highlight (as was discussed in detail in Chapter 5) that the largest proportion of these "economically active" workers are actually in informal types of work arrangements with no contracts or social security and very little predictability.

Labor participation is high in both urban and rural areas of Nepal although a greater proportion of the rural population is in the labor force. In 2008, 85.6 percent of men and 79.3 percent of women were working or actively seeking work in Nepal (Table 7.1). Even though more

Table 7.1   Economically Active Population by Gender Aged 15+, 2008 (%)

	Nepal			Urban			Rural		
	Total	Male	Female	Total	Male	Female	Total	Male	Female
Usually active	82.1	85.6	79.3	65.5	75.1	56.5	85.6	88.1	83.6
Employed	97.5	97.4	97.6	92.0	93.4	90.3	98.3	98.2	98.5
Unemployed	2.5	2.6	2.4	8.0	6.6	9.6	1.6	1.8	1.5
Usually inactive	17.9	14.4	20.7	34.5	24.9	43.5	14.4	11.9	16.4

Source: CBS 2008.
Note: Usually active and usually inactive population expressed as percentage of total population aged 15+; employed and unemployed population expressed as percentage of usually active population.

men are active participants in the labor force, women are entering the labor force at a higher rate than men (CBS 2008).

The agricultural sector in Nepal remains the largest employer, with more than two-thirds of the active labor force in Nepal (73.9 percent) still employed in the agriculture, forestry, and fishing sector. The sector with the second largest portion of the active population is the manufacturing sector with approximately 6.6 percent, followed by wholesale, retail, and trade with approximately 5.9 percent (Table 7.2).

The unemployment rate in Nepal is low, but given the weak data available on the labor market, estimates of the level of unemployment must be cautiously considered. According to the 2008 NLFS, the unemployment rate was estimated at 1.8 percent in 1998/99 and at 2.8 percent in 2008. Unemployment increased more among women (from 1.7 percent to 2.0 percent). The level of under-employment may be a more telling statistic of employment patterns given the lack of reliable unemployment data. The time-related underemployment rate[1], as a percentage of the labor force, is 6.7 percent in 2008 compared to 4.1 percent in 1998/99.

An increasing percentage of the active labor force in Nepal is finding work abroad and the flow of remittances sent back to Nepal by migrant workers constitutes a significant proportion of GDP. The main push factors behind international migration from Nepal have been high population growth rates, the civil unrest—especially after 2001—and limited private sector employment growth, reflecting the poor investment climate. In 2007/08, 229,000 official migrant departures were registered, showing a 21 percent increase over the previous four years. More than 90 percent of the migrants headed to four countries: Qatar, Saudi Arabia, the United Arab Emirates, and Malaysia (World Bank 2010g). These figures exclude migrants to India and those who use informal channels; the number of Nepalese workers in India, including seasonal workers, is believed to be between 1.5 and 2 million.

The working conditions faced by Nepalese job-seekers who decide to emigrate contrast starkly with those faced by the Nepalese who have found formal employment inside the country, in terms of protection and rights (thanks to a rigid system and highly unionized labor force in Nepal).

Labor Policy and Regulatory Environment in Nepal

Nepal has one of the most rigid regulatory frameworks in South Asia. Nepal ranks 150 out of 181 countries in the world according to Doing Business data in terms of the flexibility of labor regulations (World Bank

Table 7.2 Currently Employed Persons Aged 15 Years and Over by Sex, Locality, and Industry (%)

	Nepal			Urban			Rural		
	Total	Male	Female	Total	Male	Female	Total	Male	Female
Agriculture, forestry, and fishing	73.9	62.1	84.3	32.2	19.9	47.7	80.1	69.8	88.7
Mining and quarrying	0.2	0.4	0.1	0.2	0.3	0.1	0.2	0.4	0.1
Manufacturing	6.6	8.5	4.9	14	15.5	12	5.5	7.2	4
Electricity, gas, and water	0.9	0.7	1.1	2.1	1.5	2.8	0.8	0.6	0.9
Construction	3.1	5.9	0.7	4.9	7.6	1.4	2.9	5.6	0.6
Wholesale, retail, and trade	5.9	8.1	3.9	17.2	19.7	14	4.2	6	2.7
Hotels and restaurants	1.7	1.7	1.7	6.1	5.4	6.9	1	1	1
Transport and communications	1.7	3.5	0.1	4.2	7.1	0.6	1.3	2.8	0.1
Financial intermediation	0.3	0.4	0.2	1.3	1.6	0.9	0.1	0.2	0.1
Real estate	0.6	1	0.2	2.3	3.4	1	0.3	0.6	0.1
Public administration & defense	0.9	1.7	0.2	3.5	5.6	0.9	0.5	1	0.1
Education	2.4	3.4	1.5	5.7	5.8	5.6	1.9	3	1.1
Health and social work	0.7	0.8	0.5	2	2	1.8	0.5	0.6	0.3
Other community & social activity	0.8	1.4	0.4	2.9	3.6	2	0.5	1	0.2
Private household workers	0.3	0.3	0.3	1.4	0.8	2.1	0.1	0.2	0.1
Extra-territorial organization	0	0.1	0	0.1	0.1	0.1	0	0.1	0

Source: CBS 2008.

2009a). The government regulates the labor market through three government bodies: the Ministry of Labor and Transport Management, the Department of Labor and Employment Promotion, and Labor Offices. The Ministry of Labor and Transport Management is responsible for enacting labor laws and regulations, the Department of Labor and Employment Promotion enforces these laws, and the Labor Offices address grievances at the firm/enterprise level.

The Labor and Employment Policy 2062 (2006), the Labor Act 2048 (1992), and Labor Rules 2050 (1994) outline Nepal's labor regulatory framework. The policies apply mainly to permanent employees in larger firms, but the regulations have impacted the entire labor market, discouraging investment and growth and undermining operational efficiency and competitiveness. The Labor Act (2048) and the Trade Union Act (2049), both ratified in 1992, are the legislative foundation of the labor market in Nepal. The Labor Act covers all organized sectors employing more than 10 persons and has evolved to incorporate workers on plantations, and in construction, transport, and the service sectors.

Labor regulations in Nepal stifle productivity and growth and make it difficult and expensive to dismiss employees. Firms must obtain government approval before both hiring and laying off workers.[2] Such labor market rigidity discourages firms from hiring new workers and increases the tension between workers pushing for permanent employment and employers seeking alternatives to hiring permanent staff (such as contractual labor). Restrictive labor legislation on employment in Nepal has severely affected employment growth.[3] Table 7.3 presents the set of Doing Business indicators referring to labor market regulations, which

Table 7.3 Doing Business 2010: Employing Workers Indicators

	Rank	Difficulty of hiring index (0–100)	Rigidity of hours index (0–100)	Difficulty of redundancy index (0–100)	Rigidity of employment index (0–100)	Redundancy costs (weeks of salary)
Bhutan	12	0	0	20	7	10
Mongolia	44	11	40	0	17	9
Bangladesh	124	44	0	40	28	104
Lao PDR	107	11	0	50	20	162
Nepal	148	67	0	70	46	90
Bolivia	183	78	53	100	77	—

Source: World Bank 2009a; World Bank Doing Business Historical Database, http://www.doingbusiness.org/CustomQuery.
— = not available.

show that Nepal has especially rigid regulations in terms of hiring, firing, and in terms of redundancy costs.

The Labor Act includes a provision for a fixed minimum wage in sectors employing more than 10 persons. A committee comprised of equal numbers of representatives from the government, employers, and workers determine the fixed minimum wages. Minimum wages are fixed based on skill level (unskilled, semi-skilled, skilled, and highly skilled). Trade unions have pushed for equal wage increases across skill levels, resulting in a narrowing wage gap between skilled and unskilled workers. Wages of highly skilled workers were 24 percent higher than those for unskilled workers in 1995. In 2008, the wage differential between highly skilled and unskilled workers had declined to 7.6 percent (Table 7.4) (World Bank Doing Business Historical Database).

Labor productivity is low. As a consequence, firms tend to substitute labor with capital. Employment, domestic investment, and foreign investment data from the manufacturing sector show that enterprises in this sector tend to substitute capital for labor due to Nepal's rigid labor regulations. Between 2001–02 and 2006–07 employment decreased by 6.7 percent while investment increased 120 percent (Table 7.5). Similar results are found in foreign investment data. Between 2004–05 and 2007–08, foreign investment approvals increased significantly, by 1,295.4 percent while employment growth declined (CBS 2002, 2006).

Employment in Nepalese Enterprises

On average, manufacturing firms and automobile services are the largest in terms of number of employees with 14.1 workers (Figure 7.1). Retail and informal firms have considerably fewer workers (3.3 on average).

Table 7.4   Minimum Monthly Wages by Skill Category, 1995–2008 (Nrs)

Year	Wage category			Highly skilled	Gap (%)	Mean wage rate
	Unskilled	Semi-skilled	Skilled			
1995	1,450	1,500	1,610	1,800	24.1	1,590
1997	1,800	1,850	1,960	2,150	19.4	1,940
2000	2,116	2,166	2,276	2,466	16.5	2,256
2003	2,560	2,610	2,720	2,910	13.6	2,700
2006	3,300	3,350	3,460	3,650	10.6	3,440
2008	4,600	4,650	4,760	4,950	7.6	4,740
%	217.2	210.0	195.7	175.0		

Source: Compiled from Nepal Gazette (various years).

Table 7.5   Investment and Employment in the Organized Manufacturing Sector

Year	Investment (Nrs millions)	Employment (number)
2001–02	2,826.38	181,943
2006–07	6,223.39	169,891
% increase	120.19	−6.7

Source: CBS 2002, 2006.

Figure 7.1   Average Number of Workers by Industry in Nepal

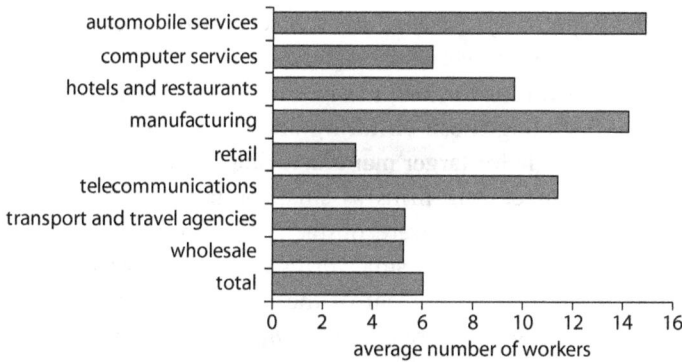

Source: Nepal Enterprise Survey 2009.

Resorting to temporary workers to cover full-time positions is much more common among manufacturing firms than among services or tourism firms. The proportion of permanent workers (among full-time workers) is 77 percent in manufacturing, 92.1 percent in tourism, 99.3 percent in retail, and 97.1 percent in other services. There is no information on the distribution of workers between temporary and permanent in informal firms, however, unpaid workers account for an average of 60 percent of workers.

The presence of women among employees is strongest in the informal sector. Women account for 31.7 percent of workers in informal firms, for 18.6 percent in manufacturing, 22 percent in retail, 24.4 percent in other services, and for 15.5 percent in tourism. Within all sectors, large firms tend to employ a higher proportion of women.

Firm growth in terms of employment in the past three years has been on average around 3.9 percent. The strongest growth was observed in the other services sector (10 percent per year on average) while average annual growth was 3 percent in retail and 1 percent in manufacturing.

Labor Market Issues Identified by Firms

Despite the established legislative and institutional arrangements, indus-trial relations in Nepal are deteriorating. Trade union activities, lockouts, and strikes are on the rise, disrupting productivity. The government's lack of capacity to enforce the arrangements and monitor compliance on the part of both employers and employees is exacerbating the problem.

Political problems are considered the most important labor market issue by a majority of firm managers in all sectors. Cross-sectorally, more firm managers in the tourism sector perceive political problems as the main labor market issue compared to manufacturing, retail, and other services (82.7 percent). Salaries are the second most commonly cited major issue by firms in every sector (Figure 7.2).

Regardless of the sector, size is what matters when it comes to labor regulations (including those on hiring and firing), which tend to be a more severe obstacle for larger manufacturing firms. More than twice as many large manufacturing firms as small or medium firms cite labor regulations as a major or severe obstacle: 59.5 percent in large firms, compared to 20.6 percent in small firms and 23.8 percent in medium firms. Also, more than 90 percent of the large service firms rated labor regulations as a major or severe obstacle. On the other hand, labor market regulations are not considered a severe obstacle to operations in tourism firms because they are mostly small-sized firms—only 5.8 percent of these firms judged it to be a major or very severe obstacle.

Figure 7.2   Most Important Labor Market Issue Perceived by Firms in Nepal

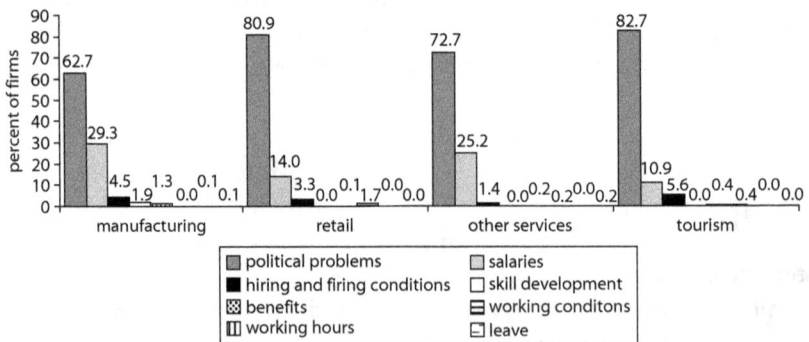

Source: Nepal Enterprise Survey 2009.

However, it should be noted that, as mentioned earlier in the report, political instability is a catch-all phrase that for many employers includes a lot of labor market issues. By political instability, many firm owners mean politically motivated *bhands*, closures, and poor labor relations with politically unionized labor. Therefore, this result should be interpreted as including other politically-motivated labor market constraints such as those related to working hours and hiring and firing (which often times become political issues if they involve hiring and firing politically unionized labor). This shows that for Nepalese firms, the "cost of the conflict" in terms of worsened labor relations linked to political instability, is pressing and high.

Skills

Skills of the workforce, just as labor regulations, are considered a major issue mainly among large firms. Indeed, 45.3 percent of large service firms, 33.3 percent of large tourism firms, and 14.8 percent of large manufacturing firms rated inadequate worker skills as a major or very severe obstacle. In terms of sectors, the greatest percentage of firms identifying an inadequately educated workforce as a major or very severe obstacle was in tourism where around 9 percent of the firms said that an inadequately educated workforce is a major or very severe obstacle to their establishment's current operations.

Large firms are also more likely to offer training opportunities. When training is made available, it is usually internal and targeted to skilled production workers in large firms. The larger the firm, the greater the amount of training opportunities offered (44.7 percent of large manufacturing firms offered training programs to their employees). Skilled production workers in large manufacturing firms received the most training, but overall, few workers in manufacturing firms are offered formal training programs. During FY2007/08, 6.7 percent of manufacturing firms offered formal training to their permanent full-time employees. Unskilled workers in small firms are more likely to be trained than unskilled workers in large manufacturing firms. Overall, 22.4 percent of the workers surveyed through the employees' survey received formal training from their current employer.

Education is likely to be the strongest predictor of compensation (wages and allowances) as both wages and allowances increase consistently with higher educational attainment. Educational attainment is also a strong predictor of employee training by their employer. Compensation tends to be higher on average in large firms, in tourism firms, and especially in services other than retail.

Nearly one half of the workforce in Nepal has a secondary education. 48.5 percent of the workers have a general or technical secondary education and 20 percent of workers have a university first degree. Regionally, about a quarter of workers from the East and Central regions have a university first degree, 25.9 percent and 23.4 percent, respectively, compared to 9.4 percent in the West (Table 7.6). Workers in the other services sector are the most educated; 43.8 percent have a university first degree and another 18.8 have a university post-graduate degree.

Trade Unions

In most firms (94.6 percent), employees do not belong to trade unions, however, large firms are strongly unionized. Ninety-six percent of large firms have unionized labor (Table 7.7). Reflecting size composition, union membership is highest in the manufacturing and tourism sectors and virtually non-existent in retail and other services. In firms where unions are present, the average participation rate is 71 percent of the employees; participation rates are again stronger in medium and large firms and in the manufacturing and tourism sectors.

Large firms suffer the greatest losses from union activities. Twenty-six percent of the firms experienced disruptions in operations due to trade union actions; 5.3 working days were lost on average in FY2007/08. Firms with 100 employees or more had much greater losses; 42 percent of them experienced disruptions, with an average of 8.4 working days lost. The total number of working days lost in the manufacturing sector was 7.1 compared to 5.9 days in the retail sector. There appears to be no correlation between the presence of trade unions or the level of trade union participation and the average number of days lost to trade union action. This suggests that trade union actions cause losses to firms not only because their employees go on strike but possibly also because strikes outside the firm do not allow employees to work (as in the case of strikes in public transportation systems) or because workers participate in general strikes even though they are not trade union members. Indeed, politically linked labor unions sometimes prevent firms from shutting down, even if they are operating at a loss.

Political problems and salaries were the main disputed issues that led to trade union action in FY2007/08 as perceived by firms (Figure 7.3).

Table 7.6 Highest Level of Education Completed by Workers (%)

	None	Primary school	General secondary school	Technical secondary school	Vocational training	University first degree	University post-grad degree
Total	**6.4**	**19.4**	**37.5**	**11.0**	**2.0**	**20.2**	**3.6**
Region							
West	3.1	25.0	49.0	11.5	2.1	9.4	0
Central	7.1	17.5	33.8	10.8	2.2	23.4	5.2
East	11.1	18.5	33.3	11.1	0.0	25.9	0
Size							
Small (5–19)	10.2	22.4	36.7	16.3	0.0	12.2	2
Medium (20–99)	8.2	15.1	37.4	10.0	1.8	22.8	4.6
Large (>=100)	1.6	25.8	37.9	10.5	3.2	18.5	2.4
Sector							
Manufacturing	7.2	22.0	38.7	11.8	2.0	16.7	1.6
Retail	0.0	0.0	50.0	12.5	0.0	25.0	12.5
Other services	6.3	12.5	12.5	6.3	0.0	43.8	18.8
Tourism	3.2	11.1	36.5	7.9	3.2	30.2	7.9

Source: Nepal Employees Survey 2009.

Table 7.7   Union Participation among Establishments' Workforce and Its Impact on Business Activity

	% firms with unionized workers[a]	Average union participation rate[b]	% firms with losses to trade union action[c]	Average losses (no. days)[d]
Total	5.4	71.0	26.0	5.3
Region				
West	6.6	85.1	27.3	4.5
Central	6.0	65.4	16.4	1.7
East	1.5	83.8	63.1	20.6
Size				
Micro (<5)	0.1	34.0	24.5	5.9
Small (5–19)	14.3	65.1	29.6	3.9
Medium (20–99)	45.7	75.6	28.3	3.3
Large (>=100)	96.4	73.5	42.0	8.4
Age				
<5 yrs	1.6	100.0	14.6	2.2
5–9 yrs	1.4	69.4	40.4	9.3
10–19 yrs	11.3	72.3	21.5	3.3
20+ yrs	13.7	76.8	13.1	2.9
Sector				
Manufacturing	29.1	73.0	47.1	7.1
Retail	0.5	31.0	26.1	5.9
Other services	1.5	48.6	11.2	2.1
Tourism	18.6	79.7	26.3	4.5

Source: Nepal Enterprise Survey 2009.
a. proportion of establishments where *some of the workers* are unionized.
b. average proportion of each establishment's workforce that are members of trade unions among firms where unions are present.
c. proportion of establishments that lost any working days to trade union actions over FY2007/08.
d. average number of days lost to trade union action over FY2007/08 among firms that suffered such losses.

The concentration of trade union activity in these two areas most likely explains the identification by firms of political problems and salaries as the main labor market issues because union action on these issues were most likely to disrupt firm operations.

Civil unrest disrupts firm operations on average more often than trade union activities. Firms reported losing an average of 44 days to civil unrest. Seventy-five percent of firms with losses to civil unrest lost 60 days or more. Micro firms and firms in the East are more affected than others by civil unrest. Average losses in the Eastern region are an astounding 119 days per year.[4] Only large firms and firms in the Central region lost less than 30 days per year to civil unrest.

Figure 7.3   Most Important Disputed Issue That Led to Trade Union Action during the Last Fiscal Year in Nepalese Firms

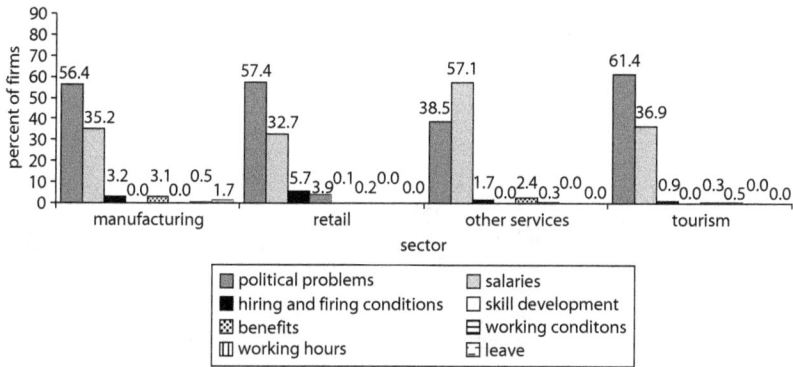

Source: Nepal Enterprise Survey 2009.

Labor Market Issues Identified by Employees

The Nepal Enterprise Survey 2009 also included an employee survey that studied the characteristics of the workers employed in the private sector, their perception of labor market issues, and their participation in trade unions. Three hundred and sixty workers employed in the firms covered by the Enterprise Survey were interviewed; between four and seven employees were randomly sampled from firms with 5 or more employees. In the sample, 37.2 percent of the workers are employed in the manufacturing sector, 30.7 percent in retail, 19.3 percent in tourism firms, and 12.8 percent in other services.[5] The structure of the Nepal Enterprise Survey 2009 allows for a comparison of employees' perception of labor market issues with the perception of their employers. Workers mostly see salaries and political issues as the main problems in their current job (Figure 7.4).

Most firms perceive political problems as the main labor market issue while most workers view salaries as the main issue (Table 7.8). However, salary was the second most cited response by firms and political problems the second most cited response by workers. Beyond that, concerns of workers cover a broad range of labor market issues.

Women earn less than men across all occupations and regions in Nepal, even when controlling for the level of workers' educational attainment. The average total monthly compensation (includes salary/wage and allowances) for women was Nrs 6,539 compared to Nrs 7,017 for men. While overall compensation is higher for men, women tend to receive a

Figure 7.4   Perception of Most Important Problem by Nepalese Workers in Current Job

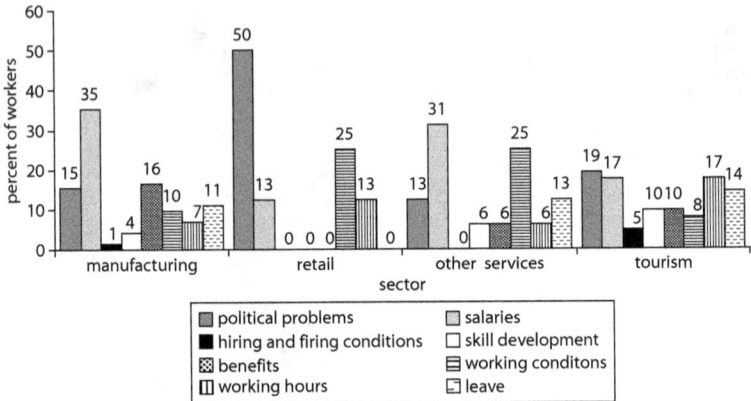

Source: Nepal Employee Survey 2009.

Table 7.8   Main Issues with Job and Main Labor Market Issues (% Workers and % Firms)

	Salary	Political problems	Benefits	Leave	Working conditions	Working hours	Skills development	Hiring and firing conditions
Workers	31.9	16.6	14.5	11.2	10.2	8.7	5.1	1.8
Firms	31.8	57.6	7.6	1.5	0.0	0.0	0.0	1.5

Source: Nepal Employee Survey 2009; Nepal Enterprise Survey 2009.

higher proportion of allowances. Allowances as a percent of total compensation was 24 percent for women and 21 percent for men.

Comparison of Employee and Firm-Level Findings

Despite the lack of skilled labor in Nepal and the premium on education in terms of wages and access to training, skills development is not perceived as much of an issue by firms and is perceived as an issue by only a small percentage of workers. Only 5.1 percent of workers view skills development as the main labor market issue (Table 7.8).

Both firms and workers also cited salaries and political issues as the main causes of union activity, although, again, workers perceived salaries to be more often the issue leading to trade union action (Table 7.9).

Firms perceived trade union membership to be higher than the level of participation reported by workers. According to employees, trade union participation among workers is on average 46.7 percent. This is

Table 7.9   Main Problem Leading to Trade Union Actions in the Opinion of Employees and in the Opinion of Employers (% Workers and % Firms)

	Salaries	Political problems	Benefits	Working conditions	Hiring and firing conditions	Leave	Working hours	Skill development
Employees	45.7	28.3	18.6	3.6	1.5	1.3	0.8	0.3
Firms	23.5	66.2	4.4	0.0	1.5	2.9	0.0	1.5

Source: Nepal Employee Survey 2009; Nepal Enterprise Survey 2009.

lower than the figure reported by firms, according to which 58.1 percent of workers are members of trade unions.

Losses from trade union participation and civil unrest are bigger for firms than for workers. Workers are able to participate in trade union activities without incurring large costs in terms of loss of working days. More than 80 percent of workers (82.5 percent) reported losing one day of work or less to participation in trade union activities. Cumulative effects of trade union activity at the firm level are high. In firms where unions are present, 64.7 percent of firms lost an average of 15.8 working days due to trade union actions.

Concluding Remarks and Recommendations

Nepal's labor laws stifle productivity and employment growth, increasing costs for firms. Labor regulations make it difficult and expensive to dismiss employees; therefore, firms are discouraged from expanding and creating more employment. Any firm employing more than 10 workers is required to have a trade union. This creates a disincentive to grow. Fixed minimum wages and a narrowing wage gap between skilled and unskilled workers (and a lack of differentiation based on skills and capabilities) discourage investments in human capital and, consequently, hamper productivity growth. Furthermore, job holders in the domestic market are generally well-protected because of the very rigid labor regulations; at the same time, such a rigid system and unionization of labor does not allow for sufficient job creation at home and forces many job-seekers to go abroad and to work in much worse conditions.

Options should be explored to reduce non-wage costs on the employer. The Bonus Act of 1973 should be reviewed to provide flexibility to employers and relax the mandatory requirements. An employment contract system should be introduced to provide employers with more options for formally employing workers and discourage the practice of

hiring workers informally without appointment letters. The current legislation does not allow broad use of contracts between employers and
employees to govern the terms and conditions of employment. To this
end, the promulgation of the Employment Contract Act would be an
alternative, which could provide a legal framework suitable to the needs
of the private sector.

**Labor flexibility should be enhanced through a review of laws, regula-
tions, and practices that stifle productivity and job creation and protect
the employed few.** Piloting flexible labor regimes in special economic
zones (SEZs) could serve as a first step, providing insight into what types
of reforms would be acceptable to both the private sector and the labor
unions. The draft SEZ bill includes provisions to establish a separate labor
regime in SEZs in cooperation with trade unions, but does not include
reforms of the procedures and costs of hiring and laying-off workers. As
potential investors (especially foreign ones) are very conscious of compliance with labor standards, reforms that promote flexibility while safe-
guarding workers' rights should be promoted.

**In the absence of government capacity and credibility, independent
(private/NGO) inspections should be considered to resolve labor disputes.** Indeed, labor relations need a wholesale re-definition in Nepal.
More dialogue with workers is needed to try to weaken the link between
their unions and politically motivated actions. This could be initially
applied on a pilot basis to one sector and/or within the SEZ where results
can be assessed before scaling up. The concept of "no work, no pay," needs
to be emphasized. The Labor Offices, which are supposed to play a
critical role in the mediation process, are deemed to be ill-equipped, with
limited expertise and experience in resolving labor disputes. They are
also severely under-staffed and under-funded. There are only 10 Labor
Offices in the country with 11 Labor Officers. An independent labor
inspections system could also increase efficiency, transparency, and
accountability in inspections.

**New labor court branches should be created to increase the efficiency
in addressing labor cases.** There is only one Labor Court in Nepal headed
by a single judge. As a result, there is a huge backlog of cases. Strengthening
labor court capacity is crucial to adequately and efficiently addressing
cases. In addition, opening new branches of labor courts in industrial
towns is equally important because of the difficulties workers have in
traveling to Kathmandu frequently for judicial proceedings.

An in-depth study should be undertaken on wages in Nepal. There
are conflicting opinions about the movement of wages over time, real

wage rates, wage structures, and wage differentials across occupations and skill levels. A scientific study on wages would provide guidelines to assess the implications of minimum wages. In particular, although workers' salaries are generally low (and thus do not cost the employers much), given that wages are the biggest problem from the employees' perspective, a slight increase in wages could potentially yield higher returns to productivity.

Actions should also be taken to encourage greater educational attainment among Nepal's workforce and to increase access to professional training and skills development. Incentives should be provided for firms to increase training provided for employees, particularly in small firms. The potential returns to higher levels of education in terms of wages and productivity serve as a strong argument for focusing on education as an integral component of Nepal's strategy to strengthen the labor market and improve competitiveness.

Notes

1. The time-related underemployment rate is defined as the currently employed who worked less than 40 hours in the reference week and who wanted to work more but did not for involuntary reasons (for the population 15 years and above).

2. Based on the provisions of the Labor Act, workers are guaranteed permanent employment after a probationary period of 240 days. Permanent workers can only be fired under exceptional circumstances, such as proof of criminal behavior on the part of the employee. A fired employee is entitled to compensation of 90 weeks of wages.

3. Mostly the Bonus Act of 1973 requires firms to pay 10 percent of profits to workers. Employers are also required to pay: i) 10 percent of a worker's wage as a contribution to the provident fund matching the 10 percent paid by the workers; ii) contribute 3 percent of profit to a workers' welfare fund; and iii) 5 percent of profits on housing and medical purposes for workers. These provisions ultimately increase costs for firms and discourage hiring.

4. This result is not driven by outliers. Reported values in the Eastern region are almost completely stratified compared to the other two regions.

5. More details about the employees' survey methodology and results are provided in Appendix 2.

CHAPTER 8

The Investment Climate for the External Sector in Nepal

The external sector in Nepal accounts for 47 percent of GDP with exports concentrated in low value added, low growth segments. Exports suffer from low productivity, high tariffs, and poor transportation infrastructure. Over 60 percent of Nepal's imports and exports are traded with India, while China is emerging as a major source of imports for the country. Reinforcing Nepal's role as a transit economy could strengthen its position as a trade partner for the two countries. Due to its poor infrastructure network and a poor investment climate, only a marginal share of the bilateral trade between India and China goes through Nepal, and Nepal lies mostly outside regional production value chains. Nepal needs policies to enhance linkages to shipment lines, improve the efficiency of customs, expand airport storage capacity, and address transport and labor issues in order to leverage its position as a transit economy.

Trends in Nepal's External Sector

The external sector in Nepal accounts for a small share of the economy—trade as a share of GDP was 47.3 percent in FY2009/10, with exports of goods and services accounting for only 9.2 percent of GDP (Table 8.1). The trade deficit in FY2009/10 increased to around 28.8 percent of GDP, following an increase in imports from 35 percent to 38 percent of GDP

Table 8.1   Trend in Nepal's Trade

	FY08	FY09	FY10
Exports (% of GDP)	12.8	12.4	9.2
Imports (% of GDP)	33.3	34.6	38.1
Trade deficit (% of GDP)	−20.5	−22.2	−28.8

Source: NRB 2009, 2010.

and a decrease in exports from 12 to 9 percent between FY2008/09 and FY2009/10. Imports as a share of GDP were almost four times greater than exports. The fall in exports was mainly due to fall in demand, and in part due to an appreciating currency. An increase in consumption fueled by strong remittance growth accounts for the increase in imports (NRB 2009, 2010).

FDI net inflows in 2007[1] amounted to a mere US$5.7 million—about 0.06 percent of GDP (World Bank 2010a). The only sectors that have recently attracted foreign investment are hydropower and tourism.

The country has diversified its export base over the years but its export markets remain extremely concentrated. By 2006, the number of exported products had almost doubled compared to the early 2000s and its Export Concentration Index had decreased from 40.8 in the late 1990s to 14.6 (World Bank 2008a). Nepal's export markets are, however, highly concentrated, with over 90 percent of exports going to three countries: India, the United States, and Germany.

The bulk of Nepal's exports consist of agricultural products and low value added manufactured goods, revealing its comparative advantage in agricultural resources and unskilled labor. Nepal is a net exporter of primary products and a net importer of manufactured goods. Semi-manufactured and agro-based products constitute the bulk of exports to India; imports from India instead mainly consist of petroleum products, high-technology products, and agricultural commodities. Merchandise exports to China mainly consist of raw agricultural and industrial materials against imports of mostly manufactured goods.

Nepal's trade dependency on China and India is overwhelming and increasing over time. This is not surprising given Nepal's geographical position and non-trade links to both countries. India accounted for around 56 percent of Nepal's trade balance over the past two fiscal years (accounting for 60 to 65 percent of Nepal's exports and 58 percent of its imports), while China has accounted for around 20 percent of Nepal's imports over the same period. On the other hand, Nepal's exports to China are very small (around 2 percent of total exports) (TEPC various years).

The composition of Nepal's top manufacturing exports is diverse. Eight goods each account for more than 3 percent of total exports. The top four export sectors reflect the country's comparative advantages, which are labor-intensive manufacturing and agriculture (Table 8.2) (World Bank 2008a).

The majority of Nepal's exports are concentrated in lower growth segments. Figure 8.1 compares each sector's performance in terms of export growth for Nepal with its performance in terms of world exports. The horizontal axis represents the growth of Nepal's exports and the vertical axis represents the growth of world exports based on their annual growth rates; the size of each point represents the sector's export share over Nepal's total exports (i.e., the importance of the sector for the country's exports). The graph shows that most exports, and the most important ones, are concentrated in sectors where global trade is growing more slowly, with the exception of organic chemicals.

The sectors for which Nepal has the largest share of world exports are losing market share worldwide. Carpet and apparels, which together account for 36.6 percent of Nepal's exports, have lost market share in worldwide exports. The segments in which Nepal has increased its share in world exports—namely organic chemicals and salt—have a relatively small share in domestic exports. The only sector that accounts for more

Table 8.2   Top 15 Exporting Sectors in Nepal

Sector	Exports as a share of Nepal's total exports in 2008 (%)
Carpets	18.04
Apparel not knit/crocheted	14.09
Animal/vegetable fats and oils	6.79
Apparel knit/crocheted	4.48
Plastics	4.40
Miscellaneous chemical products	3.25
Essential oils, perfumes, cosmetics	3.23
Iron and steel	3.16
Manmade staple fibers	2.85
Beverages, spirits, and vinegar	2.77
Coffee, tea, mate, and spices	2.64
Salt, sulphur, earth, stone, and plaster	2.37
Articles of iron or steel	1.97
Organic chemicals	1.88
Manmade filaments	1.74

Source: UN Comtrade Database, http://comtrade.un.org/.

Figure 8.1   Trade Competitiveness Map 2008: Growth of Nepal's Top 15 Exporting Sectors versus Their Growth as Worldwide Exports

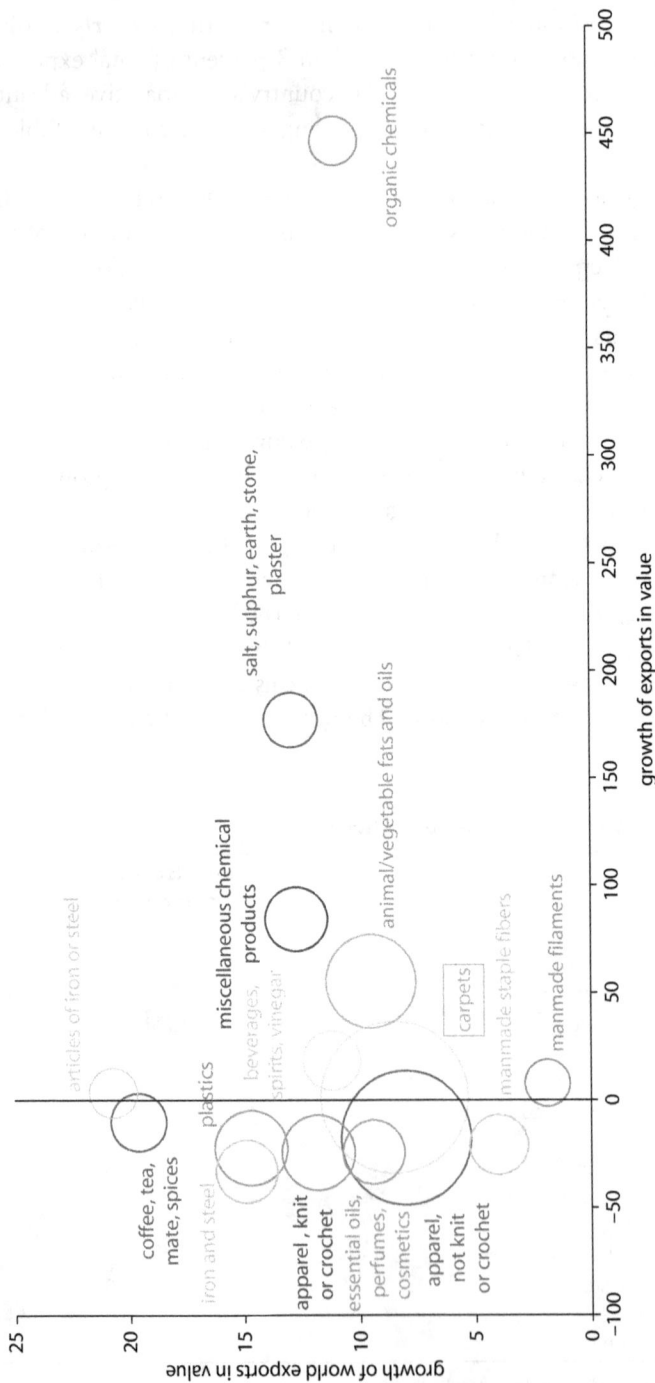

Source: UN Comtrade Database, http://comtrade.un.org/.

Note: The top 15 exporting sectors are defined as the sectors with the largest share of Nepal's export basket. Horizontal axis represents growth of Nepal exports; vertical axis represents growth of world exports; size of each bubble represents sector's export share over Nepal's total exports.

than 5 percent of Nepal's exports and has had a strong performance in world markets is animal and vegetable oils and fats (Figure 8.2).

In realizing its trade potential, Nepal faces numerous challenges relating to its geography, its economic development, and its regulatory environment. Nepal is a small landlocked country nestled between China and India, the two most populous and among the most rapidly growing economies in the world. It has a mostly mountainous and hilly terrain and poor transport infrastructure, leaving many communities with limited access to local and international markets. As a consequence, Nepal has high transport costs and almost completely depends on India for transit routes. The country's low industrialization further constrains the development of trade networks.

Characteristics of Trading Firms in Nepal

The Nepal Enterprise Survey 2009 shows that very few Nepalese firms export—only 3.1 percent of all enterprises. In the manufacturing sector, which has the highest incidence of exporters, a mere 6.7 percent of the firms export either directly or indirectly—which is low with respect to Nepal's comparator countries (Figure 8.3).

Exporters are concentrated in a few industries and among large firms (Figure 8.4). Retail traders account for 70 percent of the exporters, metals manufacturers for 7.7 percent, food and beverages and manufacturers of non-metallic mineral products account for 5 percent of the enterprises each, and garments for 4 percent. Being an exporter is also strongly correlated with firm size: while less than 3 percent of small and micro firms are exporters, 10 percent of medium firms and 28.3 percent of large firms sell their output on international markets. Older firms are also more likely to be exporters. Firms aged 20 years or more account for 70 percent of exporting firms (while they only make up 10 percent of the enterprises).

While being an exporter is associated with greater labor productivity, exporters are not characterized by a more intensive use of skilled workers. Chapter 3 shows that, as predicted by a vast body of the economic literature, being an exporter is associated with greater labor productivity. At the same time, the data show that the average education and the share of skilled production workers are not larger among exporting firms than among non-exporting ones.

Trading firms are, to some extent, more technologically advanced than others. Importers and exporters make more use of technology licensed

Figure 8.2   Growth of World Market Share for Largest 15 Manufacturing Export Sectors in Nepal (2001–08)

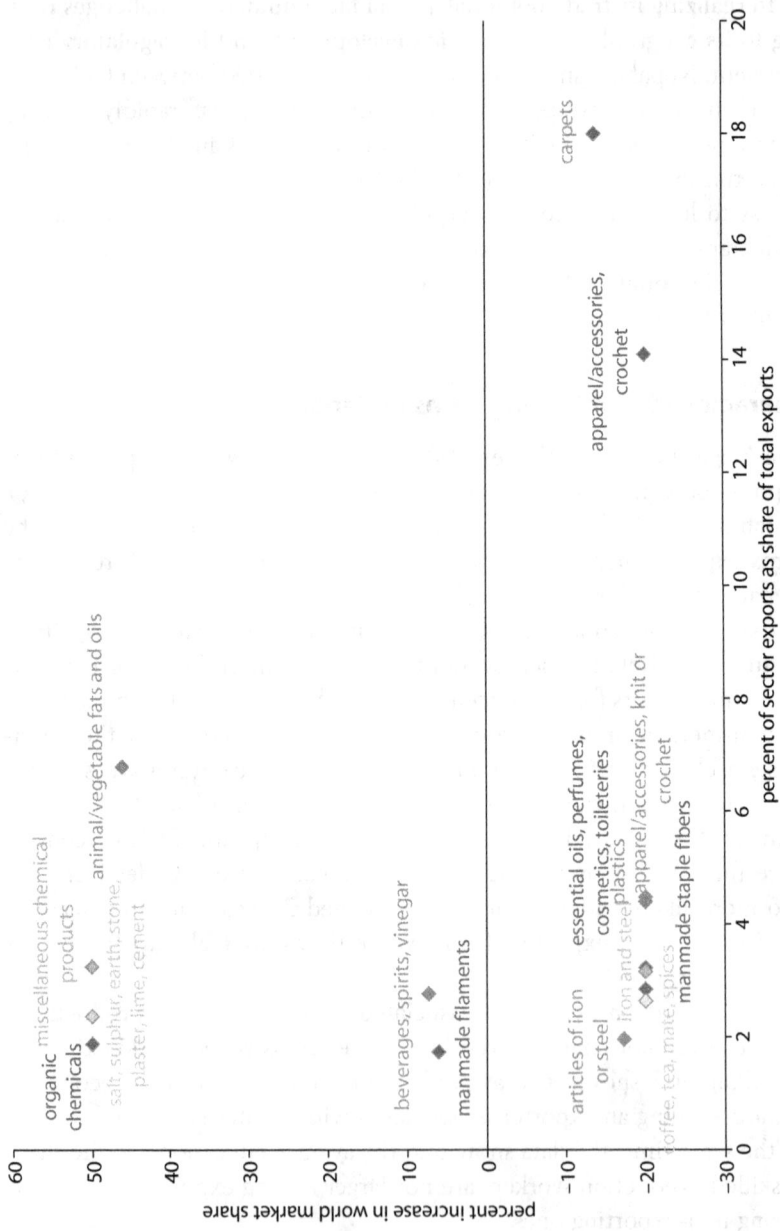

Source: UN Comtrade Database, http://comtrade.un.org/.

Notes: The top 15 exporting sectors are defined as the sectors with the largest share of Nepal's export basket. Horizontal axis represents sector's share of total exports; vertical axis represents annual growth of Nepal's share in world export for each the sector.

Figure 8.3   Percentage of Exporting and Importing Firms in Nepal and Comparator Countries

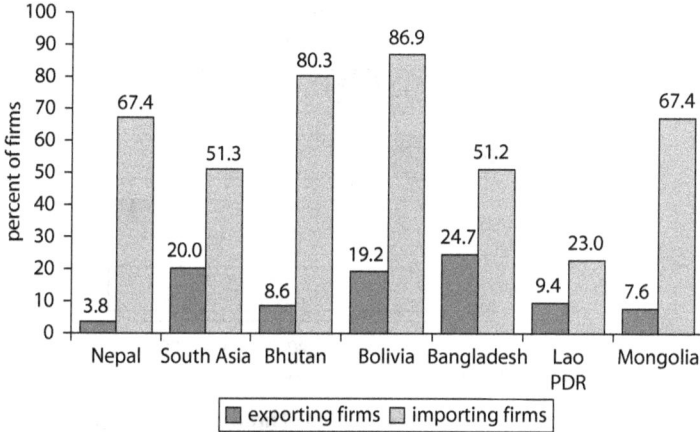

Source: World Bank Enterprise Surveys, latest available year.
Note: Comparison restricted to firms with 5+ employees in sectors surveyed in most countries in the comparator group, i.e., manufacturing, retail, wholesale, hotels and restaurants, transport, and travel agencies.

from foreign-owned companies, obtain internationally-recognized quality certifications more often, and more often have patents registered in Nepal (but not more patents registered abroad) (Table 8.3).

Roads are by far the main mode of transport used by exporters in the manufacturing industry. Manufacturing firms transported 92.2 percent of the exports by road, 2.7 percent by air, and 5.1 percent by sea (Figure 8.5). Actually, only textiles and garments rely heavily on sea transport (75 percent and 100 percent of their exports, respectively).

Air transport of exported goods is limited to enterprises located in the Central region, where the Kathmandu International Airport is located. Firms located in the Eastern region more commonly export by sea. Nepal's main access to sea is the port of Kolkata, in India, situated some 700 km from the Indo-Nepal border.

The main destination for the *direct* exporters in the manufacturing industry is India for 89 percent of the firms, followed by the United States (6 percent), Europe, China—including the Tibet Autonomous Region—and Bhutan (Figure 8.6). As most direct exports are exported to India, 94.4 percent of the firms use border crossing with India as the main point of exit for their exports. The rest of the direct exporters use the Kathmandu International Airport (2.2 percent of direct

Figure 8.4   Incidence of Exporters by Firm Size and Size Distribution among Exporters (% Firms)

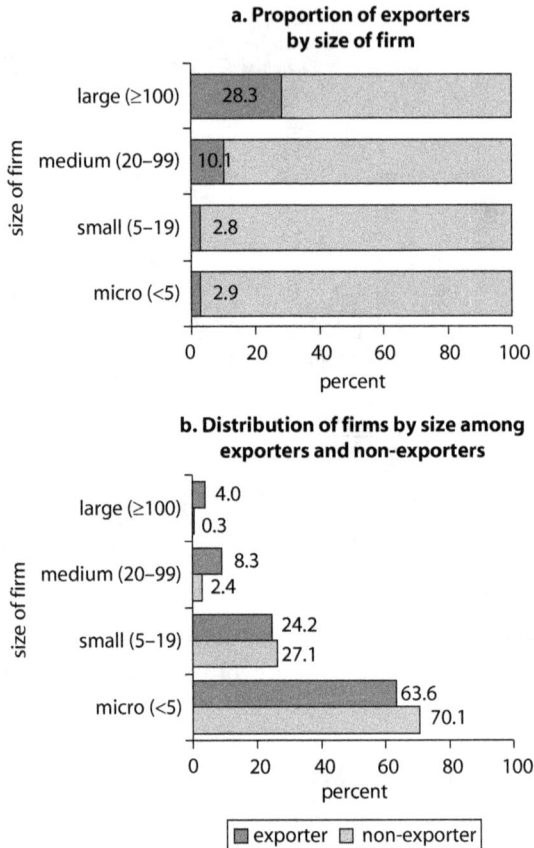

a. Proportion of exporters by size of firm

b. Distribution of firms by size among exporters and non-exporters

Source: Nepal Enterprise Survey 2009.

Table 8.3   Use of Technology (% of Firms)

	Non-exporter	Exporter	Non-importer	Importer	All firms
Internationally-recognized quality certification	0.9	1.8	0.1	1.3	1.0
Technology licensed from foreign-owned company	0.3	1.1	0.2	0.4	0.4
Patents registered abroad	0.5	0.0	0.0	0.7	0.5
Patents registered in Nepal	8.6	20.8	7.0	10.3	9.3

Source: Nepal Enterprise Survey 2009.

Figure 8.5   Proportion of Nepalese Exports Transported by Road, Air, and Sea

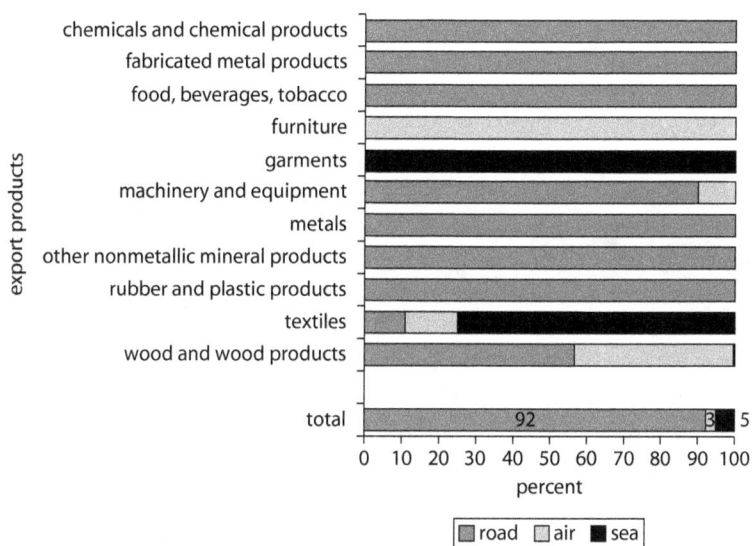

Source: Nepal Enterprise Survey 2009.

Figure 8.6   Main Destination for Direct Exporters in Manufacturing Industry in Nepal
percent of firms

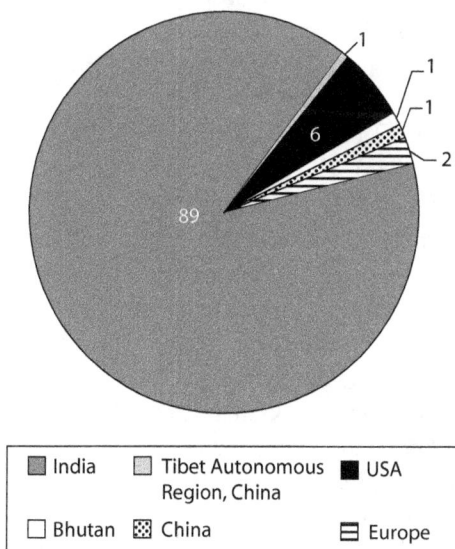

Source: Nepal Enterprise Survey 2009.

exporters) or the border crossing with China (2.9 percent of direct exporters).

Sixty-five percent of the manufacturing enterprises and all the retail enterprises import at least part of their inputs.[2] Large and older firms import more intensively than other types of firms, but more than half of the younger and smaller firms are also importers. On average, retailers import 50 percent and manufacturers 66.5 percent of their inputs. There are no strong variations across size or age of the enterprises, but there are variations between industries; textiles, telecommunications equipment, and electrical machinery enterprises import 90 percent or more of the input used.

India is the most important source country of direct imports for 77.9 percent of the firms; Thailand, Korea, and Indonesia are each the most important source country for another 5 percent of the firms. Europe, the Middle East, Singapore, China, and Malaysia account for 2 percent each or less. The vast majority of direct imports enter by road (89.7 percent) and through the border with India (94.3 percent of the direct imports transit through it); only 0.3 percent of imports transit through the Kathmandu International Airport.

Barriers to Trade

Trade policy in Nepal has become more protectionist over time. Despite a number of market-oriented reforms implemented during the 1990s, Nepal has one of the most protectionist trade policies in the world as attested by the latest Trade (Most-Favored Nation [MFN]) Tariff Restrictiveness Index (TTRI), which ranks Nepal 120th out of 125 countries (World Bank 2008a). The country's MFN applied simple tariff average in 2007 (12.6 percent) was slightly lower than in the South Asia region (14.4 percent) and comparable to the low-income group (12.6 percent), whereas the import-weighted tariff average (14.6 percent) is much higher. MFN duty-free imports accounted for less than 2.0 percent of Nepal's total imports in the early 2000s (World Bank 2008a).

Tariffs remain high despite the fact that Nepal is signatory to a number of treaties. Nepal benefits from Generalized System of Preferences treatment from a number of industrialized countries, including the European Union. Nepal also signed a Preferential Trading Agreement with India in 2002 by which the country has preferential access to the otherwise highly restricted Indian market. Nepal is also party to the South Asian Free Trade Agreement, which involves a phase-out of tariffs over 10 years starting in

2006 (World Bank 2008a). Nepal has an ongoing engagement with India and China to improve its bilateral trade arrangements.

Trading across borders is the first priority for business environment reform according to the Doing Business indicators. Trading across borders is evaluated in terms of the number of documents and the time necessary to import and export as well as in terms of the costs involved in exporting and importing a standardized cargo of goods by ocean transport. Nepal has the poorest score in the ease of international trade (161st out of 183 economies) because of increased cost and time associated with shipping/receiving goods by ocean transport in addition to the relatively larger number of documents required (Table 8.4) (World Bank 2009a). Given Nepal's landlocked and mountainous terrain, a poor score is expected; however, improvements could be made in Nepal's customs clearance processes, and trade facilitation initiatives could be undertaken to encourage trade exporting and transit trade. A cross-country comparison of the trading across borders dimension of the Doing Business indicators reveals that Nepal's disadvantage results mainly from the cost and the number of documents necessary to export by sea.

According to the Nepal Enterprise Survey 2009, exporters need a relatively short amount of time to clear customs, but not importers. It takes on average almost 6 days for direct exporters to clear customs at the main point of exit. By this standard, Nepal fares better than most comparator countries, including the average for the South Asia region. Clearing imports, on the other hand, requires on average 14 days, which is more than in all comparator countries except for Bolivia. Customs clearance takes considerably longer in the Central region, both for exports and imports (Table 8.5).

Compared to other countries, imports not only face less efficient customs, but also appear to be susceptible to informal payments. While less than 5 percent of enterprises report being asked for informal payments or gifts in reference to custom clearance for exports, 25.5 percent of enterprises report being asked for such payments in reference to customs clearance for imports. **Theft is not an issue for Nepalese exporters. Poor quality and management of transportation systems, instead, cause more losses.** Nepalese direct exporters report that they do not suffer losses during transit because of theft. Instead, losses due to breakage or spoilage, which can be ascribed to poor transport infrastructure and/or poor management of the transportation system, amount on average to 1.9 percent of the enterprises' sales—which is larger than in most comparator countries and almost the same as the regional average (Table 8.6).

Table 8.4 Doing Business 2010: Trading across Borders

	Rank	Documents to export (number)	Time to export (days)	Cost to export (US$ per container)	Documents to import (number)	Time to import (days)	Cost to import (US$ per container)
Bangladesh	107	6	25	970	8	29	1,375
Bolivia	121	8	19	1,425	7	23	1,747
Bhutan	153	8	38	1,210	11	38	2,140
Mongolia	155	8	46	2,131	8	47	2,274
Nepal	161	9	41	1,764	10	35	1,825
Lao PDR	168	9	50	1,860	10	50	2,040

Source: World Bank Doing Business Historical Database, http://www.doingbusiness.org/CustomQuery.

Table 8.5   Average Number of Days to Clear Customs in Nepal and Comparator Countries (Manufacturing Sector)

	Direct exports	Imports
Nepal	5.6	13.8
South Asia	8.4	9.9
Bhutan	2.2	5.6
Bolivia	15.3	26.1
Bangladesh	8.4	10.2
Lao PDR	7.3	10.8
Mongolia	18.6	8.2

Source: World Bank Enterprise Surveys, latest available year.
Note: Comparison restricted to firms with 5+ employees in sectors surveyed in most countries in the comparator group, i.e., manufacturing, retail, wholesale, hotels and restaurants, transport, and travel agencies.

Table 8.6   Losses from Direct Exports (% Sales)

	Due to theft	Due to breakage or spoilage
Nepal	0.0	1.9
South Asia	3.1	2.0
Bhutan	1.5	2.2
Bolivia	0.1	0.4
Bangladesh	0.0	0.4
Lao PDR	0.0	0.0

Source: World Bank Enterprise Surveys, latest available year.
Note: Comparison restricted to firms with 5+ employees in sectors surveyed in most countries in the comparator group, i.e., manufacturing, retail, wholesale, hotels and restaurants, transport, and travel agencies.

Strikes pose the greatest obstacle to road transport in Nepal, while airfreight capacity and customs at Nepal's airports are the most important obstacles for air transport. 96.4 percent of the firms identified strikes as the most important obstacle to transport by road (Table 8.7). The main obstacles to air transportation identified by the firms varied more. Airfreight capacity and customs at Nepal's airports are the most important for a little over one third of the firms each. Frequency of air traffic, distance to the airport, and time and distance to the markets were indicated as the most important obstacles by between 5 and 11 percent of the firms.

Overall, exporters appear to find the investment climate less constraining than the overall enterprise population except for labor regulations, which are found by 10 percent of exporting firms to be a major or very

Table 8.7   Main Transportation Obstacles

	Exporter	Importer	All firms
By road			
Road quality	0.0	1.9	1.3
Petrol availability	5.4	0.3	0.5
Strikes	94.6	97.2	96.4
Time/distance to market	0.0	0.6	1.8
By air			
Airfreight capacity	33.1	36.9	36.9
Frequency of air traffic	14.6	11.3	11.3
Distance to airport	0.0	11.3	11.3
Customs at Nepal's airports	45.6	35.3	35.3
Time/distance to market	6.7	5.2	5.2

Source: Nepal Enterprise Survey 2009.

severe obstacle to their business (Figure 8.7). These results are likely to be driven, or at the least co-determined, by the fact that exporters are often large firms. On the other hand, customs and trade regulations are not more problematic for exporters than for non-exporters.

Dependence on India and China

Given its location, Nepal is dependent on China and India in terms of trade, aid, investments, tourism, and remittances. This dependency has been growing over time. In particular, Nepal trades over 60 percent of its total imports and total exports with India (TEPC various years). However, these relations are lopsided with Nepal facing a huge trade deficit and attracting very little investment. India is often considered Nepal's "natural" trading partner and the two countries share a 1,800 km long open border; the port of Kolkata in India serves as Nepal's access to the sea and major transit point for Nepal's third-country trade. China is instead emerging as the major source of imports (Figure 8.8).

Preferential trade with India, which is Nepal's largest trading partner, is carried out on the basis of the Indo-Nepal Trade Treaty 1996 (renewed in 2002 and 2007). The treaty has a provision for automatic renewal every five years. However, unlike exports to other countries, Nepal's exports to India are subject to India's internal taxes; such taxes may be reimbursed to the Nepalese government but not to Indian exporters. Informal trade between the two countries is also estimated to be high due to the open border they share.

Figure 8.7   Proportion of Nepalese Exporters Identifying Investment Climate Obstacles as Major or Very Severe

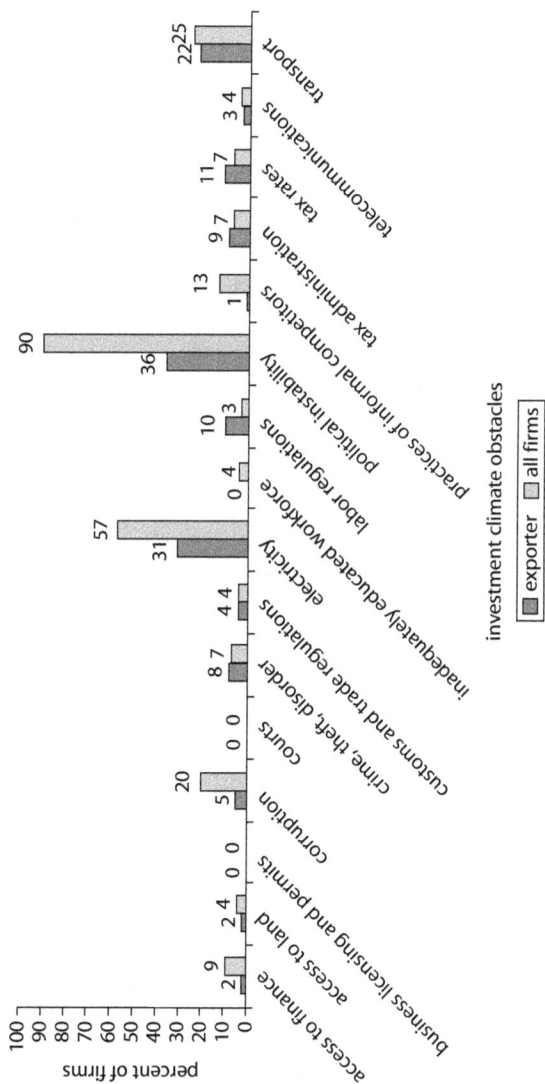

investment climate obstacles

■ exporter □ all firms

Source: Nepal Enterprise Survey 2009.

Figure 8.8   Direction of Foreign Trade in Nepal

Direction of foreign trade (total and India)

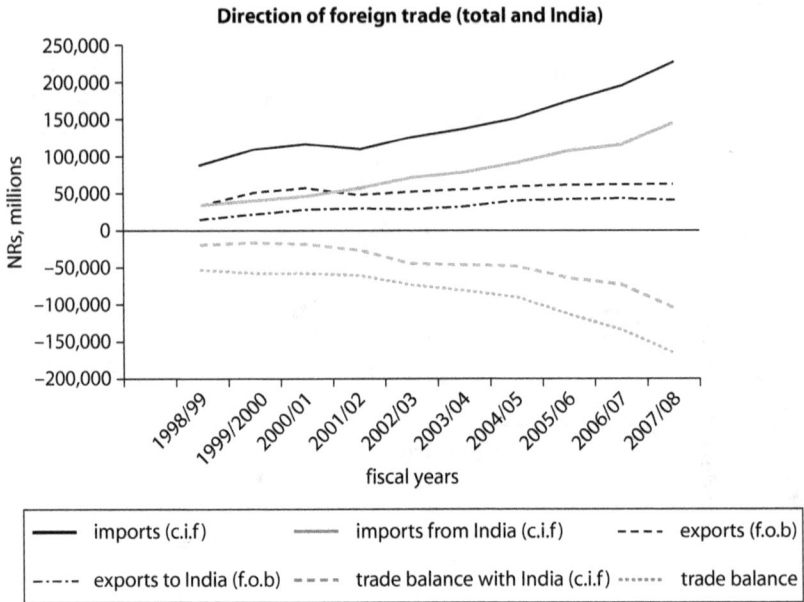

imports (c.i.f)   imports from India (c.i.f)   exports (f.o.b)
exports to India (f.o.b)   trade balance with India (c.i.f)   trade balance

Direction of foreign trade (total and China)

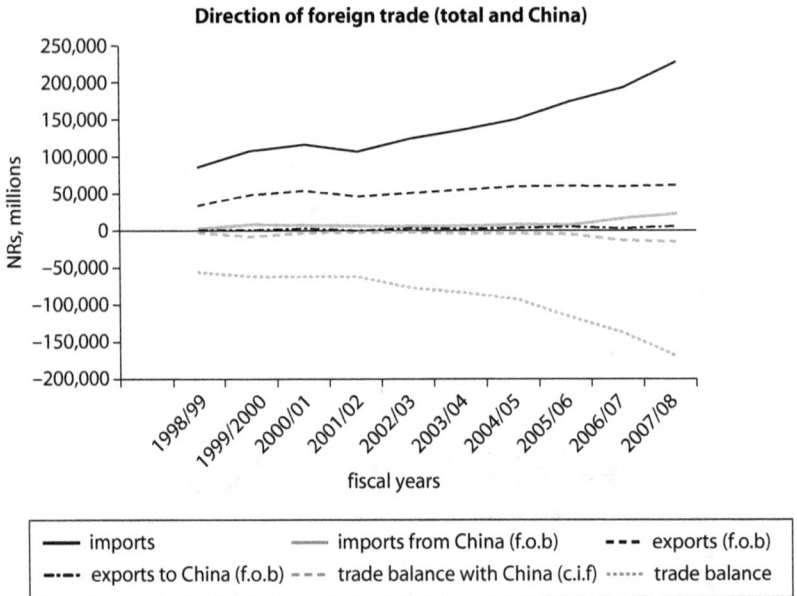

imports   imports from China (f.o.b)   exports (f.o.b)
exports to China (f.o.b)   trade balance with China (c.i.f)   trade balance

Source: TEPC various years, "Nepal Overseas Trade Statistics."
Note: f.o.b. = free on board. c.i.f. = cost, insurance, freight.

Nepal depends on India and China not only for trade in goods and services but also for investments. FDI inflows in Nepal largely originate from China and India; according to data up to mid-July 2008, 40 percent of total FDI-approved projects originated from these two countries. China mainly directs FDI toward manufacturing and real estate construction, whereas India mainly directs FDI toward minerals and real estate construction (MOICS 2008).

Tourism also largely depends on China and India. Tourism is a key service export for Nepal. In 2007, the shares of tourist arrivals from India and China were 28.2 percent and 5.2 percent—the first and fifth positions, respectively. Arrivals of tourists from India have been declining in number while arrivals from China have increased steadily (FNCCI 2008).

India is the single most important destination for work migrants: The open border between the two countries and cultural similarities make migration to India relatively easy for work migrants from Nepal. According to a recent World Bank survey, 41 percent of Nepalese work migrants, or about 0.87 million people, were in India for work in 2009. Remittances from India account for 17.2 percent of total remittances received by Nepal (i.e., 3.8 percent of GDP). Most of the remittances from India flow through informal channels (World Bank 2009c).

Both China and India are also important development partners of Nepal and have provided resources (including aid for trade) to various sectors. Grants from India helped build part of the International Airport in Kathmandu as well as national highways, bridges, cables, dams, and irrigation projects. Pipeline projects include hospitals, polytechnics, schools, integrated border check posts, and road and rail links on the Indo-Nepal border. Assistance from China has been mainly directed to roads, transport, health, sports, water resources, social development, and services sectors. Pipeline projects include a dry port at the China-Nepal border town of Tatopani, a hydropower station, and a polytechnic extension project (FNCCI 2008).

Nepal's Role as a Potential Transit Economy

Despite its proximity to these giant economies, Nepal has been unable to become part of a global production network or be inserted into regional value chains precisely because of the deterioration of its business environment. Nepal could, however, accrue the benefits of its unique location by facilitating trade and becoming a transit economy between China and India, thus benefiting from their fast economic development.

Only a marginal part of the bilateral trade between China and India goes through Nepal. Bilateral trade between India and China reached US$40 billion in 2007 (MOC 2010); most of this trade travels by sea. The land route across the Himalayas could significantly reduce the transport time for commodities, especially for trade directed to the western areas of China, and offer a cheaper alternative to transport from industrial centers located on China's eastern coast.

As discussed in Chapter Four, before Nepal can become an effective transit country, it needs to expand and improve the quality of surface transport infrastructure. At the moment, transport facilities are more oriented toward India than toward China, partly in reflection of the fact that Nepal's industrial belt lies in the Terai, which is directly connected to India by markets, roads, communications, and mobility of people. Indian Railways has a developed network on the Indian side of the India-Nepal border and a train directly connects an inland container depot in Nepal (in Birgunj) with the Indian port-town of Kolkata. The existing road linking Kathmandu and Lhasa (Tibet Autonomous Region, China), instead, does not allow for transportation of freight. Road and rail links to China need to be expanded and strengthened in order for Nepal to become a corridor between China and India.

Nepal uses Kolkata Port in western India for import and export. Nepal has an agreement with Bangladesh to use its ports, but traders generally prefer to use the Kolkata Port. Cross-border infrastructure and customs facilities are in poor condition increasing processing and transportation time; as a result, cross-border trading incurs substantial transaction costs as compared to other countries like Bangladesh, India, and Pakistan.

Some recent developments in infrastructure have enhanced Nepal's future prospects as a transit economy. China is rapidly expanding its transportation network, especially in South Asia. The highway that links China with Pakistan is situated north of the border between China and Nepal. A second road linking Nepal with the Tibet Autonomous Region of China is being constructed with Chinese assistance. There are also plans to extend the rail link from Beijing to Lhasa to Nepal's border, about 120 km northeast of Kathmandu. In 2006, China and India announced the reopening of the Nathu La pass through Sikkim (in India) for the expansion of bilateral trade.

Aside from further expanding and improving its surface transport infrastructure, Nepal needs to improve its transport management and facilities, including cargo handling, storage facilities, and procedures to deal with freight movement in transit.

Nepal could exploit its position as a transit economy in the tourism sector as well. A growing number of Chinese tourists visit Lhasa; Nepal could attract some of them. In order for this to be possible, Nepal needs to develop a good transit road, flexible visa regulations, and regular air links between Nepal and Chinese cities. Nepal could also attract Indian tourists en route to two of the holiest places for Hindus and Buddhists in the Tibet Autonomous Region, China.

Conclusions and Recommendations

Despite its proximity and deep economic relations with two of the largest and fastest growing economies, China and India, Nepal's trade outcomes have been poor and the country has not been able to become part of a global production network or be inserted into regional value chains precisely because of its deteriorating business environment. The poor investment climate and supply-side bottlenecks explain the country's limited success in attracting FDI despite liberal investment laws.

Improving terms of trade with its neighbors requires Nepal to either increase exports of existing products (in terms of both value and volume) or identify new products with export potential in China and India. The challenge for Nepal is to increase exports of commodities in sectors with rising demand in China and India and where Nepal has a comparative advantage. The Nepal Trade Integration Strategy 2010[3] (MOCS 2010) has identified 19 sectors with potential for good export performance; these are listed in Table 8.8. Functional incentives linked to employment creation, upgrading of skills, upgrading of technology, and improving export performance are more efficient than general tax incentives for encouraging the production of such specific exports. Such incentives need to be put in place. Nepal also needs to seek better terms from its trade partners. Proper market access needs to be ensured by addressing issues related to non-tariff barriers and related regulatory issues, especially when exporting to India. Further, Nepal needs to strengthen its trade sector in order to become a transit economy between India and China, taking advantage of its proximity to these two countries. The opening to international trade of the Chinese economy and the economic development of its western regions present Nepal with an opportunity to become a route for bilateral trade between India and China.

The main issues facing traders and exporters in Nepal are: power shortages, lack of freedom of transit, cost of transport, higher average time

Table 8.8   Priority Export Potential

Agro food	Craft and industrial goods	Services
Cardamom	Handmade paper	Tourism
Ginger	Silver jewelry	Labor services
Honey	Iron and steel	IT services
Lentils	Pashmina	Health services
Tea	Wool products	Education
Noodles		Engineering
Medicinal herbs/essential oils		Hydro-electricity

Source: MOCS 2010.

taken to clear imports/export, and breakage or spoilage. Lack of technical standards, phyto-sanitary measures, and intellectual property rights, as well as weak regulation of domestic services also constrain the export sector. Addressing these issues is crucial for enabling Nepalese exporters. Therefore, a number of reforms can be undertaken in the short and medium terms.

In the short term, bringing shipping lines to the Inland Clearance Depots (ICDs) is necessary. The ICD–Multi-Modal Transport Act and Regulations have been enacted recently, but are yet to be implemented. Containers should be able to go directly to Birgunj ICD. The government should initiate negotiations with shipping lines and the Indian government about this, as it has the potential to reduce the cost of import and export by up to 12 percent. **Another proposed short-term reform is improving the Kathmandu International Airport warehouse** through reduced storage charges and reduced airfreight costs.

In the medium term, a comprehensive program of capacity building should be provided for the customs department to minimize the time and documentation needed to clear customs. This program could focus on developing better procedures, training customs officers in classification and valuation, and putting in place systems and automation that would enable traders to clear their goods more expeditiously (World Bank 2007a). In the medium term, labor issues should also be addressed. The principle of "no work no pay" (e.g., when the workers leave work to participate in a political rally) should be enforced and the SEZ law should be enacted.

In terms of legal and policy reforms, the Export-Import Act needs to be amended and a Trade Promotion Act (for trade facilitation) should be enacted. The National Board of Trade should have more frequent consultations. Finally, better data coordination among the Trade and Export Promotion Centre (TEPC), NRB, Customs Administration, and the private sector is needed.

Notes

1. The last date for which accurate data are available.
2. Questions about share of imported inputs were not asked of firms in the other services survey (which includes tourism).
3. http://www.mocs.gov.np/launching-nepal-trade-integration-strategy-2010-ntis-2010-u2-en.html.

CHAPTER 9

The Tourism Sector and Potential for Future Growth

Nepal has great tourism potential because of its natural beauty; bio-diversity; ethnic, linguistic, and social diversity; and historical and cultural wealth. Tourist arrivals in Nepal have grown from just over 6,000 in 1962 to over half a million today, despite a decade-long conflict, which left prime tourist attractions damaged and underdeveloped. The sector has great potential and could contribute significantly to revenue generation. This chapter tracks the development of the Nepalese tourism sector, examines firm level characteristics and performance, as well as constraints hindering their growth, and provides recommendations for increasing the contribution of tourism to the Nepalese economy in a sustainable manner. It highlights the need for investment in tourism-related infrastructure, quality and skills enhancement, proper regulation and monitoring, and adopting a comprehensive approach to developing the sector.

Role of the Tourism Sector in the Nepalese Economy

Tourism plays a significant and growing role in the economies of many developing countries. This is especially true for Nepal, where the poor performance of the agricultural and industrial sectors has slowed the process of structural change and where living standards remain very low. The size of Nepal's tourism sector is ranked 138 out of 181 countries (in absolute terms) and 145th in terms of contribution to GDP. In 2009,

Nepal's tourism sector contributed around Nrs 53 billion (US$653 million in current prices) to GDP (6 percent) and employed 497,000 workers (4.7 percent of total employment), both directly and indirectly. Direct contributions totaled approximately 2.4 percent of GDP (US$262 million) while the sector directly employed 193,000 workers, approximately 1.8 percent of total employment (WTTC 2009) (Figure 9.1). Moreover, tourism is a key service export for Nepal; foreign exchange earnings amounted to about US$168 million (1.3 percent of GDP) in 2008. Direct and indirect contributions of travel and tourism to GDP are

Figure 9.1   Direct and Indirect Contribution of Travel and Tourism (T&T) to GDP and Employment in Nepal, 2004–09 and Projected

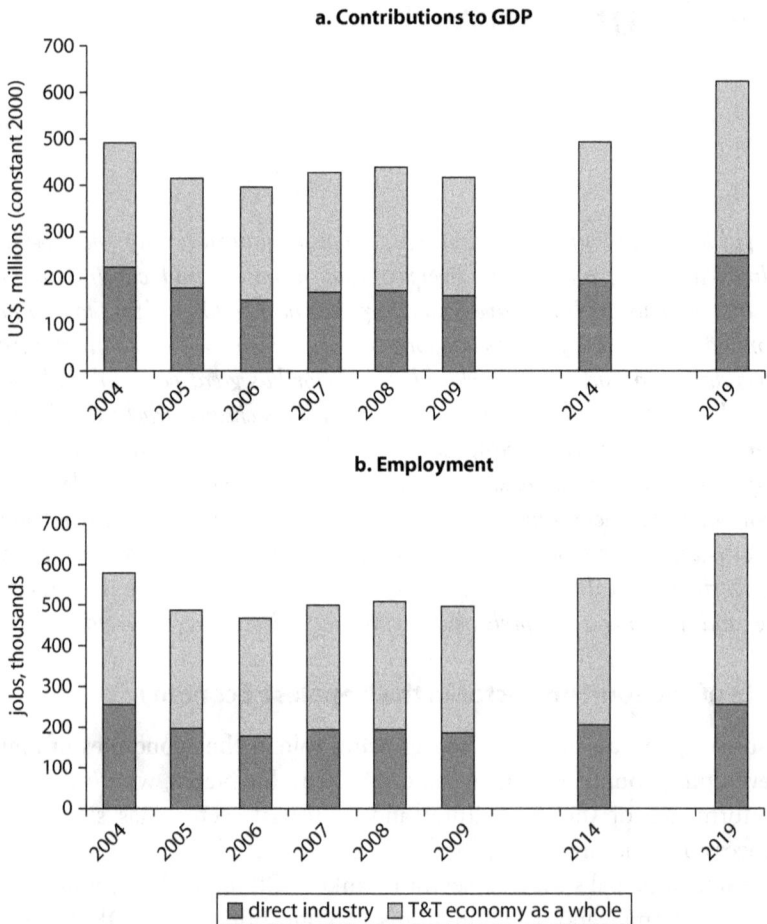

a. Contributions to GDP

b. Employment

direct industry   T&T economy as a whole

Source: WTTC 2009.

expected to rise from 6 percent in 2009 to 6.3 percent (Nrs 113.2 billion or US$1.129 billion) by 2019 (WTTC 2009).

The major sources of government revenue from tourism consist of a hotel tax, visa and trekking fees, mountaineering fees, national park entry fees, and air flight taxes. Revenue generated from national parks and conservation areas increased from Nrs 3 million in FY1988/89 to Nrs 94.6 million in FY2006/07. The royalties from mountaineering expeditions increased from Nrs 4.1 million in 1986 to Nrs 169.8 million in 2007. VAT revenues from hotels and restaurants increased from Nrs 8.4 billion in FY2000/01 to Nrs 10.1 billion in FY2006/07. Consequently, total foreign exchange earnings from tourism doubled between 1992 and 2008 from Nrs 5 billion to approximately Nrs 11 billion. However, tourism's share of total foreign exchange earnings declined during this period, from 20 percent in 1992 to 6.6 percent in 2008 (WTTC 2009). Table 9.1 gives a summary of Nepal's tourism sector statistics and growth forecasts.

Tourism Assets, Services, and Tourist Profiles

The Himalayan landscape, a wide diversity of flora and fauna, and a rich heritage of cultural and religious sites, give Nepal inherent advantages and

Table 9.1   Tourism Statistics Summary (2009) and Projections (2019)

Sector	2009			2019		
	NPR bn	% of total	Growth[a]	NPR bn	% of total	Growth[b]
Personal travel and tourism	41.7	5.9	4.2	100.6	6.7	5.1
Business travel	11.7	1.3	−3.3	24.8	1.4	3.7
Government expenditures	4.5	5.1	2.4	9.8	5.3	4.0
Capital investments	20.6	11.0	−1.1	41.7	10.7	3.3
Visitor exports	17.0	16.8	−13.6	37.2	16.0	4.0
Other exports	1.9	1.8	2.1	4.0	1.7	3.9
T&T demand	97.5	7.9	−1.5	218.0	8.8	4.3
Direct industry GDP	21.1	2.4	−6.5	46.3	2.6	4.1
T&T economy GDP	52.7	6.0	−4.1	113.2	6.3	3.9
Direct industry employment[c]	192.5	1.8	−5.1	267.8	2.0	3.4
T&T economy emploment[c]	497.1	4.7	−2.5	676.5	5.0	3.1

Source: WTTC 2009.

a. 2009 real growth adjusted for inflation (%).

b. 2010–19 annualized real growth adjusted for inflation (%).

c. '000 jobs.

a strong tourism brand. Nepal's traditional comparative advantage in tourism has been its unique natural and cultural assets resulting in an expansion in mountaineering, trekking, rafting, wildlife, and cultural preservation activities. Eco-tourism, pilgrimage, adventure, business, and special interest tourism have also been growing. The country is home to 1,310 peaks that are over 6,000 meters, including eight of the 10 highest peaks in the world. Consequently, trekking and mountaineering tourism has grown substantially since it first developed as a tourism segment in Nepal in the 1960s. In 2007, most visitors to Nepal came for holiday (41.4 percent) followed by trekking and mountaineering (19.2 percent), pilgrimage (10 percent), and business or official visits (4.6 percent) (MOTCA 2009a). Many Hindu and Buddhist pilgrims visit Nepal throughout the year.

Out of the 669 total hotel accommodations all over Nepal in 2008, approximately 54 percent were located in Kathmandu, accounting for nearly 60 percent of total available accommodations (MOTCA 2009a). Among the remaining hotel rooms, the far western and the mid-western regions had the lowest number of good quality accommodation facilities compared to the western and eastern regions of the country. The vast majority of tourist standard hotels available outside Kathmandu (285 out of a total 307 hotels) are non-star rated; they provide a total of 5,288 rooms with 10,498 beds (MOTCA 2009a).

Nepal's hospitable climate attracts tourists year round, but autumn and spring are the busiest seasons in terms of monthly visitor arrivals. However, Indian visitors come to Nepal mostly during the summer, which is a lean season for other markets. The average length of stay of a tourist in Nepal remained more or less constant at approximately 12 days during the period from 1995 to 2007 (MOTCA 2009a).

Currently, India represents Nepal's largest source for international visitor arrivals—representing around 23 percent of total air arrivals in 2009. This is due mainly to the availability of direct access, liberal travel arrangements, and the convertibility of the Indian currency in Nepal.[1] Sri Lanka has also emerged as an important source mainly driven by the attraction of the many Buddhist sites in Nepal. The EU, the United Kingdom, France, and Germany are consistent sources of long haul traffic. The United States and Canada are also important sources for Nepal in the long haul market. More recently; tourists from China and the Republic of Korea have grown rapidly from a small base. Table 9.2 summarizes the main tourism segments in 2007. The share of pilgrimage tourism rose steadily from 1.4 percent in 1995 to 10 percent in 2007. Package tours,

Table 9.2   Main Tourism Segments, 2007/08

Countries	Holiday or pleasure (%)	Trekking or mountaineering (%)	Business or official (%)	Pilgrimage (%)
India	33.6	0.9	10.8	9.9
Japan	63.7	14.5	3.1	4.2
U.K.	54.0	22.0	3.7	1.6
U.S.	49.0	14.8	4.8	4.3
France	47.3	28.5	1.7	1.9
Germany	45.1	28.6	3.2	2.7
Sri Lanka	21.1	38.4	1.9	30.8
Spain	61.2	13.4	0.7	0.6
All visitors	41.4	19.2	4.6	10.0

Source: Nepal Tourism Board (NTB) website, www.welcomenepal.com.

organized mainly by Indian tour operators, dominate this segment of the tourism market, which limits the length of stay for pilgrims.

Expenditure patterns of tourists indicate the likely impact on various economic activities in the country. Figure 9.2 gives a breakdown of average per capita expenditures by category for the period FY2002/03 to FY2006/07. Tourists staying in lower categories of accommodations are generally believed to have a greater diffusion effect on economic activities such as purchasing food and beverages locally, using local transportation, and contributing to the public exchequer in terms of taxes and fees. Tourists coming for more high-end pleasure tourism, business, religious pilgrimage, conferences, and cultural purposes, were reported as the highest spenders for accommodations followed by tourists visiting for trekking, rafting, and other more adventure oriented travel.

Characteristics of Enterprises in the Tourism Sector

The Nepal 2009 Enterprise Survey consists of a cross-section of non-agricultural firms representative the manufacturing, retail, tourism, and other services sectors of the economy. Data for 486 registered establishments in urban areas of Nepal were collected including 77 firms that reported their establishments to be "primarily associated with tourism."[2] Of these firms, 32 percent are hotels and restaurants while 63.5 percent are travel agencies; one surveyed firm identified itself as being engaged in computing and related activities. Hotels and restaurants are on average larger than all other tourism related firms; travel agencies are predominantly micro enterprises.

Figure 9.2   Average Nepal Tourist Expenditures by Category, FY2002/03–FY2006/07
percent per capita

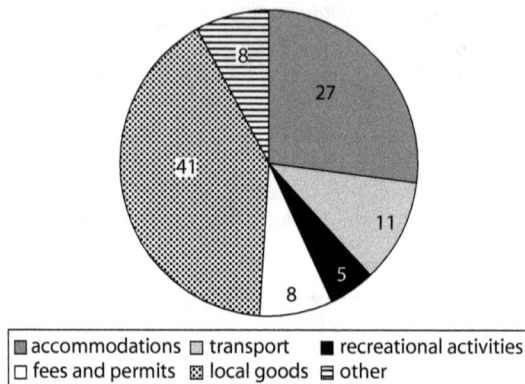

Source: Nepal Tourism Board (NTB) website, www.welcomenepal.com.

Among the surveyed tourism firms, most are located in the Central region (62 percent) and have less than five employees (52 percent). Approximately 34 percent of tourism firms have been operating for less than five years and only 8 percent for 20 years or more (Table 9.3) (Figure 9.3).

The average size of all private sector firms in Nepal is very small. However, average size varies considerably across sectors with the other services sector having the smallest average size among all sectors while manufacturing and tourism firms tend to be larger (Figure 9.4). Manufacturing accounts for a larger share of the private sector in the Central region whereas the tourism sector is larger in the West. Firms in the manufacturing sector are on average older.

Firm Performance in the Tourism Sector

Average total sales for tourism firms surveyed in FY2007/08 amounted to Nrs 10.6 million, which is higher than the average for all private sector enterprises (Nrs 7.9 million). Sales, as expected, are related to the firm's size. Annual sales-per-worker in the tourism sector amounted, on average, to Nrs 1.3 million about 1.6 times the average of the overall private sector. On average, sales-per-worker have grown by 33 percent and 9 percent per year over the past three fiscal years for the hotels and restaurants and travel agency industries, respectively (performing better than the overall private sector's growth rate of –0.3 percent). Thus, performance

Table 9.3   Tourism Survey Sample

	% Micro (<5)	% Small (5–19)	% Medium (20–99)	% Large (>=100)
West	34.5	55.4	10.1	0
Central	50.8	35.6	10.3	3.3
East	100	0	0	0
Total	51.6	37.2	9.1	2.1

Source: Nepal Enterprise Survey 2009.

Figure 9.3   Breakdown of Tourism Enterprises by Region, Size, and Age
percent

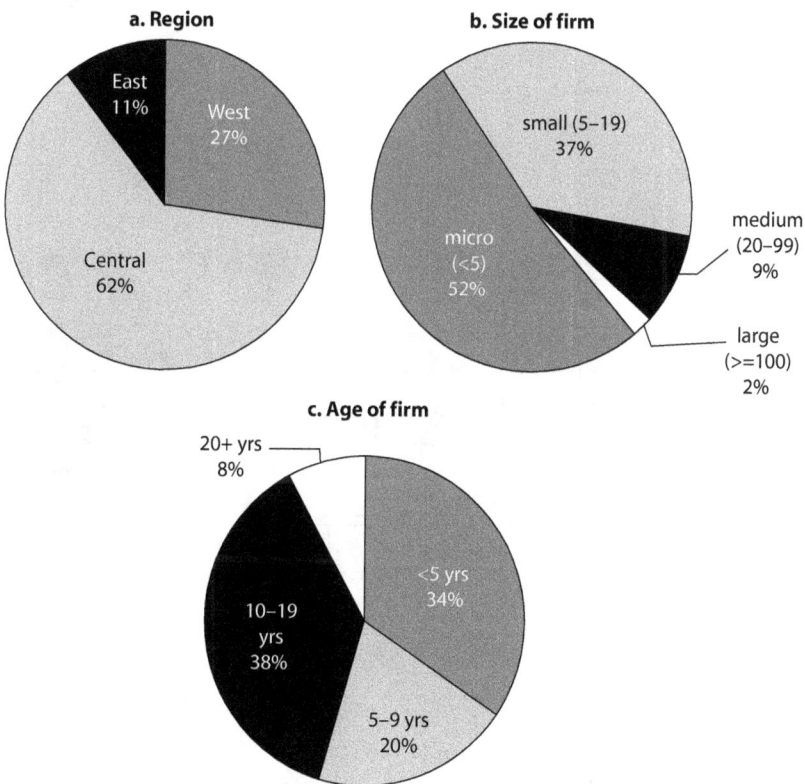

Source: Nepal Enterprise Survey 2009.

compares well with the rest of the private sector in Nepal, as can be seen in Table 9.4.

Tourism firms on average employ 14 permanent full-time workers. However, half of the firms do not employ more than 4 permanent full-time employees—this reflects the higher proportion of travel agencies and younger firms. Tourism firms in the Central region tend to employ more,

Figure 9.4   Sector Comparison of Nepal Firms by Region and Size

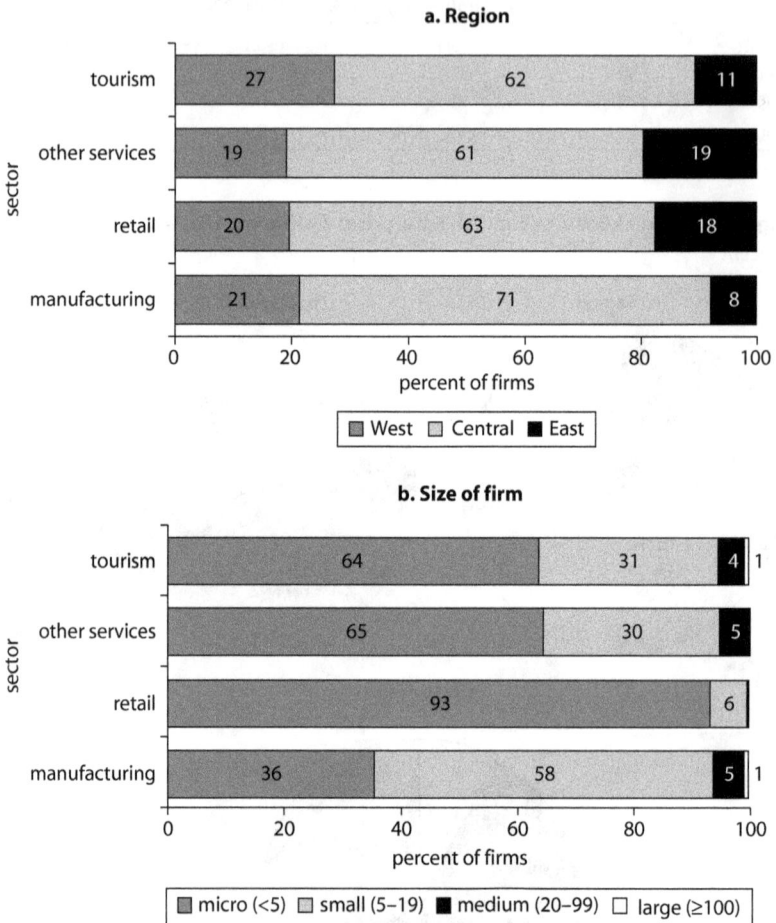

a. Region

sector			
tourism	27	62	11
other services	19	61	19
retail	20	63	18
manufacturing	21	71	8

percent of firms

☐ West ☐ Central ■ East

b. Size of firm

sector				
tourism	64	31	4	1
other services	65	30	5	
retail	93	6		
manufacturing	36	58	5	1

percent of firms

☐ micro (<5) ☐ small (5–19) ■ medium (20–99) ☐ large (≥100)

Source: Nepal Enterprise Survey 2009.
Note: In panel b, percentages for medium and large firms are both less than 1 in the retail category.

as do older firms, which employ an average of 86 workers. Hotels and restaurants are relatively large, with an average of 32 workers. On average, tourism firm employment slightly decreased (–0.4 percent) between 2005/06 and 2007/08. Employment in tourism tends to be larger than the average for the private sector.

Tourism establishments in Nepal show very limited growth in size over the life of the firms. Tourism firms have mostly remained within their initial size group. Table 9.5 gives a representation of the movements of tourism firms across size groups; the diagonal represents firms that have stayed within their initial size group.

Table 9.4   Industry Performance: Sales Growth, Labor Productivity, and Employment

	Sales & labor productivity			Employment	
	Sales average annual growth rate from 2005/06 (%)	Sales per worker average 2007/08 (thousand Nrs)	Sales per worker average annual growth rate from 2005/06 (%)	Average 2007/08	Average annual growth rate from 2005/06 (%)
Nepal	3.7	979	−0.3	6.0	3.9
Tourism overall	16.8	1,333	18.6	13.7	−0.4
Hotel & Restaurants	28.8	229	33.4	31.6	−3.7
Transport & travel agencies	9.5	1,969	9.5	5.5	1.7

Source: Nepal Enterprise Survey 2009.

Table 9.5   Tourism Firm Growth (% Firms)

	Size at time of establishment				
Present size	Micro (<5)	Small (5–19)	Medium (20–99)	Large (>=100)	Total
Micro (<5)	52.2	0.0	0.0	0.0	52.2
Small (5–19)	11.5	26.1	0.0	0.0	37.6
Medium (20–99)	0.0	4.3	4.5	0.0	8.8
Large (>=100)	0.0	0.7	0.0	0.7	1.4
Total	63.7	31.1	4.5	0.7	100.0

Source: Nepal Enterprise Survey 2009.

Tourism Investments

Over half of the tourism firms surveyed have made investments to improve their competitiveness either by upgrading their classification, significantly improving their facilities, or significantly upgrading services provided to clients—the last of these being the most common type of investment. Of the sample, 61 percent of the firms made investments to upgrade their classification, 75.9 percent to significantly improve their facilities, and 86.7 percent to upgrade services offered to clients (Figure 9.5).

The future outlook for firms in the tourism sector is overall positive. Over a half of the enterprises declared that they intended to expand their establishments' capacity over the next two years (Figure 9.6).

When measuring quality certifications, it appears that only 1.5 percent of the firms have an internationally recognized quality certification. As is often the case, quality certification is more common among older firms

Figure 9.5   Percentage of Nepalese Tourism Firms Investing to Improve Competitiveness

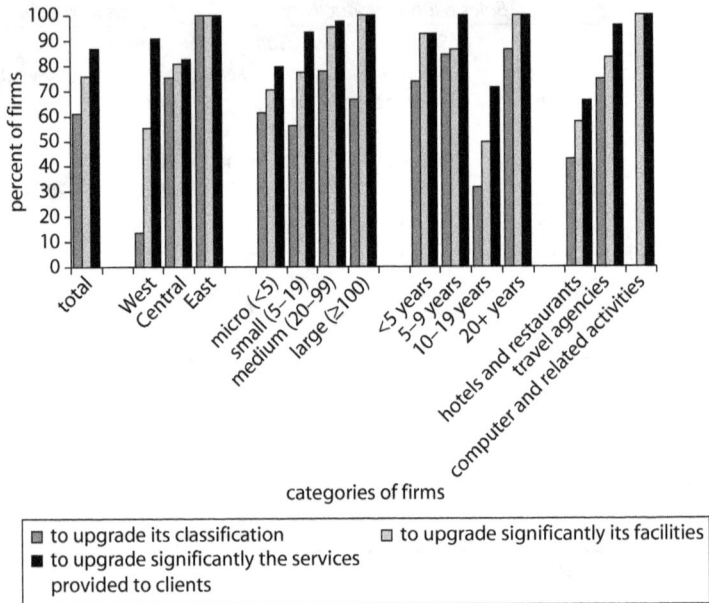

Source: Nepal Enterprise Survey 2009.

(4.3 percent) and is most common among large firms (16.7 percent). An even smaller proportion of the firms have an environmental certification, such as Green Globe or ISO 14000; only 1.2 percent of the firms have an environmental certification. These businesses are medium-sized hotels established over 20 years ago located in the Western region.[3]

Of the firms surveyed, very few (2.1 percent) applied for a construction-related permit in the past two years. Medium and large firms more commonly applied for permits, 15.8 percent and 33.3 percent, respectively. The wait for the permit to be granted, however, ranged between 14 and 120 days, while approximately half of the firms reported that an informal gift or payment was expected or requested in reference to the application. The firms surveyed do not perceive access to land as an obstacle to business, even among hotels and restaurants.

Infrastructure and the Tourism Sector

For Nepal's tourism sector to reach its full potential, it must address infrastructure constraints in the medium and long term. Nepal's road

Figure 9.6   Nepalese Tourism Firms Planning to Maintain or Expand Capacity over FY2010/11

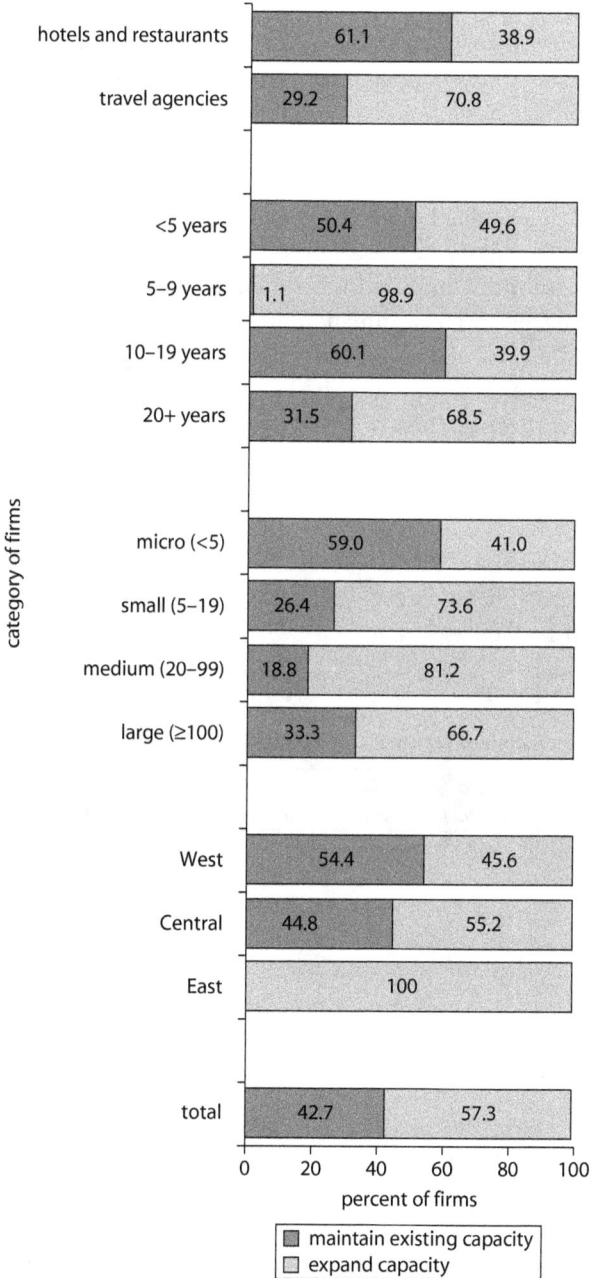

Source: Nepal Enterprise Survey 2009.

network is underdeveloped and airports in the mountainous regions are in need of further investment. The share of the national flag carrier, which once accounted for more than 50 percent of total tourist arrivals, has decreased dramatically to less than 25 percent of total tourist arrivals nowadays, as a result of inefficient and ineffective management. Other domestic carriers have stepped in demonstrating the viability of the air travel market despite impediments. Additionally, Tribhuvan International Airport (TIA), Nepal's only international airport, is in much need of investment and re-organization. Tourism infrastructure in the mid-western and far-western regions of the country is considerably weak. Five western districts are still not connected with adequate roads. There are only two direct air links between Kathmandu and other airports in the west. The airports in the mid-western and far-western regions are located at high altitudes and are ill-equipped (MOTCA 2005). Many airports in these remote destinations are also not operational due to damage of infrastructure during the decade-long armed conflict (MOTCA 2008).

Most tourism firms rate transportation as a moderate or major obstacle; transport is rated as a major or very severe obstacle by 42.7 percent of the firms surveyed (Table 9.6). It is more frequently a major problem for large firms (66.7 percent) and for younger firms (43.4 percent for firms established less than five years ago). Over two-thirds of the tourism

Table 9.6   Perception of Transport as an Obstacle in the Tourism Sector (% Firms)

	No obstacle	Minor	Moderate	Major	Very severe	Major or very severe obstacle
Total	**10.5**	**24.9**	**21.8**	**39.6**	**3.1**	**42.7**
Region						
West	26.5	26.5	5.8	30.6	10.7	41.3
Central	5.4	28.4	32.6	33.3	0.4	33.7
East	0.0	0.0	0.0	100.0	0.0	100.0
Size						
Micro (<5)	9.1	29.5	20.4	41.0	0.0	41.0
Small (5–19)	14.5	19.7	18.1	40.9	6.7	47.6
Medium (20–99)	4.8	21.7	46.1	20.6	6.7	27.3
Large (>=100)	0.0	16.7	16.7	66.7	0.0	66.7
Age						
<5 yrs	19.2	3.4	34.0	36.1	7.3	43.4
5–9 yrs	0.0	0.0	11.2	85.8	3.1	88.9
10–19 yrs	6.7	58.4	15.6	19.3	0.0	19.3
20+ yrs	17.8	22.1	25.5	34.5	0.0	34.5

Source: Nepal Enterprise Survey 2009.

firms surveyed reported that their clients face transportation difficulties getting to their establishment. Establishments in the Western region are especially concerned by transportation difficulties (87.8 percent). Moreover, virtually all firms (97.4 percent) reported suffering losses due to transportation difficulties.

Firms in Nepal face an acute shortage of electricity. Chronic power shortages, approaching 16 hours daily in 2008/09, commence in winter and last until spring, the months when tourist arrivals are at their peak. Almost all firms experienced power outages in FY2007/08. Typically, firms experienced an average of two outages a day (60 per month) and outages lasted for five hours on average. These outages resulted in losses that amounted, on average, to 31.3 percent of the firm's sales, higher than that for manufacturing and services. Within the tourism sector, losses as a proportion of sales are smaller for large firms (17 percent). As a result of these obstacles, a very high proportion of tourism enterprises find electricity to be a major or very severe obstacle to their operations (97.7 percent). In particular, firms in the West and medium and large firms found electricity to be more of an obstacle.

Internet use among tourism firms in Nepal is widespread but not universal. According to the Nepal Enterprise Survey 2009, 69.4 percent of the tourism firms use email to communicate with their clients and 53 percent of the firms have a website (Figure 9.7). Looking beyond averages, we find that all of the large firms use email and have a website while among micro firms, half use email and 29.5 percent have a website. Access to email and a website among small firms is above average.

Access to Finance in the Tourism Sector

Most tourism firms do not use banks to finance their working capital or their fixed assets, resorting instead to internal funds. Tourism enterprises finance their working capital for the most part (85 percent) through internal funds. Of the many tourism firms that purchased fixed assets during FY2007/08, 58.5 percent in total, and 83 percent of large firms, financed their purchases entirely through internal funds. Seventy-one percent of the firms have a checking or a banking account; the proportion is lower among micro enterprises (60 percent) and among hotels and restaurants (45.1 percent). This is far greater than the average of 45 percent for all private sector firms in Nepal. However, 28.4 percent of tourism firms have a credit or a loan from a financial institution, compared to

Figure 9.7   Use of Internet and Email in the Tourism Sector in Nepal

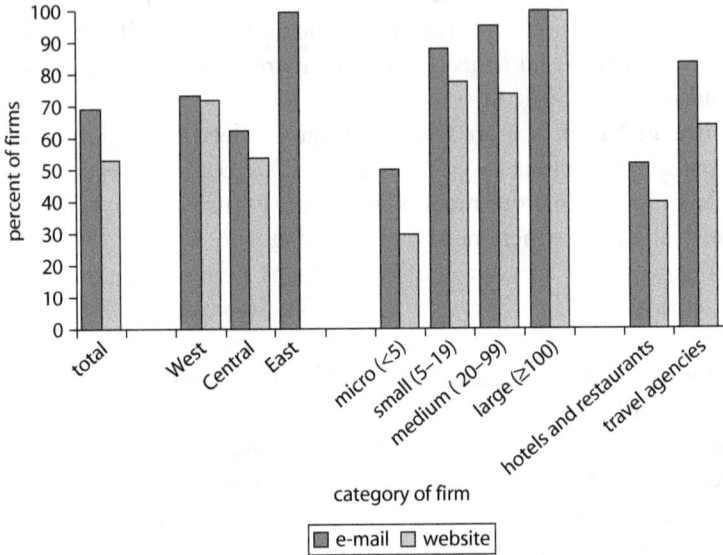

category of firm

■ e-mail □ website

Source: Nepal Enterprise Survey 2009.

29 percent for the private sector as a whole. The incidence is much lower in the Central region and among hotels and restaurants.

Of the firms sampled, only 14.3 percent applied for a new loan or line of credit in the past two years. Applications were much more frequent in the Western region (32.2 percent) and among medium firms (31.7 percent). Most of these were granted by private commercial banks (61.5 percent); the second most common source was non-bank financial institutions (27.5 percent), followed by state-owned or government banks (11 percent). The median value of these loans was Nrs 600 thousand and nearly always required collateral (92 percent). The most frequently used collateral was the owner's personal assets. Most firms reported the value of the collateral to be 200 percent of the loan's value, while some firms reported it to be 750 percent.[4] Among firms that did not apply for a loan, most did not apply because they had no need for a loan (73.4 percent), 15.2 percent did not apply because collateral requirements are too high, and 8.8 percent were discouraged by the complexity of application procedures. Collateral requirements deter micro firms and travel agencies more than others, while the complexity of procedures especially deters small firms.

More tourism firms rate access to finance as a major or very severe obstacle (10.9 percent) than the overall private sector (around 9 percent).

Firms in the Central region have more difficulty accessing finance, as do micro and recently established enterprises.

Other Investment Climate Issues

Most of the tourism firms sampled are fairly satisfied with services for immigration, tourism regulation, and tourism centers. The majority of firms rated each of these services as fairly good. The services offered by tourist information centers received the worst ratings while immigration procedures received the best. However, large firms (whose clients are the ones that use these services most often) rated such services as very or slightly poor. Immigration procedures appear to be better in the Central region while regulations and tourist centers received better ratings in the Western region.

More tourism firms consider skills of the workforce a major or very severe obstacle (8.5 percent) than firms in other sectors of the economy. Availability of an educated workforce is a significant problem in the Western region and for the categories of large firms. In the majority of the tourism firms sampled, none of the employees belong to a trade union. In those firms with trade union members, 14.9 percent of the workers are unionized.

As is the case with the rest of the private sector, tourism firms perceive political instability to be a major problem for businesses in Nepal. Corruption is viewed as a major or very severe obstacle to business activities by 29.4 percent of the tourism firms, and is especially severe for large firms and for very young ones. **On average, 32.5 percent of the tourism firms choose to pay for security. The incidence is much larger for large and older firms as well as firms in the Central region;** whereby most of these firms sustained costs of over 5 percent of their sales for security services. In the year before the survey, **4 percent of the firms in the tourism sector suffered losses due to crime and about 13 percent of the firms believe crime is a major or very severe obstacle.** Firms in the Central region and hotels and restaurants are more subject to theft, robbery, and vandalism than others.

Conclusions and Recommendations

Investment in tourism related infrastructure is needed to grow the sector and to ensure accessibility to tourism resources/establishments by road and air. Large resources, both domestic and foreign, are required to ensure the sustainable growth of the tourism sector, and the development of sound infrastructure and management facilities. For the tourism sector to reach its potential, in the medium and short term, strategic infrastructure linkages that reduce transport time between destinations have to be identified and an investment program developed and implemented, through both public and private investments. These could include selected small airfields within Nepal to encourage domestic travel and enhance the tourism product. Developing better connecting nodes between road and air travel is also needed. Given the large capital costs involved in such development, the private sector and foreign investors would need to undertake these projects. However, the issues of licensing, approvals (which at times involve Cabinet approvals, for example, for long-term leasing of land for airport development), and land titling need to be addressed first. Electricity shortages and unpredictable fuel supply, which also result in water supply shortages, are a hassle for tourists and undermine the private sector's ability to offer quality services. These constraints can be addressed through investments in energy efficiency measures (in particular for larger establishments), better water and waste management, etc., but are primarily a country-wide cross-sectoral issue.

Investment in a skilled and educated workforce is needed to provide high-value services in the face of increased competition. Availability of an educated workforce is a significant problem in the Western region and for large and small firms. In particular, investment in developing the skills of those employed in tourism enterprises can lead to higher tourism expenditures and positive spillovers in those areas that rely on expenditures beyond accommodations. This can be done through vitalizing the tourism training institutes and supporting them with better programs and teachers. In addition, there is a need to regulate and support tourism training institutes to ensure quality of their programs and encourage certification. Finally, introducing responsible tourism as a subject in high school curriculum could be considered. Given the large costs and effort involved in doing so, it could be piloted with the help of donor support in some schools.

Domestic political stability and improvement in the implementation of existing tourism laws and regulations could do much to improve support for the sector and increase its competitiveness. For example, the Civil Aviation Authority of Nepal (CAAN) subsidizes parking fees to domestic airline companies, a bias against international airlines operating in Nepal. In addition, in order to encourage FDI in a sector that requires major land/infrastructure investments, it is imperative to resolve some of the issues that occur in terms of land ownership rights and cumbersome court procedures. Capacity building in tourism related government institutions is needed to ensure the proper regulation and monitoring of the sector. Comprehensive data on hotel or guesthouse/lodge occupancy in Nepal are needed to prepare a proper marketing strategy and to monitor its implementation.

Promotion of and investment in quality and environmental certifications are part of a more general branding and marketing strategy for Nepal. With proper regulation and monitoring, these certifications can offer expanded opportunities for tourism establishments in Nepal (e.g., eco-tourism, individual high-end travelers, etc.). This has the potential to increase the spending per tourist and encourage the registration of tourism establishments, which would aid in monitoring and provide a more consistent quality brand for the sector as a whole.

Developing Nepal as an attractive, safe, and sustainable tourism destination requires a holistic approach wherein the *government, the private sector, and public-private partnerships* work collectively to meet stated objectives. Nepal's rich cultural and natural heritage brings tourism to the forefront, as it is capable of generating high economic growth and contributing to a rapid rise in living standards resulting from increased sustainable employment. The government's new tourism policy highlights the need to identify new tourism destinations, develop tourism-related infrastructure, provide reliable service delivery to tourists, and enhance the quality of those services—easy access, a safe stay, and an increased length of stay. To implement this policy, public-private partnership is needed to:

- Develop a tourism master plan that focuses on sustainable tourism development;
- Build the capacity of tourism related public institutions to ensure competitive airline regulation, tourism marketing, licensing of tourism establishments, etc.;
- Support micro and small enterprises, which bear the burden of infrastructure constraints and instability disproportionately (and spend time and resources addressing those issues instead of focusing on upgrading their skills and service offerings).

Notes

1. The Nepalese Rupee is pegged to the Indian Rupee.
2. Not all "Hotels and Restaurants" identified themselves as "primarily associated with tourism." Therefore, average sales per person for tourism "hotels and

restaurants" in this chapter differs and is greater than that for all "hotels and restaurants."

3. When asked to describe the certification they obtained, one business did not respond, another reported "Consumer Cleaner Production" and the third reported "Fewa B Pach & Environment Protection."

4. There are not enough observations to have representative statistics within groups.

Methodology of the Nepal Enterprise Survey 2009

The Nepal Enterprise Survey 2009 is a representative survey of registered firms in the manufacturing and services sectors in urban Nepal and covers a broad range of business environment topics including access to finance, corruption, infrastructure, crime, competition, and performance measures. Information on firm characteristics and their performance, and measures of objective data on the business environment is also collected. In addition to the Enterprise survey, an Employee Survey and Informal Survey were conducted.

Overall, data were collected for 486 registered establishments, 120 unregistered establishments, and 392 employees in urban areas of Nepal between March 8, 2009 and June 15, 2009[1] through a sampling process stratified by industry, region, and size (Table 1A.1).

Enterprise Survey

Sampling Frame and Sampling Strategy

The Enterprise Survey is a representative survey of the manufacturing and services sectors of the economy. It comprises: all manufacturing sectors according to the ISIC Revision 3.1 group classification (group D), construction sector (group F), services sector (groups G and H), transport, storage, and communications sector (group I), and sub-sector 72, which

Table 1A.1   Nepal Enterprise, Informal, and Employee Surveys 2009—Achieved Sample

Survey	Micro (<5 employees)	Small (5–19 employees)	Medium (20–99 employees)	Large (100+ employees)	Total
Manufacturing	49	46	70	21	**186**
Retail	37	98	12	3	**150**
Other services	26	19	27	1	**73**
Tourism	6	29	36	6	**77**
All formal sector	**118**	**192**	**145**	**31**	**486**
Informal sector	**77**	**42**	**1**	**0**	120
Employee survey		49	219	124	392

Source: Nepal Enterprise, Informal, and Employee Surveys 2009.
Note: UN-weighted number of observations; one observation has missing information on the industrial sector and another has missing information on its age.

is IT firms. The following sectors are therefore excluded: financial intermediation (group J), real estate and renting activities (group K, except sub-sector 72, which is IT firms), and all public or utilities sectors.[2] The sectors included in the sample by two-digit ISIC code are:

- Manufacturing: 15, 16, 17, 18, 19, 20, 21, 22, 23, 24, 25, 26, 27, 28, 29, 30, 31, 32, 33, 34, 35, 36, 37
- Services: 45, 50, 51, 52, 55, 60, 61, 62, 63, 64, 72

The Enterprise Survey for Nepal targeted 480 registered establishments: 120 establishments with less than five employees and 360 establishments with five or more employees. For Nepal, registered firms were defined as being registered with the Inland Revenue Department, i.e. having a PAN/VAT number.

The survey sample for establishments was selected using stratified random sampling with replacement. Three levels of stratification were used in the sample: industry, firm size, and geographic region.

First, the universe was stratified into manufacturing, retail, and other services industries. Other services were further divided into tourism and non-tourism in order to allow specific analysis of the tourism sector. The initial sample design of 480 observations had a target of 180 interviews in manufacturing, 150 interviews in retail, 75 interviews in other services—tourism, and 75 interviews in other services—non-tourism.

Size stratification was defined following the standardized definition used for the Enterprise Surveys: micro (less than five employees), small (five to 19 employees), medium (20 to 99 employees), and large (100 or more employees). One hundred and twenty interviews were targeted for the micro survey and 360 for small, medium, and large firms with an oversampling of large firms, given the high prevalence of micro and small firms in Nepal.

Regional stratification was defined in terms of the geographic regions with the main cities of economic activity in the country. Western Nepal included Butwal, Dhangadhi, Nepalgunj, and Pokhara; Central Nepal included Banepa, Bhaktapur, Bharatpur, Birgunj, Hetauda, Kathmandu, Lalitpur, and Simara; and Eastern Nepal included Bhadrapur, Biratnagar, and Itahari.

The sample frame was initially based on lists of firms provided by the GoN and by appropriate trade associations; the lists obtained, however, were deemed incomplete and potentially out of date. It was, therefore, decided to undertake block enumeration, by which lists of establishments were created through visits. In total, the contractor enumerated 6,755 establishments for the survey fieldwork; the block enumeration elicited firms for both the Enterprise Survey and the Informal Survey.

In an initial stage, 6,652 firms were enumerated in the three regions; in a second stage of block enumeration, 103 manufacturing firms were enumerated in two industrial estates in the Central region—Simara and Hetauda. Ninety-two out of 103 of these firms were medium or large sized. It was decided that these two industrial estates should be enumerated because manufacturing firms, especially larger ones, had been shutting down as a result of excessive load shedding, and so some additional manufacturing firm listings were needed in order to meet survey targets. It was not feasible to fully enumerate all the blocks/clusters available in large cities such as Kathmandu, so randomly chosen clusters and blocks were enumerated within selected clusters.

Since the sampling design was stratified and employed differential sampling of the strata, individual observations should be properly weighted when making inferences about the population. Weights are computed as the inverse of their probability of selection, dividing universe cell estimates by the achieved cell counts.

Final Sample Size

The Enterprise Surveys, along with all other surveys, suffer from both survey non-response and item non-response. The former refers to refusals to participate in the survey altogether, whereas the latter refers to refusals to answer some specific questions. Different strategies were used to address these issues. The overall survey response rate for the Nepal Enterprise Survey was 95 percent (486 completed interviews / 513 attempted interviews).

The contractor achieved a higher number of employee surveys than originally targeted. The contractor successfully interviewed 392 employees in 68 firms. Four to seven employees were interviewed per firm.

Informal Survey

An Informal Survey is similar to an Enterprise Survey but has fewer questions; questions are also tailored to the characteristics of the country's informal sector.

The Nepal 2009 Informal Survey targeted 120 unregistered firms across a range of sectors and geographic regions.

The sampling frame for the Informal Survey was obtained through the same block enumeration process undertaken for the formal enterprises. Sampling was stratified by sector and geographic region. Since many informal firms are likely to operate within a household setting, the sample frame is not likely to be a representative list of informal firms since informal firms operating exclusively within the household setting were not enumerated. As a consequence, the Nepal 2009 Informal Enterprise Survey is not strictly representative of the Nepalese informal sector as a whole but is a fairly robust selection of informal firms in physical proximity of formal firms.

Sampling weights were not computed for the Informal Survey because the block enumeration was likely not to capture informal firms working within houses and thus the sample could not be considered as representative of the universe of informal firms in urban Nepal.

Notes

1. Registered firms were defined as being registered with the Inland Revenue Department, i.e., having a PAN/VAT number.
2. The full classification is available on the United Nations Statistics Division website (http://unstats.un.org/unsd/cr/registry/regcst.asp?Cl=17).

Methodology and Results of the Employee Survey

Employee Survey Methodology

The Employee Survey targeted 360 employees from the larger formal firm sample. The sampling process consisted of extracting a random sample of firms from the formal firms survey that was—at the same time—representative in terms of industries. Following the selection of firms, four to seven employees were randomly sampled from the obtained firm sample. In this case, sampling had to reflect composition by type of occupation.

The achieved sample consisted of 392 employees in 68 firms. The majority of the employees in the survey work in a medium-size firm (Figure 2A.1). The industrial composition of the sample, which consists of a cross-section of 486 firms—is rather diverse (Table 2A.1). In terms of industry coverage, 37 percent of the sample is in the manufacturing industry, followed closely by the retail industry with 31 percent of the sampled firms. The telecommunications industry has the least number of firms, only three, with two in the Central region and one in the East. The other two industries that also have smaller numbers of firms are the automobile services industry and the computing industry. Within the manufacturing sector, the main product mix of firms includes apparel, furniture, plastic, and basic metals. In terms of geographical distribution, the survey

Figure 2A.1   Employee Survey Sample Breakdown by Firm Size
percent

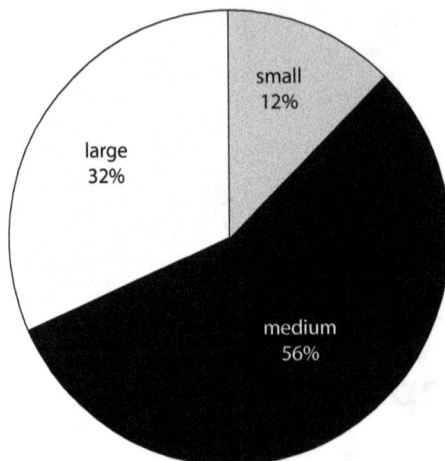

Source: Nepal Employee Survey 2009.

Table 2A.1   Nepal Employee Survey 2009—Achieved Sample

	Employee survey sample				Overall sample[a]
	No. of workers	% workers	No. of firms	% firms	% firms
Total	392	100.0	68	100.0	100
Survey					
Manufacturing	305	77.8	51	75.0	37.2
Retail	8	2.0	2	2.9	30.7
Other services	16	4.1	3	4.4	12.8
Tourism	63	16.1	12	17.6	19.3
Region					
West	96	24.5	17	25.0	17.9
Central	269	68.6	47	69.1	73.4
East	27	6.9	4	5.9	8.7
Size					
Small (5–19)	49	12.5	9	13.2	52.2
Medium (20–99)	219	55.9	41	60.3	39.4
Large (>=100)	124	31.6	18	26.5	8.4
Firm's age					
<5 yrs	24	6.1	4	5.9	19.3
5–9 yrs	55	14.0	10	14.7	20.7
10–19 yrs	157	40.1	28	41.2	36.8
20+ yrs	156	39.8	26	38.2	23.2

Source: Nepal Employee Survey 2009.
Note: a. sample distribution of manufacturing, retail, other services, and tourism firms obtained by excluding micro enterprises (i.e. enterprises with less than 5 employees).

covers the Western, Central, and Eastern regions of Nepal: about 69 percent of the firms are from the Central region, 25 percent from the West, and 6 percent from the East.

Employee Survey Results

Approximately two-thirds of workers (77.8 percent) in Nepal are employed in manufacturing. Tourism is the second largest sector employing 16.1 percent of workers. Retail and other services employ only 2 percent and 4.1 percent of workers, respectively. The average age of workers is 32, and about 20 percent of workers are women.

Education

There is a broad range of educational attainment among workers in Nepal; however, overall levels of formal education are low with nearly two-thirds of the workforce with secondary education or less. About 20 percent of workers have only a primary school education. Workers with either general or technical secondary education make up nearly half of the workforce (48.5 percent). About 20 percent of workers in the sample have completed a university degree.

Regionally, education levels are lowest in the East and highest in the Central region sectorally, workers in the manufacturing sector have less formal education than workers in retail and other services.

Compensation

The average total compensation for workers in Nepal is Nrs 6,924 per month. Total compensation includes a salary and allowances that amount on average to 21 percent of the total compensation. Compensation and both its components, wages and allowances, are higher on average for managers, in large firms, in tourism, and particularly in other services. The average salary is Nrs 5,443 per month. Wages tend to be higher the longer an employee has been working for their current employer, with older, more senior workers earning higher wages, but not higher allowances.

Average monthly compensation for full-time production workers was Nrs 8,000. Production workers in the West earned nearly four times as much as workers in the East. Production workers in the mineral industry have the highest average monthly compensation. Average monthly compensation is highest in small firms.

Women earn less than men across all occupations and regions in Nepal, even when controlling for the level of workers' educational

attainment. The average total monthly compensation (includes salary/wage and allowances) for women was Nrs 6,539 compared to Nrs 7,017 for men. While overall compensation is higher for men, women tend to receive a higher proportion of allowances. Allowances as a percent of total compensation was 24 percent for women and 21 percent for men.

Education is likely to be the strongest predictor of compensation (wages and allowances). Both wages and allowances increase consistently across levels of education attainment.

Skills and Training

Educational attainment is also a strong predictor of employee training by their employer. The proportion of workers who received training is directly proportional to the level of education completed by the worker.

Workers with a higher average wage are also more likely to be trained by their employer with almost no difference between full-time workers with a permanent contract and workers with a temporary contract. Skilled workers are more likely to be trained than unskilled non-production workers. Training is also more common in the East than in other regions, and in the other services sector. No workers surveyed in the retail sector reported having been trained by their employers.

Training is proportional to the age of the firm and the age of the worker, which may be an indication that employee training is declining over time. Overall less than one-fourth (22.4 percent) of workers surveyed received formal training from their current employer.

Issues in the Labor Market

Workers in Nepal perceive salaries and political problems as the main labor market issues (31.9 percent and 16.6 percent, respectively) but benefits, leave, working conditions, and working hours are also often cited as main concerns (Figure 2A.2). The retail sector is the only sector where more workers said political problems are the main problem in their current job, rather than salary. Retail workers also tend to see working conditions rather than salary as a problem in their job. Benefits and leave were not a concern for retail workers. Salary was the biggest issue for manufacturing and other services.

Trade Unions

Almost half of workers in Nepal report participating in trade unions (46.7 percent). There are no significant regional variations in union membership but significant variations across sectors. Manufacturing and

Figure 2A.2   Perception of Most Important Problem by Nepalese Workers in Current Job

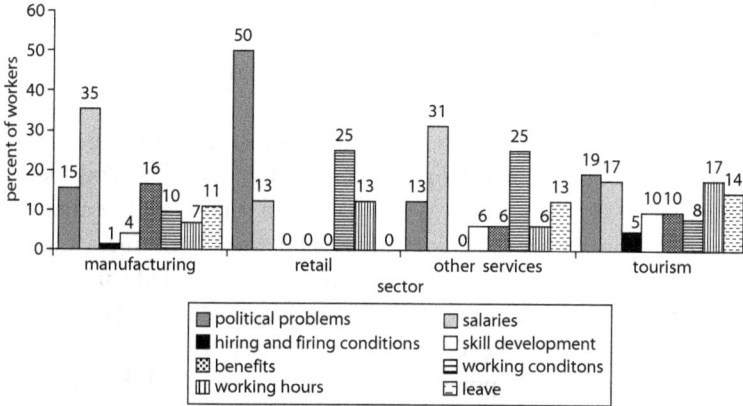

Source: Nepal Employee Survey 2009.

tourism sectors have the greatest number of union membership, 51.5 percent and 42.9 percent, respectively. Very few employees in the retail or other services sector are members of trade unions.

Workers with less education and employed in lower skilled jobs are more likely to be union members. Among trade union members, males are more likely to participate in trade union actions than women. Union activity tends to increase with worker seniority. Participating in trade union actions does not necessarily require taking off working days. About 20 percent of workers reported having participated in trade union actions without missing a day of work; 57.7 percent of workers who missed work to participate in trade union actions reported missing one day of work.

Most workers do not think there should be more trade union action initiatives than currently take place. Forty-three percent of workers think there should be less trade union action initiatives. Thirty-five percent of workers think that the number should stay the same. Less educated workers, younger workers, and workers with lower skill occupations are more likely to wish for more trade union initiatives. Eighty-eight percent of retail workers think that there should be less trade union activity.

The main problems leading to trade union actions in the opinion of employees were salaries (47 percent of workers), political issues (28.3 percent of workers), and benefits (18.6 percent of workers). Workers in medium and large firms more often attributed union activity to political issues. Workers in small firms more often cited salaries as the main reason for union actions. A larger share of managers, professionals, and more educated workers consider political problems as the main reason for trade union actions. Workers in the East cited political problems most often as the main reason for union action. This is the only region where more workers felt that political problems were a bigger issue than salaries (44.4 percent in the East, compared to 28.6 percent in the Central region, and 22.9 percent in the West).

Trade union activities may not fully reflect the range of labor and employment issues concerning workers. When asked to consider their own job, workers cited political problems and salaries as the main issues, but benefits, leave, working conditions, and working hours are also significant concerns for workers more often than for trade unions. Trade unions, however, act almost exclusively on political and salary issues.

As underlined by the Global Competitiveness Report 2009–2010 (WEF 2009), the development of the private sector and the competitiveness of a country depend on three key dimensions of infrastructure: transport, electricity, and telecommunications. An effective transport infrastructure enables entrepreneurs to access input and output markets and facilitate the movement of workers. An adequate and reliable electricity supply is essential for enterprises to be able to produce without interruptions, in a timely fashion, and without excessive costs for electricity. Finally, the telecommunications infrastructure increases the productivity of the economic system by making relevant information available in the decision making process of all economic actors.

Other Aspects of the Labor Market

Job satisfaction is high in Nepal with most workers reporting being at least "fine" with their job and their employer (61 percent and 64 percent, respectively). Only 12 percent of workers report being dissatisfied with their jobs and only 6 percent are dissatisfied with their employers (Figure 2A.3). Male and female workers report about the same level of satisfaction with their employer; however, twice as many female workers as male workers report being satisfied with their jobs (20.8 percent and 10.1 percent, respectively). No clear conclusions regarding employee satisfaction can be drawn across education levels or occupations.

More than half of workers in Nepal report being fine with skills developed on the job although more male workers are satisfied than female workers (12 percent and 7.8 percent, respectively) (Figure 2A.3).

Workers in Nepal tend to live close to their jobs with the majority commuting to work by foot or bicycle. Most workers need on average 23 minutes to travel from home to work. About 64 percent travel to

Figure 2A.3   Nepalese Worker Satisfaction with Current Job, Employer, and Skills Developed on the Job

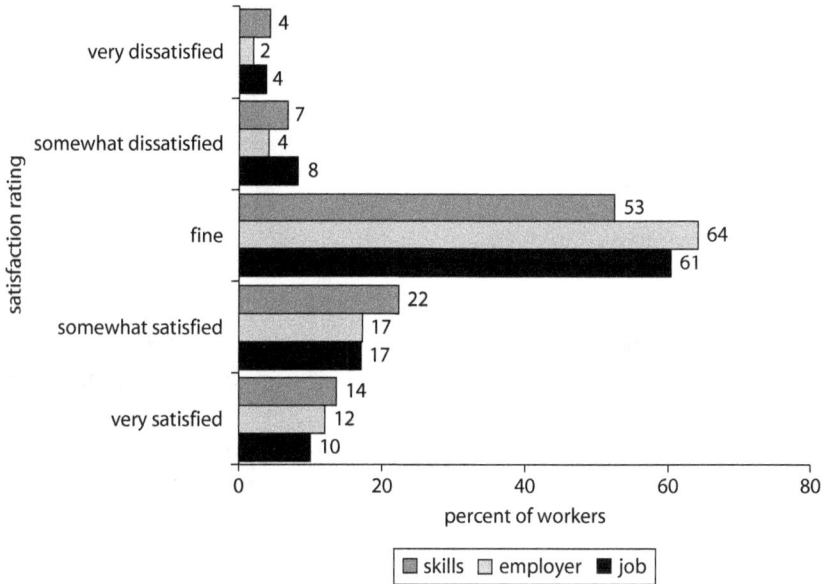

Source: Nepal Employee Survey 2009.

work on foot or by bicycle, and another 23 percent reach work by public transport. Use of public transport was lowest in the East where only 3.7 percent of workers used this mode of transportation for their commute. In the Central region, 29.4 percent used public transportation to get to work.

Transportation is not a major issue for employees. Nearly two-thirds (61.5 percent) answered that transportation used to reach the workplace presents no noteworthy problems. Transportation at the firm level was a more severe problem, with 44.2 percent of firms citing transportation (mostly of goods) as a major or very severe issue. Strikes were identified as the main transportation problem by firms, except in the East where fuel availability is the main issue. Correspondingly, only 1.5 percent of firms find transportation to be the most important investment climate obstacle.

The Central region of Nepal attracts the most workers from other regions. Nearly 30 percent of the workforce in Nepal has migrated from their region of origin. Workers born in the Central region of Nepal tend

Table 2A.2   Distribution of Employee Sample by Region of Origin and Region of Current Employment (% Workers)

Region where currently working	Region of origin					
	West	Central	East	Terai	Outside Nepal	Total
West	19.4	1.5	1.5	1.5	0.5	24.5
Central	7.7	34.7	14.0	10.5	1.8	68.6
East	0.8	0.0	5.4	0.0	0.8	6.9
Total	27.8	36.2	20.9	12.0	3.1	100.0

Source: Nepal Employee Survey 2009.

to stay and work there, and workers from other regions tend to migrate there. Among Nepalese workers, 96 percent born in the Central region continue to work there, and 82 percent of migrant workers moved to the Central region. People from the West migrate less for work. Seventy percent of workers in the West are originally from the region. Two-thirds of workers born in the East are currently working elsewhere, mostly in the Central region (Table 2A.2).

Migrant workers in Nepal are most often men, are more frequently employed in the manufacturing sector, and have relatively lower levels of education. Seventeen percent of workers are currently considering migrating for work—35 percent within the country, 5 percent to India, and 66 percent elsewhere. More than one-third of workers in the East are considering migration. About a quarter of workers with university level education are reportedly willing to migrate. Younger workers are also more willing to migrate. The majority of workers considering migrating are looking for better salaries.

Bibliography

Agarwal, M., and R. Dhakal. 2009. "Socio-economic Determinants of Income Generation in the Informal Sector of Nepal. A Case of Chitwan District." Paper prepared for the Special IARIW-SAIM Conference "Measuring the Informal Economy in Developing Countries," Kathmandu, Nepal, September 23–26.

Asian Development Bank. 2008. Volume 1 of *TA 6362-REG: South Asia Subregional Economic Cooperation (SASEC) Tourism Development Project Draft Final Report.*

Banerjee, A., and E. Duflo. 2008. "Do Firms Want to Borrow More? Testing Credit Constraints Using a Directed Lending Program." Department of Economics Working Paper 02-25, Massachusetts Institute of Technology, Cambridge, MA.

Beck, T., A. Demirgüç-Kunt, and V. Maksimovic. 2005. "Financial and Legal Constraints to Firm Growth: Does Firm Size Matter?" *Journal of Finance* 60: 137–77.

CBS (GoN Central Bureau of Statistics). 1996. *Nepal Living Standards Survey 1995/96.* Kathmandu: National Planning Commission Secretariat, CBS.

———. 1999. *Nepal Labour Force Survey Report 1998/99.* Kathmandu: National Planning Commission Secretariat, CBS.

———. 2002. *Census of Manufacturing Establishments 2001/02.* Kathmandu: National Planning Commission Secretariat, CBS.

————. 2003. Volume 1 of *Population Monograph of Nepal*. Kathmandu: National Planning Commission Secretariat, CBS.

————. 2004. Volumes 1 and 2 of *Nepal Living Standards Survey 2003/04, Statistical Report*. Kathmandu: National Planning Commission Secretariat, CBS.

————. 2006. *Census of Manufacturing Establishments 2006/07*. Kathmandu: National Planning Commission Secretariat, CBS.

————. 2007. *Statistical Year Book 2007*. Katmandu: National Planning Commission Secretariat, CBS.

————. 2008. "Report on the Labor Force Survey." Government of Nepal Central Bureau of Statistics, July.

Claessens, S., and L. Laeven. 2003. "Financial Development, Property Rights, and Growth." *Journal of Finance* 58 (6): 2401–36.

De Loecker, J. 2007. "Do Exports Generate Higher Productivity? Evidence from Slovenia." *Journal of International Economics* 73 (1): 69–98.

Djankov, S., C. McLiesh, and A. Shleifer. 2007. "Private Credit in 129 Countries." *Journal of Financial Economics* 84 (2): 299–329.

Doing Business Historical Database. World Bank, Washington, DC. http://www.doingbusiness.org/CustomQuery.

Economist Intelligence Unit. 2009–10. "Political Instability Index." http://viewswire.eiu.com/site_info.asp?info_name=social_unrest_table&page=noads&rf=0.

Escribano, A., and J. L. Guasch. 2005. "Assessing the Impact of the Investment Climate on Productivity Using Firm-Level Data: Methodology and the Cases of Guatemala, Honduras, and Nicaragua." Policy Research Working Paper Series 3621, World Bank, Washington, DC.

FACD (GoN Ministry of Foreign Aid Coordination Development). 2008. *Nepal: A Profile of Development Partners*. Kathmandu: Ministry of Finance, Foreign Aid Coordination Development.

Fernandes, A. 2008. "Firm Productivity in Bangladesh Manufacturing Industries." *World Development* 36 (10): 1725–44.

Ferrari, A., G. Jaffrin, and S. Shrestha. 2007. "Access to Financial Services in Nepal." World Bank, Washington, DC.

FNCCI (Federation of Nepalese Chambers of Commerce and Industry). 2008. *Nepal and the World: A Statistical Profile 2008*. Kathmandu: FNCCI.

Grameen Bank. 2007–08. "Banking for the Poor."

Guiso, L., P. Sapienza, and L. Zingales. 2004. "Does Local Financial Development Matter?" *Quarterly Journal of Economics* 119 (3): 929–69.

ILO (International Labour Organization). 2005. "Decent Civil Works in Nepal: From Research to Action Planning." International Labour Office, Nepal.

———. "The Informal Sector." International Labour Organization, Regional Office for Asia and the Pacific, Bangkok. http://www.ilo.org/public/english/region/asro/bangkok/feature/inf_sect.htm.

IMF (International Monetary Fund). 2010. "IMF World Bank Debt Sustainability Analysis." World Bank, Washington, DC.

International Telecommunication Union. 2009. ICT Indicators Database. http://www.itu.int/ITU-D/ict/publications/world/world.html.

Jütting, J., and J. R. De Laiglesia. 2009. *Is Informal Normal? Towards More and Better Jobs in Developing Countries.* Paris: OECD Development Centre.

Kee, H. L., and K. Krishna. 2008. "Firm-Level Heterogeneous Productivity and Demand Shocks: Evidence from Bangladesh." *American Economic Review* 98 (2): 457–62.

Laeven, L. 2003. "Does Financial Liberalization Reduce Financing Constraints?" *Financial Management* (Spring): 5–34.

Levine, R. 2005. "Finance and Growth: Theory and Evidence." In *Handbook of Economic Growth*, ed. P. Aghion and S. Durlauf. Amsterdam, The Netherlands: Elsevier Science.

Majagaiya, Kundan Pokhrel. 2009. "FDI in Nepal's Hydropower Sector: A Focus on the Product." *Nepal Monitor.* http://www.nepalmonitor.com/2009/01/fdi_in_nepals_hydropower.html.

Melitz, M. 2003. "The Impact of Trade on Intra-Industry Reallocations and Aggregate Industry Productivity." *Econometrica* 71(6): 1695–1725.

MOC (China Ministry of Commerce). 2010. "Bilateral Trade of India and China." http://english.mofcom.gov.cn/aarticle/subject/ciecf/lanmuc/201001/20100106760350.html.

MOCS (GoN Ministry of Commerce and Supplies). 2010. *Nepal Trade Integration Strategy 2010.* Kathmandu: MOCS.

MOF (GoN Ministry of Finance). 2007. "Economic Survey."

MOICS (GoN Ministry of Industry, Commerce and Supplies). 2004. *Nepal Trade and Competitiveness Study.* Kathmandu: National Planning Commission Secretariat, CBS.

———. 2008. *Industrial Statistics Fiscal Year 2064/065 (2007/2008).* Kathmandu: MOICS, Department of Industry.

MOPPW (GoN Ministry of Physical Planning and Works, Department of Roads). 2006. *Road Statistics.* Kathmandu: National Planning Commission Secretariat, CBS.

MOTCA (GoN Ministry of Tourism and Civil Aviation). 2005. *Civil Aviation Policy 2063*. Kathmandu: National Planning Commission Secretariat, CBS.

———. 2007. *Nepal Tourism Statistics 2007*. Kathmandu: National Planning Commission Secretariat, CBS.

———. 2008. "Draft Report on Tourism Strategic Plan for Khaptad Area and Surroundings of Far Western Region of Nepal (2009–2018)." Khaptad Area Tourism Development Committee, Kathmandu.

———. 2009a. *Nepal Tourism Statistics 2008*. Kathmandu: National Planning Commission Secretariat, CBS.

———. 2009b. *Tourism Policy 2065*. Kathmandu: National Planning Commission Secretariat, CBS.

NEA (GoN Nepal Electricity Authority). 2008. *Fiscal Year 2007/08—A Year in Review*. Kathmandu: National Planning Commission, CBS.

Nepal Gazette. Various years. http://nepalgazette.com/.

NPC (GoN National Planning Commission). 2007. "Three Year Interim Plan (2007/08–2009/10." National Planning Commission, Kathmandu.

NRB (Nepal Rastra Bank). 2009. "Economic Report 2008/09." Recent Macroeconomic Situation Report, Nepal Rastra Bank.

———. 2010. "Macroeconomic Indicators of Nepal, July 2010." Recent Macroeconomic Situation Report, Nepal Rastra Bank.

OECD (Organisation for Economic Co-operation and Development). 2009. "Promoting Pro-Poor Growth: Employment."

Qian, J., and P. Strahan. 2005. "How Laws and Institutions Shape Financial Contracts: The Case of Bank Loans." *Journal of Finance* 62 (6): 2803–34.

Rajan, R., and L. Zingales. 1998. "Financial Dependence and Growth." *American Economic Review* 88: 559–87.

Sophastienphong, K., and A. Kulathunga. 2010. *Getting Finance in South Asia*. Washington, DC: World Bank.

Suwal, R., and B. Pant. 2009. "Measuring Informal Sector Economic Activities in Nepal." Paper prepared for the Special IARIW-SAIM Conference "Measuring the Informal Economy in Developing Countries," Kathmandu, Nepal, September 23–26.

TEPC (GoN Trade and Export Promotion Centre). Various years. *Nepal Overseas Trade Statistics*. Kathmandu: Trade and Export Promotion Centre.

Transparency International. 2009. "Corruption Perceptions Index 2009. Regional Highlights: Asia-Pacific."

Tuladhar, I. 1996. "Factors Affecting Women Entrepreneurship in Small and Cottage Industries in Nepal." International Labour Organization working paper, International Labour Office.

United Nations (UN) Comtrade Database. United Nations, New York. http://comtrade.un.org/.

United Nations Economic and Social Council. 2006. "Poverty and the Informal Sector." Economic and Social Commission for Asia and the Pacific, Committee on Poverty Reduction, Third session, November 29–December 1, Bangkok, note by the secretariat.

United Nations (UN) Millennium Development Goals Indicators Database. United Nations, New York. http://mdgs.un.org/unsd/mdg/Default.aspx.

World Bank. 2000. *The Business Environment and Manufacturing Performance in Nepal.* Washington, DC: World Bank.

———. 2003. *Nepal Trade and Competitiveness Study.* Washington, DC: World Bank.

———. 2006. "Nepal Resilience amidst Conflict. An Assessment of Poverty in Nepal, 1995–96 and 2003–04." World Bank, Washington, DC.

———. 2007a. *Nepal. Mini-Diagnostic of the Investment Climate.* Washington, DC: World Bank, Foreign Investment Advisory Service (FIAS).

———. 2007b. "Nepal: Transport at a Glance, 2007." World Bank, Washington, DC.

———. 2007c. *Finance for All? Policies and Pitfalls in Expanding Access.* Washington, DC: World Bank.

———. 2007d. Reaching Out: Indicators of Access to and Use of Banking Services across Countries [Database]. http://go.worldbank.org/EZDOBVQT20.

———. 2008a. *Nepal: Trade Brief.* Washington, DC: World Bank.

———. 2008b. *Banking the Poor.* Washington, DC: World Bank.

———. 2009a. *Doing Business Report 2010.* Washington, DC: World Bank.

———. 2009b. *Nepal Economic Update, September 2009.* Washington, DC: World Bank.

———. 2009c. "Labor Migration Survey." World Bank, Washington, DC.

———. 2009d. *World Development Indicators 2009.* Washington, DC: World Bank.

———. 2010a. World Development Indicators Database. World Bank, Washington, DC. http://data.worldbank.org/data-catalog/world-development-indicators.

———. 2010b. *Nepal Economic Update, April 2010.* Washington, DC: World Bank.

———. 2010c. *Getting Electricity. A Pilot Indicator Set from the Doing Business Project.* Washington, DC: World Bank.

———. 2010d. *South Asia Getting Finance Indicators.* Washington, DC: World Bank.

————. 2010e. "Doing Business. Nepal." World Bank, Washington, DC.

————. 2010f. *Doing Business. Reforming through Difficult Times.* Washington, DC: World Bank.

————. 2010g. "Large-Scale Migration and Remittances in Nepal: Issues and Challenges." World Bank, Washington, DC.

World Bank and CBS (GoN Central Bureau of Statistics). 2010. "2010 National Living Standards Survey." Preliminary report.

World Bank Demographic and Health Surveys. 2009. EdStats. World Bank, Washington, DC.

World Economic Forum (WEF). 2009. "The Global Competitiveness Report 2009–2010." World Bank, Washington, DC.

WTTC (World Travel and Tourism Council). 2009. *Travel and Tourism Economic Impact 2009: Nepal.* London: WTTC.

www.ingramcontent.com/pod-product-compliance
Lightning Source LLC
Chambersburg PA
CBHW061147220326
41599CB00025B/4382